What is cool?

Elvis was cool, but so is Elvis Costello. Sinatra is cool, but so is Blondie. *Naked City* was cool, but so is *Dallas. Lolita* was cool, but so is *The Godfather.*

True cool is eternal. Neither fad nor fashion, trend nor taste, the concept links past and present with a snap of the fingers. Zap! Gillespie and Dylan. Cool is the essence of style — daring, personal, rare. Yet, in a world of ever-encroaching uncool, it has become harder and harder to distinguish the real thing.

Cool stands as your ultimate guide, leading you to those rare and enduring items, the coolest of the cool.

COOL

A Hipster's Directory

Edited by Gene Sculatti

Vermilion

London Melbourne Sydney Auckland Johannesburg

Vermilion and Company

An imprint of the Hutchinson Publishing Group

17-21 Conway Street, London W1P 6JD

Hutchinson Group (Australia) Pty Ltd
30-32 Cremorne Street, Richmond South, Victoria 3121
PO Box 151, Broadway, New South Wales 2007

Hutchinson Group (NZ) Ltd
32-34 View Road, PO Box 40-086, Glenfield, Auckland 10

Hutchinson Group (SA) (Pty) Ltd
PO Box 337, Bergvlei 2012, South Africa

First published in Great Britain 1983

Grateful acknowledgement is made to the
following for permission to quote from songs:

Warner Bros., Inc., for "Highway 61" by Bob
Dylan. © 1965 Warner Bros., Inc. All rights
reserved. Used by permission. Plangent
Visions Music for "Man Called Uncle" by Elvis
Costello. Copyright © 1979 USA and Canada
Plangent Visions Music, Inc. Lord Buckley's
poem "Hipsters, Flipsters, and Finger-Poppin'
Daddies" is reprinted by permission of City
Lights Books. Copyright © 1980 by the Estate
of Lord Buckley.

Printed in Great Britain by The Anchor Press
and bound by Wm Brendon & Son Ltd
both of Tiptree, Essex

British Library Cataloguing in Publication Data

Sculatti, Gene
  Cool.
  1. United States—Popular culture
  I. Title
  306'.1'0973   E169

ISBN 0 09-152391-5

Edited by Gene Sculatti

Associate Editor: Richard Blackburn
Assistant Editor: Marsha Meyer
Contributors: Joe Goldberg
               Perry lane
               Byron Laursen
               Joe McEwen
               Andy Meisler
               Richard Meltzer
               Bob Merlis
               Steve X. Rea
               Davin Seay
               Ronn Spencer
               Swamp Dogg (Jerry Williams, Jr.)
               Nick Tosches
               Jim Trombetta
               Gregg Turner
               Tom Vickers
               Sal Zero

Design: Harry Chester & Associates
Photography (including all frontispieces and
production setups): Chuck Krall
Additional Photography: Mike Koehn
Models: Annie Nisbet, James Valley

For the late great Bobby Mitchell,
then as now the Boss of the Bay

Acknowledgements

Thanks go to several cool people, specially to Chuck Thegze, who believed in it enough to help me sell it, and to Nansey Neiman, who bought it. And to Mar Mar for inspiration and advice. And, as they say, to a host of others without whom this would've been just another "good idea" . . .

Rick Abramson
Buddy Bob Alpert
Hope Antman
Ken Barnes
Jim Bickhart
Mr. "C"
Larry Caffo
Crescenzo Capece
Leigh Charlton
Don Chowder
Al Collins
Sidney L. Davis
El Cholo Restaurant
Jim Fishel
Gregg Geller
Jeff Gold
Rick Griffin
Terri Hinte
Eric & Hollywood Book and Poster

Humble Harv & Mama's Closet
David Leaf
Leah, Harriette & Joe
Mark Leviton
Major Bill Liebowitz
Hudson Marquez
Jim Marshall
Russ Meyer
Eric Monson
Tony Pipitone
The Pumping Piano Gang
Gabrielle Raumberger
Peter Reum
Bill Shinker
Gary Stewart
Theresa Volpe
Tom Zito

G.S.

CONTENTS

Notes on Cool
The Book Starts Here

**Now the roving gambler
he was very bored
Trying to create a next
world war
He found a promoter who
nearly fell off the floor
He said "I've never
engaged in this kind of
thing before"
—Bob Dylan,"Highway 61"**

Right now, we feel a little like that promoter. Not that we're up to anything here as earth-shaking as the next world war, but we may drop some bombs, light a few fires. And Bob Dylan's a good place to start when cool's the topic.

At his peak, writing and wailing "Highway 61" and "Like a Rolling Stone" at the world back in '65-66, Dylan occupied a cool place like no one else. Rebellious, flip, overflowing with mystery, he stood there on the backs of those album jackets in stovepipes and fruitboots, feeling behind those sunglasses like "some combination of sleepy john estes, jayne mansfield, humphrey bogart/mortimer snurd, murph the surf and so forth." Disengaged, out of time, resembling nothing that had come before, he stood alone, an incomparable icon of fresh style—cool.

But to get back to that promoter. We've never engaged in this kind of thing before, assembling all these personalities and pieces in one place and inviting everyone over. It's a pretty presumptuous gig. But somebody's got to do it.

"Hipsters, Flipsters and Finger-poppin' Daddies, knock me your lobes!" roars the late great rapper Lord Buckley in his hip-talk tribute to Shakespeare's *Julius Caesar.* "I came here to lay Caesar out, not to hip you to him!"

The Catalog of Cool comes to hip you to hundreds of items of enduring cool—books, magazines, movies, records, clothes, cars, diversions. Some may be familiar. Others have collected too much dust and not enough deserved attention and will come as surprises. There are lots of opportunities for discovery. You'll be formally introduced to the cool world of "correct" sunglasses; to the Cadillac Ranch, Cabazon's dinosaurs, and Louis Prima's "gleeby rhythms"; to customized Levis, paper dresses, Plastic Man; to Lenny Bruce's greatest riffs and Raymond Loewy's 1953 Studebaker Starliner coupe, "the most beautiful car ever

1

made in America" (see Chapter 8, Wheels).

The Catalog has a practical side, too. Each of the book's eight sections contains a "Shop Around" guide, offering where-to-buy leads, addresses, and advice. If you discover something here, we're assuming you'll want to learn more about it.

LOST THEIR COOL: San Francisco's Grateful Dead, preferable as proto-punks in '66 than as terminal hippies later. See Sounds for "Psychedelic Music."

So, just what is cool anyway?

Well, one look around will tell you what isn't cool: sponge-soft record charts, soapy translated-from-the-TV movies, non-books and non-magazines.

It's no secret. American culture is up to its pectorals in mediocrity, swamped with the second-rate. Brooke Shields passes for beauty. Humor is snickering en masse at sly marijuana references passed back and forth between lame disc jockeys and "hip" comedians.

Individual expression? Cal Klein and Jordache haul out a tire pump, inflate the image of a basic low-fashion garment (blue jeans) to bursting, then sell you the airburger as instant style. Here, have a bite.

In such an uncool world, true style—actions committed with some flair and cut with an edge, deeds that throw sparks or dare to display wit publicly—is hard to find.

Cool is not a fad or a fashion. Therefore, cool's enemies are not "preppy" or "punk" or next month's unearthed or invented sensibilities. Cool's beef is with misapplied style, false expression—attitudes and tastes that have nothing to do with the person who adopts them. Thousand-buck cowboy ensembles, idle jet-setters who send nanny out to find them New Wave togs for the cocktail party, "Fatigue chic." (You want khaki parachute pants? Enlist.)

To the outsider, the manifestations of cool may look arbitrary. That's because cool is selective in the way it reveals itself. It isn't elitist, but it knows its own. Cool never takes to the streets or billboards to proselytize; if you've got the goods, the mountain will eventually come to you.

True cool is eternal. Its independence from prevailing tastes is just one indication that cool follows its own mind for a reason. Like any deep faith, cool's flame burns, vanishes, reappears. Cool runs underground much of the time, but it never slows up. Like lightning, it links its past practitioners to its present with a flash and a fingersnap. Duchamp shakes hands with Dizzy Gillespie. Lenny Bruce cracks a line, Dylan cribs it in scribbling a song. A hundred years later, some seventeen-year-old girl poet will name a magazine after the song and publish a photo of Diz and Duchamp slapping five at Birdland. Cool reinvents its own wheel. It's a groove.

Cool has nothing to do with being "with it" or "in" by contemporary standards. If anything, like the holy fool, cool is often out of step. It's misunderstood (see our profile on George Hunter), persecuted (Bruce), or simply ignored in its time. True cool is nothing more (or less) than the fullest expression of what it is that's different or unique about a person. That's how the cool books get written, the cool movies away from here and invent your own version of cool.

That's what most of the characters celebrated in the *Catalog* did. That's why they're here, portrayed (hopefully) at the top of their distinctive forms. We'll hip you to Sam Peckinpah's warped Western series (see Chapter 7, Tube), to the Shanels' Japanese doowop music (Chapter 1, Sounds). Our Ink chapter clues you in to Doris Piserchia's

COOL REGAINED: *Batman,* twice as much fun in reruns. See *Tube* for "The Gone Shows."
Hamerschlagg Collection

made. Someone taps his uniqueness and liberally invests his creations with it. When those creations or expressions achieve maximum impact, that's cool. Imagination counts.

"Uniqueness"? "Fullest expression"? We'd better stop now, before we devolve into pop psych and start soliciting memberships and taking up collections.

The point here should be fairly obvious: Learning everything that's between these covers won't *make you cool,* any more than it's made any of us cool. (Just look!) You are cool if you go

sci-fi P.I. Mr. Justice and to that Terry Southern story about Boris and Priscilla and their pals pushing that gone globe of mercury around the floor.

We start, appropriately, at the beginning—with jazz. In New York. In the late Forties. Our man was there and wants to tell you about it in an essay entitled "The Birth of the Cool."

It falls to the grand Lord Richard Buckley to provide our invocation. As Mr. Rabadee said to the All Hip Mahatma, "Straighten me, 'cause I'm ready!"

—G.S.

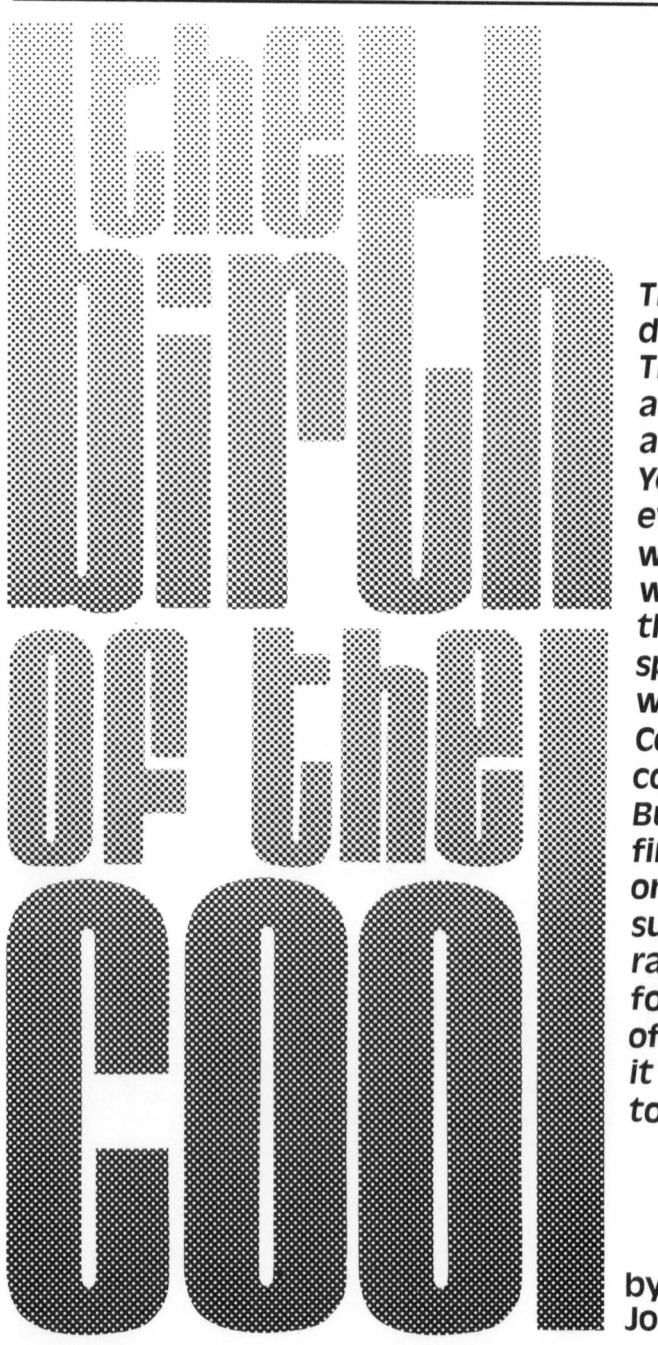

the birth of the cool

The A Train
departs.
The world
awaits
a new lick.
Years later,
everyone else
will find a
way to put
their own
spin to the
word "cool."
Cool this,
cool that.
But when it
first arrives,
on a
subterranean
rail headed
for the heart
of Bop City,
it belongs
to jazz alone.

by
Joe Goldberg

Jazz musicians were probably the first people to use the word *cool* who weren't talking about the weather.

You can probably get an argument about it, as you can about most things involving jazz slang (and therefore jazz sociology), but it seems likely that the use of the word *cool* to describe a desirable attitude or mode of behavior goes back to the beboppers. Anything but cool, they were in revolt against Louis Armstrong and his epoch-making recordings of a scant 20 years before, recordings made by a group that called itself "Louis Armstrong and His Hot Five," expanded on occasion to a "Hot Seven." In the interim Armstrong had become synonymous with "hot jazz," so obviously musicians concerned with overturning Armstrong's primacy couldn't call themselves "hot," no matter how blazing they were.

Slang, and the in-group behavior it stems from, are both based on that principle of exclusion. So it is probably no accident that early recordings by the two founders of bebop have *cool* in the title: Charlie Parker's *Cool Blues* and Dizzy Gillespie's *Cool Breeze*. Both were recorded in 1947.

The principle of exclusion may have been operating in the music, too. Drummer Kenny Clarke, who played in the after-hours Harlem sessions at Minton's Playhouse and Monroe's Uptown House where bop began, has been quoted as saying that he and his colleagues adopted the new, complex chord progressions as a way of assuring that unwanted outsiders wouldn't be able to sit in with them. But the late Thelonious Monk, for so long mistakenly thought of as a bebopper because he was the house pianist at Minton's at the time, was probably closer to the truth when he told jazz journalist Nat Hentoff, "I was just trying to play a gig, trying to play music. While I was at Minton's anybody sat in if he could play. I never bothered anybody. I had no particular feeling that anything new was being built. It's true modern jazz began to get popular there, but some of these histories and articles put what happened over the course of ten years into one year. They put people all together in one time in one place. I've seen practically everybody at Minton's, but they were just there playing. They weren't giving any lectures."

As usual, Monk is probably right. A Columbia University student named Jerry Newman, who may have been the first record bootlegger, used to go to the nearby Harlem clubs with a wire recorder (tape wasn't invented yet), and some of what he captured has since been commercially released. Among the treasures is a recording of Monk playing with the great guitarist Charlie Christian at Minton's in 1941; from the same year, there is a Gillespie recording made at Monroe's and named for another Columbia student who used to hang out there. The eponymous student, since better known, was Jack Kerouac.

I know why Kerouac was there. Some years later, on summer vacations from high school and college, I was there myself. Not at Monroe's or Minton's, but at the Royal Roost (so called because it featured chicken-in-a-basket), Bop City, Birdland (when it opened), and, most especially for me, an upstairs room of a Chinese place on West 52nd Street

There is a Gillespie recording made at Monroe's and named for another Columbia student who used to hang out there. The eponymic student, since better known, was Jack Kerouac.

called—and I beg you to believe it—the Sing Song Room of the Confucius Restaurant. I hasten to add that this was not the 52nd Street of song and story; it was three blocks over from that, next door to the ANTA Theatre.

I remember the Sing Song Room mostly because Lennie Tristano was there on occasion. In the days when *cool, hip,* and *cerebral* were all vaguely synonymous terms, no one was more any of those things than Tristano, a white, blind jazz pianist whose group usually included alto saxophonist Lee Konitz.

Kerouac wrote of following Konitz around, and, years later, I was amazed to learn that Konitz was only five years older than me. In those days, I thought he was a god. He was the first musician I ever got up nerve enough to speak to.

Our great meeting took place in the men's room of The Royal Roost, into which I had followed him for what I think were asexual, if worshipful reasons.

We both looked our best—he, I now realize, because he was proud to be playing with Tristano in the hippest club in the hippest city in the world, and him barely old enough to work in a joint where they sold booze. And me, because I was there.

Let me tell you what we looked like.

Konitz looked like a scholarly young businessman. A lot of that effect came from his heavy horn-rimmed glasses, also known as bop glasses because Dizzy Gillespie wore them. (Dizzy Gillespie was such a trend setter that many young musicians with excellent eyesight bought heavy horn-rimmed frames with window glass in them. In fact, he was such a trend setter that when a picture in a jazz magazine showed him with the top button of his trousers accidentally unbuttoned, many young musicians started going around that way, in danger of losing their pants.) Konitz also wore, as I recall, a

white Oxford cloth shirt, a black knit tie, and a light garbardine suit. He could have been a young stockbroker.

I was in my uniform, the basic component of which was a camel's hair cardigan jacket lacking both collar and lapels, with wide stitching on all the edges. It was what the Woody Herman band wore, and I think now that anyone not holding a horn in hand would probably look ridiculous in one. But in those days you had to have one, and I did. You also had to have a spread-collar shirt, one whose collar points were so wide apart that they were almost parallel to the ground. (If the collar also had a large roll, it was called a Mr. B after Billy Eckstine, who popularized that version.) The reason for the wide spread was to accommodate a Windsor knot, named for the Duke of Windsor, who had supposedly invented it.

The Windsor knot looked like a symmetrical V, rather than the regular lopsided four-in-hand. Some necktie manufacturers embellished on this by making solid-knot ties—ties that were patterned except in the part where you tied the knot. There they reverted to a single background color. You had to tie the knot just so, or you wouldn't get the right effect. The alternative to the solid-knot was an open-weave knit tie with a white stripe down the middle and a different color on each side.

The shirts invariably had French cuffs, with cufflinks of metal that went all the way *around* the cuff like a clasp, to end on the other side. The really hip New York shirtmakers, like John Blye, went to outrageous excess. They would make wide *button-down* spread-collar shirts with French cuffs. Can you imagine? Button-downs with French cuffs. Talk about dichotomy, boy.

The pants were pegged, of course, and a lot of them extended above the belt line. The belt itself was as narrow

**Cooled Out, Circa 1950.
Uniform for the complete
hipster.**
From the top:
1. Bop glasses
2. Spread-collar shirt. Points
   parallel to the ground, please.
3. Lapel-less, collar-less
   Cardigan jacket. Two-button.
4. Solid-knot tie.
5. Solid-color handkerchief. No
   points.
6. Narrow belt, worn to one side.
7. Pegged, pleated trousers, with
   cuffs.
8. Clasp cufflinks.

Optional: keychain, attached to
belt loop, tucked in pocket.

**There were several stores
along Broadway
displaying these
wonders. The hippest of
them all but, sadly, a
world I never made, was
Phil Kronfeld. In the
conformist Fifties, Phil
Kronfeld used to show a
suit in his window that
looked like a Lenny Bruce
parody of the regimental
banker's gray flannel.**

as possible, and the buckle was worn
off to the side, to show that you didn't
really need the belt. The socks were
Argyle, and the shoes could come from
only one place, Flagg Brothers. They
were called flaps, which I suspect is a
corruption of Flaggs, and they were the
heaviest, squarest-toed, deadliest
things you ever saw, with thick, wide
soles and a capacity to do great injury.
There were several stores along
Broadway displaying these wonders.

The hippest of them all but, sadly, a world I never made, was Phil Kronfeld. In the conformist Fifties, Phil Kronfeld used to show a suit in his window that looked like a Lenny Bruce parody of the regimental banker's gray flannel. It was gray, all right, but not the dark Wall Street-shadowed gray. It was light gray, as light as your mother's hair, and it was single-breasted, in a time when double-breasteds were still the thing. Most outrageous of all, it only had one button. *One button!* Do you understand what that means? Can you visualize how deep the cleavage went, how much of your solid-knot tie it showed? One thing that will bother me until the day I die is that I never owned a Phil Kronfeld suit.

Anyway, there we were, Konitz and I, side by side at the Roost, pissing in the john. I don't remember what I said to him, or, far more important, what he said to me. It probably doesn't matter anyway. All I wanted was to be in the Presence, and I hoped the power would rub off.

And that's not quite the adolescent fantasy you might think. Power does rub off. Cool jazz was growing out of white-hot bebop even as I was standing around wondering how I should dress, and with some of the same practitioners. Gillespie and Parker, like other revolutionaries, were learning that they would be foolish to think the revolution stopped with them.

There is a collection of 78's made for Capitol under Miles Davis' name that has been released on LP, with some justice, as *Birth of the Cool.* Certainly the great names are there. Besides Miles and Konitz, there are Gerry Mulligan, John Lewis, Kenny Clarke, and Gil Evans, among others. These tracks are the outgrowth of a nine-piece rehearsal band that played one live engagement for two weeks at the Roost in 1948. Miles Davis was called the leader, and that by virtue of the fact

that, having played with Parker, he was the best known. Lewis and Clarke—and yes, they were explorers—were part of the rhythm section of Dizzy Gillespie's big band and would later become half of the Modern Jazz Quartet. But even before that, in 1947, Gil Evans, arranging for the big band of Claude Thornhill, did three charts on Charlie Parker tunes that featured solos by Konitz, as startling now as they were then. These were the initial (and are probably the continuing) standard by which to define cool jazz.

Charlie Parker died in 1955, so that is considered the landmark year of the decade. But he had done his major work a good bit before then, and the two halves of the music he spawned split like an amoeba in 1954. Parker was half Kansas City (cool Lester Young) and half blues honkers. His influence was greater than anyone's before or since—"Behold, he doth bestride the narrow world like a Colossus," as the fella said—and musicians were taking off chunks of his style and fashioning entirely new things from it. Miles Davis, his protege, had announced them both, one with the *Birth of the Cool* LP, the other with a down-home blues called "Walkin'."

"Walkin'" spawned a movement that was at first called hard bop, to distinguish it from bebop, and, sometime after that, funk. It was bop stripped to its basics, with the several intricate tones that Parker had employed removed and only the blues changes remaining. Art Blakey and Horace Silver were two of its earliest proselytizers. Sonny Rollins came in there too, and later there was "Cannonball" Adderley. Not accidentally, all of them had worked with Miles, who, like Walt Whitman, contradicted himself and contained multitudes.

At the same time, a reaction to this trend was growing, one that eventually became known as cool jazz, but which must now be considered as primarily white backlash. In a way, its spiritual father was saxophonist Lester Young, whose light, floating, horizontal lines were the prime influence on the "Four Brothers" sound of the Woody Herman saxophone section—containing at various times Stan Getz, Zoot Sims, Jimmy Giuffre, and Herbie Steward. That makes Young, who says he was influenced by Frank Trumbauer, the C-melody saxophonist who worked with Bix Beiderbecke, a rare instance of a great black musician influenced by a white who primarily influenced whites.

That Herman band sound was one origin of cool, with Getz probably the single greatest influence on saxophonists of the time. Gil Evans and those Miles Davis Capitol recordings are others, but the greatest breeding ground for cool players was the Stan

For a while, cool and West Coast were practically synonymous terms. "White faggoty jazz" was another description applied to the new sound by a well-known East Coast black bebopper.

Kenton orchestra.

For a while, *cool* and *West Coast* were practically synonymous terms. "White faggoty jazz" was another description applied to the new sound by a well-known East Coast black bebopper. Most of its best-known practitioners were in the Kenton band at one time or another. Shelley Manne, Shorty Rogers, Bob Cooper, Gerry Mulligan, Frank Rosolino, Howard Rumsey . . . the list goes on. The entire band was white, so it should have come as no surprise when Kenton, in the last years of his life, advocated the presidency of

George Wallace. Eventually, the movement succumbed to terminal preciousness, as when Bob Cooper and Bud Shank recorded a quintet LP that featured flute and oboe, but before it went down, cool spawned its mavericks, who are (no surprise either) still around. These include Gerry Mulligan and his instant star trumpeter, Chet Baker; guitarist Jim Hall, who first became known playing with the quintessentially cool Chico Hamilton Quintet; and John Lewis. And Lee Konitz. But perhaps the most remarkable and, in his diffident way, unsung of these is the great alto saxophonist Paul Desmond, who spent so much of his professional life with Dave Brubeck and always sounded as though his basic method had been derived from the few records Lester Young made on clarinet.

It's not altogether that easy to pin down cool, which went out of fashion about as quickly as the extreme Ivy League clothing most of its practitioners wore. At one time, one of its Great White Hopes was Kenton altoist Art Pepper, who emerged from the cleansing fires of dopes, prison, and Synanon as the Great White Survivor, sounding a lot like John Coltrane and canonized as a kind of cross between George Burns and Richard Pryor.

And I remember something else: a single released in the late Forties by the intermission singer at the Royal Roost, Harry Belafonte, called "Lean On Me." It featured an instrumental break by a tenor saxophonist named Brew Moore that was as light, dancing, lovely, and Lester Young-derived as anything to come out of the cool movement.

So maybe I have no more idea of the origins of cool than I have of the subsequent career of Brew Moore.

I do know one thing, though. If Brew Moore is around, he would no more want to feel responsible for Kool and the Gang than Charlie Parker would for Bebop Deluxe.

Lives of the Hipster Saints:

AL "JAZZBEAUX" COLLINS

It's late.
In the background,
a piano plays a
drowsy blues.
Then a voice.

"People ask me what it looks like down in the Grotto, and I haven't really said too much about it lately, I guess, but one of the main things is that in order to get here you've got to come down a long kind of underground tube that leads in from street level. At Forty-second and Third. You crawl in on a tube over which there's a burlap sack hanging down. That's to keep the wind and cold air from blowing in. And then you are immediately in the main cave room, which is hemispherical and looks almost vaulted at the highest point . . . about twenty feet above the Grotto floor, which is flat and dry.

"And the Big Ben stalagtite, which is

10

the largest one of several, comes down fifteen feet from the ceiling. And then there are smaller ones growing up from the floor of the Grotto—and one is about five feet, six feet high—and those are stalagmites. If they ever connect, they're called columns, and we have three of these, where a stalagtite and a stalagmite have . . . grown together. It's very rare, but we have 'em."

The piano shimmers. The voice resumes. " And at the top of the Grotto it's very dark purple, almost black. And then it starts getting progressively light as it goes down the side, [piano] getting into the various shades of purple, mauve, magenta, taupe, and all those. And then if you look over to the left side you will see a mushroom patch growing there of the Purpulus grottus variety, and they're about four feet in diameter. They're huge. And that's where I got the idea to have Purple Grotto-burgers. I was gonna have a series around town underneath the ground where you go in and have a Grotto-burger. 'Cause mushrooms . . . are very much like steak—filet mignon . . . if you get a good mushroom. And these are the best . . .

"Over on the extreme right there's a pit of fluid that's almost like a small lake. And it's a fluid that has not been analyzed as yet. It's thick, and we've plumbed the depths to about two

hundred fifty, three hundred feet with lead weights and wire, and there's no sounding the bottom. So that's one of the reasons no people are allowed down in the Grotto. I just can't get insurance for a place like this . . ."

What? Where are we? For all the sense it's making, it might as well be Mars in 2856, or maybe 7680. But we're in New York City, in 1982. It's four in the morning; we're tuned to radio station WNEW, and the piano, the voice, and the way-out word jazz belong to Al "Jazzbeaux" Collins.

Cool may not even be the word for Collins. He's of it, inside it, beyond cool. Just ask the Jazzbeaux multitudes, Al's Pals —they must number in the hundreds of thousands by now—gathered around radios in San Francisco, Salt Lake, and L.A., where they're waiting for him to return, as if to ask, "Did it really happen?" It did. It does, week-nightly, midnight to 5:30 A.M., now in New York, just as it did from 1950 to 1960.

Back then they turned to Jazzbeaux for jazz. He was in the clubs, at Birdland and the Hickory House, down at the downbeat offices, digging, and he was on the air laying a taste on the ears—Dizzy Gillespie, Charlie Parker, Sinatra and Shearing and Peggy Lee, and Slim Gaillard doing that whole "mello-roony" rap about "Ce-ment mix-er, putty putty."

But if it's music that brought 'em in, it was Jazzbeaux (then "Jazzbo") who kept them coming back, with an announcing style so laid back it was four winks west of Sominex, but so hip. Snooze and you lose, 'cause what he's saying at that crazy half-speed is twice as gone as any other disc jockey you've ever heard.

It all started at the University of Miami in 1941 with the line "What's new at the 'U'? This is Al Collins, and here's Professor Hoo-ha." Subbing for a fellow student, Collins made his radio debut on the college station by accident. No matter. After reading the line, standing for the first time in the studio control room "with the lights, the 'On the air' signals, the engineer, the mike, the drama of the thing hit me with a bursting brilliance. And I said to myself, 'Hey. Whew! What a scene. I think I would like to do this.' "

At Chicago's WIND a few years later, his engineer suggested Collins use something with the word *jazz* to title his program, which was, after all, a jazz show. A product of the day, a clip-on bow tie called Jazzbows, did the trick. "I went on the air that night," Collins remembers, "and said, 'Hi, this is Jazzbeaux here with some really fine music.' And the phones started ringing and everybody wanted to know 'Who's Jazzbeaux?' I said, 'Heck, it's a really good handle."

The handle helped get Collins to WNEW in 1950. He recalls a night there, too.

"I started my broadcast in Studio One which was painted all kinds of tints and shades of purple on huge polycylindricals which were vertically placed around the walls of the room to deflect the sound. It just happened to be that way. And with the turntables and desk and console and the lights turned down low, it had a very cavelike appearance to my imagination. So I got on the air, and the first thing I said was, 'Hi, it's Jazzbeaux in the Purple Grotto.' You never know where your thoughts are coming from, but the way it came out was that I was in a grotto, in this atmosphere with stalagtites and a lake and no telephones. I was using Nat Cole underneath me with 'Easy Listening Blues' playing piano in the background."

For fun, Collins gave the Grotto its own bestiary—Harrison the Tasmanian Owl, who dug Paul Desmond and Brubeck; Jukes, a female chameleon who went for swing; Clyde, a Dixieland-digging crow; and a flamingo named Leah, who, Jazzbeaux told his listeners, liked "music to fly by."

The combination hit hip Manhattanites like a saucer from the spheres; within days, fans began showing up at 'NEW demanding to be taken down-

> # For fun, Collins gave the Grotto its own bestiary—Harrison the Tasmanian Owl, who dug Paul Desmond and Brubeck; Jukes, a female chameleon who went for swing; Clyde, a Dixieland-digging crow; and a flamingo named Leah, who, Jazzbeaux told his listeners, liked "music to fly by."

stairs to the Purple Grotto.

Collins capitalized on his radio fame in 1954, cutting a series of "Great Moments in Hipstery" bop-talk records for Capitol. "Little Red Riding Hood" was his hit, but "Discovery of America" had some choice lines. On Columbus, "hanging out at the royal court in Spain": "Chris has been on the scene for months and there's one thing on his mind: boats. It was then that he met Queen Isabella, who had only one thing on her mind: (ahem). In short, she had bulging eyes for our man. In fact, she was verily flipping her coronet for Mr. C . . ."

Jazzbeaux split for San Francisco in 1960 (where he was to stay until 1969). He kicked things off at KSFO there with the "Collins on a Cloud" show. To the accompaniment of dreamy harp

music, Collins "floated" over the city, looking down and grooving on the bridges, ships, and scenes.

From '60 to '62 he had his own TV show on the local ABC affiliate, mornings at 8:30 right after the *Crusader Rabbit* cartoons and before Jack La-Lanne's warmups. Many viewers (this one included) couldn't quite believe their eyes or ears. Here was Collins, in sky-blue jumpsuits, interviewing celebrities, politicians, sheikhs, musicians, and Third Street bums as they sat in a barber chair. Here were impromptu studio performances by the entire Count Basie Band, Louis Prima, Jackie Mason, and others.

"The producer of the show and I would drive down the street in San Francisco. If we saw anybody that looked like a character—or anybody that looked different from everybody else—we'd yell at them, 'Seven o'clock tomorrow morning at Channel Seven. Be there!' We got great guests—one pirate-looking guy with a wooden leg who walked around like Captain Hook."

A central part of the TV program was the (sometimes multiple) screening(s) of the scene from *Treasure of the Sierra Madre* where Mexican actor Alfonso Bedoya tells Bogart, "Badges? [pronounced botches] I don't have to show you any stinking badges!" The line has delighted Collins for twenty years. He liked it so much, in fact, that in 1970,

while at Los Angeles' KFI, he convinced city fathers in suburban Sierra Madre to help him stage a festival for the faithful. Twenty-five thousand showed up to nosh with their hero, attend art exhibits, and enjoy round-the-clock showings of the movie at the town's Humphrey Bogart Theatre.

Late in 1981, Jazzbeaux left Frisco's KGO to return to 'NEW. Re-ensconced in the Purple Grotto, he's once again mild and woolly in New York—fading out a Coleman Hawkins side to deliver an impromptu dissertation on the virtues of egg-drop soup ("A lot of people misunderstand it. It's best when it gets into a gelatinous kind of feeling, if you know what I mean."), plugging a small-press poetry mag, inviting character-callers like the Baron of Bleecker Street to phone in.

The Baron is the head of Società Mangione ("the society of people who love to eat"), the first New York chapter of Al's Pals, more than three hundred individual special interest clubs formed by Jazzbeaux buffs across the country.

"That whole thing started in San Francisco," says Al. "We were having a bad drought, and one night this lady called up the show. Her name was Olga, and she talked like Zsa Zsa Gabor. She was off the wall, to put it mildly. She'd go out in the morning in Bodega Bay, where she lived, and greet the tide with a sign that said 'Welcome In, Tide,' and she'd perfume some of the flowers that had no original scent. She went out with a pitch pipe and gave the hummingbirds the right note so they wouldn't be out of tune. So she called one night and said, 'Jazzbeaux dahling, if you want to have water, you must have frogs. Everybody knows that where frogs are, there's water, so if everybody gets a pair of frogs and puts them in their back yards, soon we'll have water.'

"So I said, 'Gee, that's a great idea, Olga.' And I hung up. About ten minutes later a guy named Mike calls and says 'Al, I have an albino frog with pink eyes, and I'd like to be a member of the frog club.' So I said, 'Listen, Mike, if you've got a pink frog with red eyes or whatever, I think you should be the president of the Frogonians.' He agreed, I gave his address, and in a week he had about forty-five letters from people. And today it's still going and he's got over ten thousand registered members."

She'd go out in the morning in Bodega Bay, where she lived, and greet the tide with a sign that said 'Welcome In, Tide,' and she'd perfume some of the flowers that had no original scent. She went out with a pitch pipe and gave the hummingbirds the right note so they wouldn't be out of tune.

Jazzbeaux's Directory of Majuberized Presidents lists names and addresses of them all, from barbed wire collector chapters and members of the Bridge Toll-Takers Association to the "Show Me Your Town Postcard Exchange" chapter and the Tobacco Chewers of America. "People who collect spatulas, people who are ex-fighter pilots . . . for a stamped, self-addressed envelope they can get in touch with other people who have the same interests." (Would-be Sharkonians and False Eyelash fanciers can get the *Directory* by sending the SASE and a one-buck donation to Al's Pals, P.O. Box 9999, Walnut Creek, California 94596.)

Jazzbeaux seems pleased just to keep it all spinning, from behind his pickle barrel in the Grotto. The calibrated candle's white and purple rings tick off the minutes in a slow burn beneath Forty-second and Third. On the turntable something cool from the West Coast spins. The lights dim.

". . . And then there are three lesser caves that you can see in the background if you look straight ahead in the Grotto. These are occupied by Doctors Hunyati, Cherumbolo, and Caligari. As a matter of fact, Caligari is up tonight, sanding down some of the small cabinets he's making. Dr. Hunyati, of course, is the famous piano tuner who developed that pinkie cream for pianists, and Dr. Victor T. Cherumbolo you know as the fellow who helps out at the planetarium . . . and shows people where the different planets are, 'cause he's from there."

A number of commercial Jazzbeaux projects are currently in the works or already in the stores and on the shelves. These include *The International Jazzbeaux,* an updating of his Fifties hip-talk records on a new album; *Just a Little Taste,* a Collins recipe book published by Al's Pals; and *Tales from the Purple Grotto: Cool Jazz and Good Times in Broadcasting,* an autobiography with a foreword by Steve Allen. *Just a Little Taste* is available in stores or direct from the publisher: $12, to Betty Graham, 947 Pinole Valley Road, Pinole, California 94564 (allow four to six weeks for delivery). *Tales from the Purple Grotto* is likewise on the shelves; for more information, write Troubadour Press, 385 Fremont Street, San Francisco, California 94105.

So Spector starts drumming on the big coffee table there with the flat of his hand in time to Susskind's voice and says, "What you're missing is the beat." Blam blam!

— Tom Wolfe
The Kandy-Kolored Tangerine-Flake Streamline Baby

Blam! Can't miss the beat. It starts here, with the following list and lowdown on music creatures who count. Half a dozen different schools of cool are represented in the all-purpose grooves-guide called

who's COOL MUSIC in

ABBA ★ Sweden's frosty foursome has poured the best since '73: bubblegum on ice, from "Waterloo" and "S.O.S." to "Dancing Queen" and "Fernando." Polar pop.

Best buy: *The Magic of Abba* (K-Tel, sixteen hits, '73-79). Wholesome goodness: *Arrival; Waterloo; The Visitors* (Atlantic).

JOHNNY ACE ★ Bang bang. Rock and roll's first suicide played his last game of Russian roulette on Christmas Eve 1954 in Houston. Posthumous hit "Pledging My Love" was his biggest.

Johnny Ace Memorial Album (MCA).

MOSE ALLISON ★ Arguably the first hip honky, Tippo, Mississippi's fave son favored laid back piano blues with titles like "Crepuscular Air" and "Your Mind Is on Vacation (and Your Mouth Is Working Overtime)." Eminently cool.

17

Best of Mose Allison (Atlantic); Local Color and Back Country Suite (both Prestige).

SYD BARRETT ★ Britain's first "acid genius" touched down long enough to found Pink Floyd (1967), then flipped his wig. Bent classics: "See Emily Play" (and the rest of Floyd's first LP), Barrett solos "Dominoes" and "Baby Lemonade."

Budget two-fers: A Nice Pair (Pink Floyd's Piper at the Gates of Dawn/Saucerful of Secrets); Madcap Laughs/Barrett (all Capitol).

BEACH BOYS ★ None cooler on the Coast, 1962-66.

Essential: Surfin' USA; Little Deuce Coupe; All Summer Long; Today; Pet Sounds; Wild Honey (Capitol). Dessert: Summer Days and Summer Nights; Friends; 20/20 (Capitol); Sunflower (Reprise). Past Blasts: Beach Boys/Brian Wilson Rarities (Australian EMI). Cheap Introductions: Endless Summer; Spirit of America; Greatest Hits (Capitol budget sets).

BEATLES ★ For their first album they created the Anti Beatles ("I Wanna Be Your Man" was the Stones' first hit). Last cool record: Revolver, which did not need a lyric sheet.

CAPTAIN BEEFHEART & HIS MAGIC BAND ★ "Equal parts Howlin' Wolf and Albert Ayler," Rolling Stone said. Unsaid: how humans could generate song-noise as radiant as "Electricity" or "Sheriff of Hong Kong." "Harry Irene," says C.B., "is about four lesbians and a tavern." Do the Candle Mambo.

Latest: Ice Cream for Crow (Virgin); Doc at the Radar Station (Virgin, 1980). Greatest: Trout Mask Replica (Reprise); Safe as Milk (Buddah); Shiny Beast (Warners). Rarest: Clear Spot; Lick My Decals Off, Baby (Reprise).

ARCHIE BELL & THE DRELLS ★ "I got ten notches on my shoes," brags the terpischorean topcat of "(There's Gonna Be a) Showdown" (1969). Dancin' fools.

Deleted LPs: Tighten Up; I Just Can't Stop Dancing; (There's Gonna Be a) Showdown (Atlantic).

Beach Boys

B-52's

B-52'S ★ They sing of lava, lobsters, strobes, and space. Their "52 Girls" lists only twenty-three. They do all sixteen dances. Extra cool: on "Cake," Cindy Wilson sounds like Morgan Fairchild.

The B-52's (featuring "Rock Lobster"); *Wild Planet* ("Private Idaho"); *Mesopotamia* (EP, includes "Cake") (all Warners).

BLONDIE ★ In the Seventies, they were the most efficient Sixties trash compacters ("X Offender," "Denis"). Now they make their own, sometimes demented ("Victor"), always coolly detached (*Autoamerican,* Deborah Harry's underrated *Koo Koo*). Pass the irony.

Best: *Blondie; Parallel Lines; Eat to the Beat; Koo Koo.* Rest: *Plastic Letters; Autoamerican; Best Of* (Chrysalis).

GARY U.S. BONDS ★ Bonds parties so far out of bounds, his best tracks ("Quarter to Three," "Dear Lady Twist") resemble dancehall brawls put to tape. Volume and spirits exceed allowable limits, even for 1961. Uncoolest cuts: '81's comeback LP *Dedication.*

Rock's Revolution: The Roots (Legrand) includes five Bonds hits. *Certified Soul* (Rhino) offers strong Bonds R&B from '68–70.

JAMES BROWN ★ Unmeasurably cool for making dance music with titles like "Funky Watergate (People It's Bad)" and "Get Up, Get into It, Get Involved, Part I." Soul Bro Number One's best is newly available on two Solid Smoke

Deborah Harry

19

The Byrds

lps: *Live and Lowdown at the Apollo, Volume 1* and *Can Your Heart Stand It — James Brown's Greatest Hits.*

ROY BROWN ★ The late New Orleans bluesologist who gave Elvis "Good Rockin' Tonite" swung like sixty. The urgency of punk, the passion of the boss balladeers, it's all in *Laughing but Crying* and *Good Rockin' Tonite* (Route 66 imports).

JERRY BUTLER ★ Chicago's Ice Man delivered almost daily between 1960 and 1970: polished pre-Soul on "He Will Break Your Heart" and "Make It Easy on Yourself," Philly class on "Moody Woman" and "What's The Use of Breaking Up."

Early times: *Up on Love* (Charly R&B import). Modernist: *Ice on Ice* (Mercury).

BYRDS ★ "The first really outrageous, long-haired group in America," Nik Cohn says in *Rock from the Beginning.* "Their stance was classic West Coast cool, deadpan and remote." Their folk-rock ('65–67) buzzed with beauty and wonder.

Recorded by THE CAPITOLS on Karen Records

COOL JERK

"They know I'm the hippest cat..."

Joe King Carrasco

Nice-priced originals: *Mr. Tambourine Man; Turn! Turn! Turn!; Younger Than Yesterday; Fifth Dimension* (Columbia).

JOHN CALE ★ Always an iconoclast, the Velvet Underground's brooding Welshman was ready for war before Haig ("Mercenaries," off 1979's *Sabotage/Live*). His *Guts* LP contains "Pablo Picasso (Was Never an Asshole)."

Fear; Slow Dazzle (Island); *Vintage Violence* (Columbia); *Sabotage/Live* (IRS).

JOE "KING" CARRASCO & THE CROWNS ★ His stated aim is "to write a song as good as '96 Tears.'" Not only do the guitarist and his Texan "Mexi-punk" group succeed ("Houston El Mover"), in 1982 they gave the wildest rock 'n' roll shows going. Keep on dancin'.

Latest: *Synapse Gap (Mundo Total)* (MCA); *Joe "King" Carrasco & The Crowns* (Hannibal).

GENE CHANDLER ★ Wearing cape and top hat, he proclaimed himself Duke of Earl in 1962 with one majestic single. His "dukedom" once included weather itself ("Rainbow"). The deposed Duke now makes dull funk.

Just Be True (featuring "Duke of Earl," "Nite Owl," "Rainbow") (Charly R&B import).

CLIFTON CHENIER ★ Beans 'n' rice aside, Louisiana's greatest cultural contribution may be an accordion-playing black Cajun who wears gold crowns on his teeth and his head. French patois meets bayou backbeat and all's well on the dance floor.

Louisiana Blues and Zydeco (Arhoolie); *Zydeco 'n' Boogie* (Maison du Soul); *Clifton Chenier Live* (Arhoolie).

EDDIE COCHRAN ★ Too young to vote, a bad white boy in blue suedes and pink pegged slacks. America's first punk ('58) was somethin' else.

Eddie Cochran — Legendary Masters Series #4 (United Artists), double LP featuring "Summertime Blues," "C'mon

Everybody," "Nervous Breakdown," and all the rest.

SAM COOKE ★ Too cool to cop a handle like "the Godfather of Soul," he nonetheless paved the way for the changes that came. Still sending, as long as there are ears to hear the voice of a lifetime. R.I.P.

The Legendary Sam Cooke feat. "You Send Me," "Another Saturday Night,"

Sam Cooke

"Cupid," "Chain Gang," "Bring It on Home to Me," "Only Sixteen," etc. (RCA Special Products).

ELVIS COSTELLO ★ Pressure-cooked cool. Later for Bowie, Springsteen, Seger. The only true original the Seventies coughed up wore white knuckles, Holly's specs, and wailed on the couplet "Look at the man that you call Uncle/Having a heart attack 'round your ankles."

Trust; Get Happy!; Armed Forces; This Year's Model (Columbia).

THE CRAMPS ★ The Munsters walk into Sears and split with axes and amps. Monsterbilly rhythms at their insane, insatiable best, all for you in '82. Great goo-goo muck: "I Was a Teenage Werewolf," "Zombie Dance," "Sunglasses after Dark."

Songs the Lord Taught Us; Psychedelic Jungle (IRS).

THE DAMNED ★ The brazen apex of British punk circa '76–77, sighted, fixed, then torched in one vaingloriously destructo album *(Damned)*. They still make great noise, but how do you top the hilarious fury of "New Rose" or "Born To Kill"?

Damned (Stiff import); *Machine Gun Etiquette* (Chiswick import); *Damned (The Black Album)* (IRS).

BOBBY DARIN ★ He couldn't decide if he wanted to be Ray Charles ("Irresistible You") or Frank Sinatra ("Mack the Knife"). Bonus cool: he also got to be Buddy Holly (he penned Holly's hit "Early in the Morning"), the Mormon Tabernacle Choir (his Christmas LP *25th Day of December*), and an exceptional actor *(Captain Newman, M.D., Pressure Point)*.

The Legendary Bobby Darin: greatest hits (Candlelite Music, Box 2, Town Center Branch, West Orange, New Jersey 07052). Worth hunting down: *This Is Darin; Twist with Bobby Darin* (Atco).

BO DIDDLEY ★ Rock's seminal silly man was also its first overweight guitarist hero. In a cowboy hat and leather breeches, he invented British R&B (the Stones cut "Mona" and "Roadrunner" in '64) and American rap ("Say Man," 1959) and patented a beat that has yet to stop.

Legends of Rock — Bo Diddley, double LP, German Chess import.

DION ★ In 1962 he gave the world the Cool Guys' national anthem, "The Wanderer." Ten years later, on the Bel-monts' Madison Square Garden *Reunion* album, after delivering the line "I get around," he tops himself, interjecting, "Jack, get around!" Hear it and know the meaning of cool.

Dion's Greatest Hits (Columbia); *60 Greatest of Dion & The Belmonts* (Canadian Prom-tel); *Reunion* (Warner Brothers). Dion's hits are available on Columbia's Hall of Fame singles series.

THE DOORS ★ Jim Morrison had the courage to make a fool of himself, often and in public. See "Land Ho!" and "Peace Frog." Lizards unite.

Real goods: *The Doors; Morrison Hotel; L.A. Woman; 13* (Elektra).

DOOWOP ★ grew in the street, right up through the concrete, to become the

Dion

Michael Ochs Archives

23

sound of the cities in the Fifties. Babbling towers of harmony were erected by the unlikeliest architects: adenoidal crooners, pimply mooks in fluorescent cardigans, underage tenors. By '63 they were all gone — but not forgotten. Today, doowop's resurging. Relic and Crystal Ball have released dozens of vintage compilations, while Ambient Sound cuts old groups anew and brandishes the slogan "The Sound of Human America."

Cheap intro's: Lost-Nite offers twenty-five budget ten-inch mini-albums featuring the Five Satins, Teen Chords, El Doradoes, and others. Ambient Sound's best: the sampler *Everything New Is Old,* plus the Capris' *There's a Moon Out Again!,* Jive Five's *Here We Are,* Randy & the Rainbows' *C'mon Let's Go!* Due soon: the Flamingos (Solid Smoke).

THE EVERLY BROTHERS ★ They made hillbilly music cool, through genetic engineering and gobs of pomade.

The Magical Golden Hits of the Everly Brothers, double mail order LP (Candlelite Music), covers from '57 ("Bye Bye Love") to '67 ("Bowling Green").

THE FLAMINGOS ★ Sometimes "I Only Have Eyes for You" (1959) sounds like a transmission from outer space. Sometimes it sounds like the spookiest record ever made.
Flamingo Serenade (End reissue).

THE FLESHTONES ★ Fuzztone, maracas, and grown-out Sixties roots make them New York's coolest combo these days. Sharp: penning "Theme from 'The Vindicators'" to accompany a flick that doesn't exist. Extremely boss.
LP: *Roman Gods* (IRS). EP: *Up-Front* (featuring "Vindicators") (IRS).

GIRL GROUPS ★ Wondering where Johnny had gone consumed lots of young gals' time between '58 and '64. Back then, packs of Jelly Beans, Dixie Cups, Cookies, and Raindrops bared their hearts over the airwaves. Today their hairdos survive in Debbie Harry and the Go Go's, and Rita Coolidge raids their canon for songs. Don't hang up.

Best: *Super Girls,* triple LP by Warner Special Products, featuring "Leader of the Pack," "Johnny Angel," "He's So Fine," and more.

DYLAN ★ From '64 to '66, Mr. Maximum Utmost. How did it feel?

Monotones

BUTCH HANCOCK ★ Professionally, this Texan folkie writes (good) songs for Joe Ely. On off hours, he produces the most deranged Dylan plagiarism since P. F. Sloan: "Mario y Maria (Cryin' Statues/Spittin' Images)," "Long Road to Asia Minor." Love minus zero.

The Wind's Dominion (Rainlight Records).

BUDDY HOLLY ★ did not need 20-20 vision to see he was pioneering a unique version of rock cool: bow tie and horn-rims. Rave on.

Buddy Holly & The Crickets: 20 Golden Greats (MCA).

HOWLIN' WOLF ★ There are others, but his Fifties and Sixties blues were best. "I asked for water," sings the original Back Door Man, "she gave me gasoline..."

Chester Burnett AKA Howlin' Wolf, Chess double LP feat. "Spoonful," "Smokestack Lightning," "I Asked for Water," "Wang Dang Doodle," etc.

ETTA JAMES ★ The real Lady Soul takes no crap ("Tell Mama," "The Pushover"). Her ballads rattle walls ("All I Could Do Was Cry," "I'd Rather Go Blind"). In "The Pickup," she's accosted by a tenor sax and gives in, after a juicy sax break, with "All right, but I have to be home by two."

Out of print, out of sight: *Peaches* (Chess double album).

MAJOR LANCE ★ Following Gene Chandler's appointment to Duke ('62), this ex-boxer from Chicago promoted himself to top brass with such hip moves as "The Matador" and "Monkey Time."

Featured on Epic's newly released *Okeh Soul* compilation.

JERRY LEE LEWIS ★ Whole lotta hellfire goin' on. The Killer awoke at dawn. He wants a drink.
Original Golden Hits, Volumes 1, 2 (Sun); *"Live" at the Star Club — Hamburg* (Philips, Dutch import); *Best Of, Volume II* (Mercury).

LITTLE WILLIE JOHN ★ He fronted Basie's band as a teenager, wrote pop history with "Fever" (1956), and in his day shared the Cool Soul mantle only with Sam Cooke. "His music was an expression of longing and desire beyond physical love," wrote Joe McEwen in *Stranded.* "Little Willie John understood."
Free At Last: twenty-one cuts, including "Sleep," "Fever," "I'm Shakin'," and "All Around the World" (Gusto).

THE LOUNGE LIZARDS ★ New York's arch art-rockers gave the world "fake jazz" in '81, blowing bogus blues ("Incident on South Street") and punk Monk ("Epistrophy"). In 1982 they scored two films, *The Loveless* and *Subway Rider.* Like wow.
The Lounge Lizards (Editions EG).

HENRY MANCINI ★ Aliquippa, Pennsylvania, may look like Squaresville, and Hank may come on like Mr. Middle-of-the-Road, but he scribed the bossest themes: "Mr. Lucky" and "Peter Gunn." Titles with the latter on the same LP: "Dreamsville," "A Profound Gass." Wiggy.
The Best of Mancini; Music from "Peter Gunn" (RCA).

ROGER MILLER ★ Anyone who thought Waylon and Willie's "outlaw Country" ever posed a threat to established Nashville law 'n' order never heard the word from this crazed Okie poet: "Kansas City Star," "My Uncle Used to Love Me but She Died."
Golden Hits ("King of the Road," "Dang Me," nine more) (Smash).

THE MONOTONES ★ Lead singer Charles Patrick cribbed the riff off a toothpaste commercial ("You'll wonder where the yellow went / When you brush your teeth with Pepsodent!") to come up with 1958's dumb rock classic "Book of Love."

"Book of Love" available in Chess Records' Blue Chip singles series.

BUCK OWENS ★ Never one to pass up a trope ("I've Got the Hungries for Your Love and I'm Waitin' in Your Welfare Line"), the *Hee Haw* superstar responded to pop's acid-rock craze with "Who's Gonna Mow Your Grass" (1969).
The Best of Buck Owens, Volumes 1–6 (Capitol).

GENE PITNEY ★ Rock as opera, long before the Who turned it into a bad joke. From '62 to '64, the Connecticut Yank was stalked by pain, anguish, and Kleenex on such boss weepers as "Only Love Can Break a Heart," "It Hurts To Be in Love." Horse opera: "(The Man Who Shot) Liberty Valance."
Gene Pitney's 20 Greatest Hits (Phoenix).

ELVIS PRESLEY ★ Distinguished by ultra-coolish behavior throughout his career, the man who shook up the Western world also took the time to record "No Room to Rhumba in a Sports Car."

Most thorough: *Elvis Elvis Elvis; 50 Gold Award Hits, Volume 1* (RCA). Rawest: *The Sun Sessions* (RCA). Rarest: *Elvis' Christmas Album* (released and withdrawn in '57 by RCA, who found it "blasphemous.") Silliest: *Harum Scarum.* (RCA).

P.J. PROBY ★ Bombastic Texas balladeer whose British success rivaled the Beatles ('64-65). Lennon said Proby "sounded like Elvis in a bottle." Fell from grace when he split his skintight breeches from knee to crotch during a London concert. Lennon and McCartney wrote "That Means a Lot" for him.

Out of print: *P.J. Proby* (featuring "That Means a Lot"); *Enigma; Phenomenon* (Liberty).

PSYCHEDELIC FURS ★ Not necessarily "psychedelic," this current Brit outfit *does* utilize a light show, mindbending sax runs, and an acid sense of humor to get its point across.

Psychedelic Furs; Talk Talk Talk (Columbia).

PSYCHEDELIC MUSIC ★ In the Eighties, as in the Sixties, it follows punk rock like the seasons. Now, as then, most of the people tossing the term around wouldn't know the Blues Magoos from the Blues Brothers. At its best, "acid rock" was a bracing blitz of jangling mood music — LPs like *The Grateful Dead* (Warners WBS 1689, to distinguish the group's first album from their other eponymous efforts); *Moby Grape* and the Byrds' *Fifth Dimension* (both CBS); *Spirit* (Epic); *Quicksilver Messenger Service* and QMS' *Happy Trails* (Capitol), and the Blues Project's *Projections* (Verve). Psychedelic by association: Captain Beefheart's *Safe as Milk* (Buddah).

These days, psychedelic rock is championed by bands like the Unclaimed, the Salvation Army, the Plimsouls (all L.A.), and Britain's Barracudas, whose *Drop Out with the Barracudas* (EMI import) is a cosmic must. The import sampler *A Splash of Colour* (WEA) gets you the 'cudas, plus the Marble Staircase, Mood Six, and the Earwigs. Groovy!

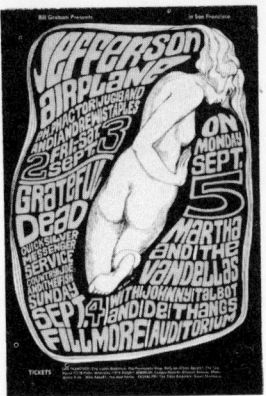

PUNK ROCK (SIXTIES) ★ They came from garages, from the suburbs. Wearing paisley and fruit-boots, brandishing handles like the Standells, Seeds, Shadows of Knight, and Chocolate Watch Band. Inspired by the Rolling Stones and other aggro units, legions of snotty kids grabbed guitars and took aim at the Top Forty. Some hit with irresistibly imbecilic records: Count Five's "Psychotic Reaction," the Leaves' "Hey Joe," and "I Had Too Much to Dream (Last Night)" by the immortal Electric Prunes.

As practiced between 1965 and 1967, punk rock was the twilight of primitive American rock 'n' roll: brash, undisciplined hard stuff. (While punk's Seventies namesake was British-born, England birthed but two punk clans in the Sixties: the Pretty Things and the transcendent Troggs of "Wild Thing" fame.)

Though the Standells' "Dirty Water" and "It's a Happening Thing" by the Magic Mushrooms may never again scale the tunedecks, Sixties punk is alive and well on record. The *Nuggets* compilation, released by Elektra in 1972 and later by Sire, offers such immortals as the Seeds, Standells, Strangeloves, and Amboy Dukes in one bonanza double album.

Angry Samoans

Then there's *Wild Thing,* a TV mail-order package featuring the Gentrys, Bobby Fuller Four, ? & the Mysterians, Troggs, Human Beinz, and Swingin' Medallions (Lakeshore Music, 930 Remington Road, Schaumberg, Illinois 60195). And *The Seeds* (GNP); the Sonics' *Boom* and *Original Northwest Punk* (Etiquette); the Pretty Things' *Vintage Years* (Sire), and the not-quite-legal Pebbles anthologies, available in hipper record shops.

PUNK (SEVENTIES-EIGHTIES) ★
New York started it ('76), London came in swinging, and L.A. mopped it up. When it was all over (any week now), punk had kicked rock out of its tie-dyed Seventies torpor, produced hundreds of tuff sides, and fallen flat on its face.

Punk's failure to completely rearrange the face of American pop is hardly its own fault. Squares still rule the world, and if they prefer musical wallpaper to wild ideas, so be it. Rumors persist about virulent outbreaks of the crazy rhythm in places like D.C., but more and more, punk '82 sounds like less, and less, and less. The music's finest minutes are probably behind it, but they're here for good ...

New York's Finest: any and all Ramones albums (Sire); *Dictators Go Girl Crazy!* (Epic); Heartbreakers, *L.A.M.F.* (Track import); Johnny Thunder's *So Alone* (Real Records import).

English Version: The Clash, *Give 'Em Enough Rope, The Clash* (Epic); *Never Mind the Bollocks, Here's The Sex Pistols* (Warners); Sham 69, *Tell Us the Truth* (Sire); Vibrators, *Pure Mania* (Epic); *Punk and Disorderly* (Poshboy).

California: *Adolescents* (Frontier); The Alleycats *Nightmare City* (Time Coast); Angry Samoans, *Inside My Brain* and *Back from Samoa* (Bad Trip); Black Flag, *Damaged* (SST); Circle Jerks, *Group Sex* (Frontier); Channel 3, *Fear of Life* (Poshboy); Fear, *The Album* (Slash); Gears, *Rockin' at Ground Zero* (Playgems); Germs, *G.I.* (Slash); *Hell Comes to Your House* (Bemisbrain sampler); The Last, *L.A. Explosion!* (Bomp); UXA, *Illusions of Grandeur* (Poshboy); X, *Los Angeles* (Slash); *Avengers* (White Noise); Young Canadians, *Hawaii* (Quintessence).

More Info: *Flipside* magazine ($6 for four issues: P.O. Box 363, Whittier, California 90608); *Volume,* 256-page punk/New Wave discography ($7.95

from One Ten Records, 110 Chambers Street, New York, New York 10007).

THE RAMONES ★ Forest Hills' four great guys, championing rock 'n' roll's three greatest chords. Gabba gabba hey! See discography under "Punk (Seventies-Eighties)."

THE RAYBEATS ★ Ventures and Venusians meet for discreet instrumental sessions. Surf music from the Twilight Zone.

Guitar Beat (PVC).

PAUL REVERE & THE RAIDERS ★ "Oregon's answer to Liverpool" wore tricornered hats and pantyhose. Kicks just keep getting harder to find.

Good Thing: *All Time Greatest Hits* (Columbia double LP).

JONATHAN RICHMAN & THE MODERN LOVERS ★ Idiot-savant hipster of the Seventies. "Hey There Little Insect," "Abominable Snowman in the Market" — he writes 'em, sings 'em, and is not embarrassed. Hear the Sex Pistols learn JR's "Roadrunner" on *The Great Rock 'n' Roll Swindle*.

The Modern Lovers (Home of the Hits); *Jonathan Richman & The Modern Lovers* (Beserkely).

NELSON RIDDLE ★ He made Sinatra swing and touched TV with class, theming both "Route 66" and "The Untouchables." And he did the beaut title piece to Kubrick's *Lolita*.

Budget buy: *Best of Nelson Riddle* (Capitol).

ROCKABILLY ★ From '54 to '56 they prowled the shadows cast by Presley,

Raybeats

Laura Levine

crazed rednecks hefting fat guitars and waterfall pompadours. Crazy, man, crazy.

Craziest: *Johnny Burnette Rock 'n' Roll Trio — Tear It Up* (including "Honey Hush," "Train Kept A-Rollin," "Rock Billy Boogie" (Solid Smoke).

Rockabilly Stars, Volumes 1-2, featuring Carl Perkins, Johnny Cash, Link Wray, Collins Kids, Ronnie Self (Epic); *Original Memphis Rock & Roll,* with Roy Orbison, Jerry Lee Lewis, Charlie Rich (Sun); Ray Campi, *Rockabilly; Wildcat Shakeout* (Rollin' Rock); *King-Federal Rockabillys* (Hank Mizell, Mac Curtis, Charlie Feathers); *Put Your Cat Clothes On* (Billy Lee Riley, Warren Smith, Jerry Lee Lewis, Harmonica Frank Floyd) (Philips UK import); Gene Vincent; *The Bop That Just Won't Stop* (Capitol).

ROLLING STONES ★ Once upon a time. Dead from the neck down since '67.

The Rolling Stones; 12 X 5; Now!; Out of Our Heads; December's Children; Between the Buttons; Metamorphosis (London).

NINO ROTA ★ Who but an opera-writing teenager could grow up to orchestrate Fellini's fractured flicks? His compositions for *8½, La Dolce Vita,* and *Juliet of the Spirits* set rinky-dink standards. Life is a carnival.

La Dolce Vita (RCA); *Juliet of the Spirits* (United Artists).

New: *Amarcord (I Remember Nino Rota),* featuring Carla Bley, Jaki Byard, Chris Stein, etc. (Hannibal).

THE SHANELS ★ Formerly the Chanels. They smoke Luckies and drink Bud. They wear black leather and gold lamé. They harmonize on old Coasters hits and wear black-face and pompadours. Japan's foremost doowop group is out of this world.

Shanels

Import LP (Japanese Epic): *Mr. Black* (featuring "Sh-Boom," "Zoom," and "Shama Lama Ding Dong").

FRANK SINATRA ★ Proto-cool. No chump, this Chairman takes his sugar to tea, swings at photographers, and whispers in presidents' ears. Ring-a-ding-ding.

Come Fly with Me; Sinatra's Sinatra; Nice 'n' Easy (Capitol); *It Might as Well Be Swing* (with Count Basie); *Francis A. & Edward K.* (with Duke Ellington); *Watertown; Trilogy* (Reprise).

THE SONICS ★ Seattle tough guys (see Sixties Punk). You want drug songs? Singer Gerry Roslie eschewed wine, water, and other solvents in favor of straight "Strychnine." All this in 1965.

PHIL SPECTOR ★ The first tycoon of teen copped the inscription off his dad's tombstone for his first hit ("To Know Him Is To Love Him," 1958). The road grew wild and wiggy, with the Ronettes, Darlene Love, Crystals, the Righteous Brothers, Ike and Tina Turner, John Lennon ("Instant Karma," "Happy Christmas," "Cold Turkey"), and the Ramones *(End of the Century).* He hits you and it feels like...

Phil Spector's Greatest Hits (Warner-Spector); *Christmas Album* (Warner-Spector); *Phil Spector Wall of Sound, Volumes 1–6* (Phil Spector International UK import).

SWAMP DOGG ★ As Jerry Williams, he produced Gene Pitney, toured with Ben E. King and Sergeant Barry ("Green Berets") Sadler. As Swamp Dogg, he's toured with Jane Fonda, won raves from the *New York Times* and cut such uncut gems as "California Is Drowning and I Live Down by the River" and "Eat the Goose (Before the Goose Eats You)."

I'm Not Selling Out/I'm Buying In (Takoma); *Rat On* (Elektra); *Swamp Dogg's Greatest Hits???* (Stone Dogg); *Total Destruction to Your Mind* (Canyon); *Best of: 13 Prime Wieners* (Warbride).

Sinatra

SOUNDS

THE TRASHMEN ★ Some have argued that the greatest rock 'n' roll song is also the stupidest. Behold the "Surfin' Bird" and those who gave it life.

Featured on *Golden Summer* surf music anthology (United Artists).

JOE TURNER ★ The eternal Kansas City star shook, rattled, and rolled (1954), flipped, flopped, and flew, and begged for prime time from his "TV Mama."

His Greatest Recordings (Atco).

VELVET UNDERGROUND ★ *Variety* called them "a three-ring psychosis." "Not since the Titanic ran into that iceberg," opined the *L.A. Times*. As created by Warhol, New York punk's parents were evil mothers.

The Velvet Underground & Nico (Verve); *Loaded; Live at Max's Kansas City* (both Cotillion); *1969 Live* (Mercury).

The Ronettes

Phil Spector

Michael Ochs Arc

TOM WAITS ★ Born late, he finally brought his beatnik lust home, scoring Coppola's glowing "cocktail landscape" *One from the Heart.*

Heat Attack & Vine; The Heart of Saturday Night (Asylum).

MARY WELLS ★ Before giving in to that schizo in "Two Lovers," Motown's toughest broad told cream puffs in no uncertain terms where to get off ("Bye Bye Baby," 1961).

Budget priced: *Mary Wells' Greatest Hits* (Motown).

JACKIE WILSON ★ Soul in a tux. In the late Fifties/early Sixties, the classest black act, with a big boss line of living hits: "Lonely Teardrops," "Baby Work Out," "Am I the Man." Along the way, helped invent Van Morrison and Otis Redding.

Solid Gold (Brunswick double LP).

YACHTS ★ Their '79 debut (*Yachts,* Radar Records) effortlessly tosses words like *dross* and *tantamount* into the music mix. Clever. Cole Porter punk.

ZACHERLE ("THE COOL GHOUL") ★ The real Count Floyd. Founded fiend-rock in '58 with "Dinner with Drac." (See also "Monster Mash," "Werewolf of London.") Igor?

"Drac" available on Abkco single, and on *American Dream — The Cameo Parkway Story* (UK import).

THE ZOMBIES ★ Breathy Brit combo ('65-69) "starred" in Otto Preminger's *Bunny Lake Is Missing* by appearing on TV in the background of a barroom scene that lasted four seconds.

Nice priced twofer: *Time of the Zombies* ("Tell Her No," "Time of the Season," "She's Not There") (Epic).

Mary Wells

Michael Ochs Archives

33

The Coolest Jazz Records

by Joe Goldberg

The Very Best of Bird. Charlie Parker's best sides, the Dial sessions, newly released by Warner Brothers on a double LP.

'Round About Midnight (Columbia). Miles Davis and John Coltrane on their first album, making the most influential jazz since Armstrong.

European Concert (Atlantic). The Modern Jazz Quartet's finest hour, a two-LP set featuring leader John Lewis' "Django," generally thought to be MJQ's best work, and nonmember Ray Brown's "Pyramid," which was.

Duke Ellington is the Great American Composer, as well as one of the coolest men who ever lived. But he might not have achieved what he did without the recordings he made in the late Twenties with the short-lived trumpeter Bubber Miley, co-composer of the seminal Duke classics "East St. Louis Toodle-Oo," "Black and Tan Fantasy" and "The Mooche." See **Hot in Harlem — Duke Ellington & His Orchestra (1928-29)** (MCA). Ellington's best period is supposed to have begun in 1940, but check into the small group recordings he made just before under the names of sidemen Johnny Hodges, Barney Bigard, and Cootie Williams.

The Complete Genius (Bluenote). The iconoclastic Thelonius Monk, perhaps the purest jazz musician we've had, at his greatest.

Sidney Bechet was jazz's most rhapsodic soloist, as shown on his versions of "Summertime" and "Blue Horizon." Try **Sidney Bechet Jazz Classics, Volumes 1-2** (Bluenote).

Joaquin Rodrigo's **Concierto de Aranjuez** entered the jazz lexicon when cut by Miles and Gil Evans. Its finest realization remains Jim Hall's on CTI, done with Paul Desmond and Chet Baker.

The Tatum Group Masterpieces — Art Tatum & Ben Webster (Pablo). Perhaps the most erotic jazz record ever made.

Crosscurrents (Capitol). The most cerebral, hence coolest, jazz group was pianist Lennie Tristano's, with sax accompanists Lee Konitz and Warne Marsh.

Count Basie made some records with sidemen he called the Kansas City Seven (1939, 1944), which featured saxophonist Lester Young occasionally on clarinet. The best of these is "I Want A Little Girl"; even the worst is superb. Originally cut for Commodore, the KC7 sides have since been sold to Columbia and licensed out repeatedly. Check liner credits.

Dizzy Gillespie with Don Byas recorded the ultimate single, "I Can't get Started." A better jazz record doesn't exist. Now available on the Smithsonian twofer **Evolution of an American Artist: Dizzy Gillespie.**

COOL COUNTRY

by Nick Tosches

Forget about Willie and Waylon. The following albums and singles contain within their grooves the bottom-line fundamentals of all that ever was, is, and will be cool in country music. Unless otherwise noted, all these records are either still in print or obtainable without much trouble. (For information regarding the rarer cool country stuff, drop six bucks for a copy of **Country** by yours truly.)

LEFTY FRIZZELL. **Lefty Frizzell's Greatest Hits** (Columbia). This anthology contains much of the best work by the man who in many ways was greater than his contemporary Hank Williams. (Took him longer to drink himself to death, for one.) Pay special attention to "If You've Got the Money, I've Got the Time."

GEORGE JONES. **George Jones** (United Artists). This two-record Super-

pak album features two of George's finest cuts, "The Warm Red Wine" and "Open Pit Mine."

JERRY LEE LEWIS. **Another Place Another Time** (Smash). 'Nuff said.

JIMMIE RODGERS. **My Rough and Rowdy Ways** (RCA). This is one of the best and raunchiest collections of early country that can be heard. "In the Jailhouse Now No. 2" is still as strong and cool as it was in 1930.

ED SANDERS. **Sanders' Truckstop** (Reprise). Though this 1970 album is not easy to come by, it is probably the only truly hep pseudo-country record ever made.

LESTER "ROADHOG" MORAN & THE CADILLAC COWBOYS. **Alive at the Johnny Mack Brown High School** (Mercury). These characters are actually the Statler Brothers, and this album is the only really cool country comedy you'll ever hear.

HANK WILLIAMS. **I Saw the Light** (MGM). This set of Hank's cool Christian country sides proves that a man can pray and sway at the same time. Listen closely to "The Angel of Death."

DICK CURLESS. "Chick Inspector" (Capitol). This 1973 single is so cool that it contains the only reference to pantyhose in the history of country music.

TOMPALL GLASER. "Texas Law Sez" (MGM). Hard to get, due to its partial suppression in 1974, but well worth the effort.

JIM MUNDY. "I'm a White Boy" (ABC-Dot). Merle Haggard wrote this song, but he didn't have the nerve to cut it.

WYNN STEWART. "I'm Gonna Kill You" (Playboy). This 1975 single was the last country song to be nationally banned from airplay.

PORTER WAGONER. "The Cold Hard Facts of Life" (RCA). The best cheatin' record in all of country. Hear it and discover the meaning not only of pathos, but also of Porter's hairdo.

THE HAYWIRE HALL OF FAME

The Top Ten Flipped Discs of All Time

Compiled by Richard Blackburn

1. "PSYCHO" by Jack Kittel (GRC). Honky-tonker Leon Payne penned this champ of all sick ditties just before his suicide, and Kittel's 1974 version captures the dementia praecox best — obviously hipping Elvis Costello, who put "Psycho" on the flip of 1981's "Sweet Dreams" (Columbia). The song's narrator calmly tells his mother how he iced his ex-wife and her lover, his own son and a neighbor girl, and dreamed of strangling his son's puppy, then asks rhetorically, "Ya think I'm psycho, don't ya, mama? Well...

2. "WILD HOG HOP" by Bennie Hess (Major). Manic panic from the Fifties, too rushed for even an instrumental break. Chased by a wild hog through briars and across rivers (with appropriate snorts and splashes), the singer collapses, safe, at his baby's door. "You're my man," she crows, "'cause you did the Wild Hog Hop!" Available on the import LP **Gonna Rock and Roll Tonight** (Collector).

3. "PENCIL NECKED GEEK" by Fred Blassie. The man who wrote the rulebook on dirty wrestling stepped out of the ring in 1976 to wax this tirade against less-than-100 percent males. Beyond macho, Blassie groin-kicks "scum-suckin' peaheads with a lousy physique," then stomps the record's engineer to death. Available on the EP **Blassie — King Of Men** (Rhino).

4. "THE FANG" by Nervous Norvus (Dot). Following his haywire hits "Transfusion" and "Ape Call," Norv flipped out in '56 and wired bop-talk to sci-fi. "The Fang" concerns an "outer space papa" who gets "earthbound" so he can "hit the chicks with a Martian jolt!" (See also Buchanan & Goodman's "Flying Saucer" novelties and Jessie Lee Turner's "Little Space Girl" on Carlton.)

5. ESQUERITA AND THE VOOLA (Capitol LP). Under the impression that

WHEN I SAY ROCK'N'ROLL IS HERE TO S[TAY]

QUERITA!

deciphering "sweet words of pismotology" and "the pulpitudes of love" from the Medallions' "The Letter" (Roulette **Golden Goodies** Volume 15).

8. "I PUT A SPELL ON YOU" by Screamin' Jay Hawkins. This cacaphony of screams, moans, and inarticulate gargling was actually a hit for Hawkins, who topped himself with such weirdies as "Constipation Blues" and "She Put the Whammy on Me" (in which he takes his revenge on a lost girlfriend with a shotgun). "Spell" is included on the new **Okeh Rhythm & Blues** LP (Epic).

9. "BE FAIR" by the Gallahads (Del Fi). Fifties love paranoia (as in the Rays' "Silhouettes") reaches an all-time high in this fable of "a blind boy and his girlfriend." As she walks him home, he accuses her of kissing his best friend. "It's no fun being blind." Right.

10. "ROCKIN' BONES" by Ronnie Dawson (Rockin'). Forget the Showmen's ode to rock "It Will Stand." This is

if a half-maniac like Little Richard could succeed, then surely a total loon would do twice as well, Capitol in the late Fifties signed Esquerita. They were wrong. None of his records clicked, and this LP is one of the rarest in collectordom. On its cover, Esquerita looks like the front of a '59 Continental with a tumbleweed process and rhinestone shades. Inside: wordless voodoo chants, falsetto shrieks, and chaos called "Juicy Miss Lucy," "Batty over Hattie" and "Hole in My Heart." Reissued recently: a double Esquerita LP (French Capitol).

6. "THE BIG MACHINE" by Gene Savage (Big West). The ultimate hot rod song. Savage's machine "don't use gasoline" mainly because it's a big M-60 tank. In competition with conventional dragsters, it blasts them with a cannon, then flies away. Bye bye 409.

7. "RUBBER BISCUIT" by the Chips (Josie). Covered by the Blues Brothers, this doowop novelty shares honors with dozens of nonsensical classics. Frank Zappa and a crew of linguists are still

Michael Ochs Archives

Screamin' Jay Hawkins

it! Ronnie asks to be buried with his records and requests someone "put a phonograph needle in my hand" so he can rock into the promised land. Covered by the Cramps on **Psychedelic Jungle,** but no one touches Dawson for demonic weirdness. In photos, he resembles a waxed, brushcut Dorian Gray with eye makeup.

Bop City

"MANHATTAN FABLE" by Babs Gonzales (Bruce). One of the great bop comics, Gonzales outdoes himself on the Harlem jive talk here. "One morning about a deuce of ticks ago, a cat from the lowlands hit the Apple" and so forth, including someone named Congolene Freddy. Real gone! Also high in the hipsters hall of fame: Slim Gaillard, whose Forties classics "Slim's Jam," "Flat Foot Floogie," and "Cement Mixer (Putty Putty)" place him alongside Lord Buckley. Gaillard, who still occasionally performs, coined such deathless hipsterisms as "mellareenie" and "vootie" while singing the praises of "avocado seed soup." Gaillard's coolness can still be caught on the LPs **Slim's Jam** (Alamac) and **Black California** (on Arista's Savoy Series.)

When he wasn't playing piano behind Jack Kerouac **(Poetry for the Beat Generation,** Hanover, out of print), Steve Allen in the mid-fifties read some of his **Bop Fables** on Coral Records. Harry the Hipster Gibson's priceless 78's "Who Put the Benzedrine in Mrs. Murphy's Ovaltine" and "Four-F Ferdinand the Frantic Freak" legitimately deserve the description "far out." Scheduled for release shortly is **International Jazzbeaux,** Al Collins' overdue followup to his 1954 "Hip Little Red Riding Hood," which should include some surprise riffs played off "Jack and the Beanstalk" and "Goldilocks." Like wild, man!

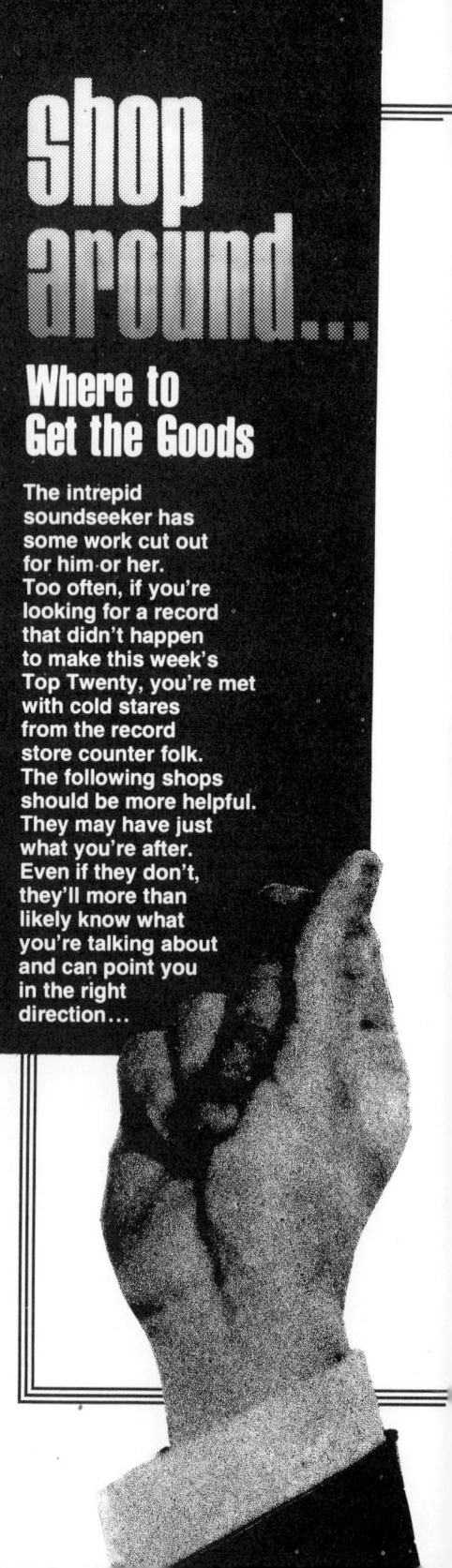

shop around...

Where to Get the Goods

The intrepid soundseeker has some work cut out for him or her. Too often, if you're looking for a record that didn't happen to make this week's Top Twenty, you're met with cold stares from the record store counter folk. The following shops should be more helpful. They may have just what you're after. Even if they don't, they'll more than likely know what you're talking about and can point you in the right direction...

Camelot Music, Atlanta Highway and Oporto Avenue, Birmingham, Alabama
Roads To Moscow, 6102 North 16th Street, Phoenix, Arizona
Sac's Wax & Tape, 620 West 14th Street, Little Rock, Arkansas
Rasputin Records, 2377 Telegraph Avenue, Berkeley, California
Down Home Music, 10341 San Pablo Avenue, El Cerrito, California
Aron's Records, 7725 Melrose Avenue, Los Angeles, California
Rhino Records, 1720 Westwood Boulevard, Los Angeles, California
Tower Records, 8801 West Sunset Boulevard, Los Angeles, California
Tower Records, 2500 16th Street, Sacramento, California
Arcade Music Co., 4904 Voltaire, San Diego, California
Magic Flutre, 510½ Frederick, San Francisco, California
Tower Records, 2525 Jones Street, San Francisco, California

Wax Tracks, 638 East 13th Street, Denver, Colorado
The Finest Store, 2406 Eighth Avenue, Greeley, Colorado
Festoons Records, 23 Whitney Avenue, New Haven, Connecticut
Record Museum, Blue Hen Mall, Dover, Delaware
Record & Tape Exchange, 2349 M Street NW, Washington, D.C.

Scorpio Records & Tapes, 1935 NW Second Avenue, Boca Raton, Florida
Classic Wax, 237 85th Street, Holmes Beach, Florida
Turtles Records & Tapes, 124 Alps Road, Athens, Georgia
Wax-N-Facts, 432 Moreland Avenue NE, Atlanta, Georgia
Brass Ear, Inc., Country Club Shopping Center, Idaho Falls, Idaho

Wax Trax, 2449 North Lincoln, Chicago, Illinois
Co-op Tapes & Records, 1203 25th Street, Des Moines, Iowa
Hastings Books & Records, 1010 South Kansas, Liberal, Kansas
Gold Mine Records, 6469 Jefferson Highway, Harahan, Louisiana
Leisure Landing, 5500 Magazine St., New Orleans, Louisiana

Deorsey's, 663 Stillwater Avenue, Bangor, Maine
Yesterday & Today Records, 1327-S Rockville Pike, Rockville, Maryland
Cheapo Records, 645 Massachusetts Avenue, Cambridge, Massachusetts
Bonzo Dog Records, 522 East Williams, Ann Arbor, Michigan
Zodiac Records, 6343 GD River, Detroit, Michigan

Oar Folkjokeopus, 2557 Lyncale Avenue South, Minneapolis, Minnesota
Pied Piper Music, 507 West Howard Avenue, Biloxi, Mississippi
Vintage Vinyl, 6354 Delmar, University City, Missouri
Music Man Studio, 725 Lafayette Road, Hampton, New Hampshire

Cheap Thrills, 382 George, New Brunswick, New Jersey
Sound Warehouse, 2511 San Mateo Boulevard NE, Albuquerque, New Mexico
Big Hit Oldies, 170 Bleecker Street, New York, New York
Colony Record & Radio Center, 1619 Broadway, New York, New York

Record Hole, 3017 Hillsborough Street, Raleigh, North Carolina
Record Head Inc., 510 East Main, Bismarck, North Dakota
Stiff Records, 1828 Coventry, Cleveland, Ohio
Chrystal Ship, SW 10th and SW Morrison, Portland, Oregon
Third St. Jazz, 10 North Third Street, Philadelphia, Pennsylvania

Looney Tunes II, 85 Tower Hill Road, Wakefield, Rhode Island
Collectors Record Lane, 1387 Elvis Presley Boulevard, Memphis, Tennessee
Inner Sanctum, 504 West 24th Street, Austin, Texas
Bip Bop Boom Records, 916 Clay Street, Houston, Texas

Pure Pop, 115 South Winooski, Burlington, Vermont
Memory Lane Records, 15394 Warwick Boulevard, Newport News, Virginia
Second Time Records, 4141 University Way NE, Seattle, Washington
Leslie's Record Lane, West Washington Street, Charles Town, West Virginia

Record Head, 7418 West Hampton Avenue, Milwaukee, Wisconsin
The Record Shop, 113 West 17th, Cheyenne, Wyoming

Music by Mail
There are a number of competent mail order record services capable of locating hard-to-find records. These two are the best:
    Disques du Monde, P.O. Box 836, New York, New York 10159
    The Record Obsession, P.O. Box 69577, Los Angeles, California 90069

Keeping Abreast
Since most of the music that gets heard (on the radio) these days is hopelessly square, it stands to reason there must be lots of good stuff falling between the cultural cracks. That's where **OP** comes in. A tabloid quarterly, it covers all the hip missed links — local and regional, old-time and New Wave, and lots of independently produced unheard music. Send $8 for eight issues to: Lost Music Network, P.O. Box 2391, Olympia, Washington 98507.

Goldmine plumbs those historical depths (formerly called "oldies") in a monthly tabloid full of info and record ads. Send $20 for twelve issues to: P.O. Box 187, Fraser, Michigan 48026.

GEORGE HUNTER

George Hunter took paisley, Victoriana, Maxfield Parrish, Marvel Comics, the Wild West, and rock and roll and synthesized something so unique, so patently new and wonderfully appropriate that it overnight became the de rigueur aesthetic of San Francisco's flowering Golden Age.

The CHARLATANs

by Davin Seay

It was 1965 and, sure, something was happening. But it wasn't only Mr. Jones who didn't know what it was—no one had the foggiest idea, out there on the hilly ascents of Frisco's Barbary Coast, what this new and verging scene looked or sounded like. Fact was, ripe as the Sixties were to *happen,* scant few at this halfway point in the decade had the imagination or simple chutzpah to manhandle all that seething energy and make of it style, attitude, and history.

George Hunter knew. What he knew gave grand design and color to the age. George Hunter took paisley, Victoriana, Maxfield Parrish, Marvel Comics, the Wild West, and rock and roll and synthesized something so unique, so patently new and wonderfully appropriate that it overnight became the de rigueur aesthetic of San Francisco's flowering Golden Age. What he created—a gaslight aura lighting the mysterious, the marvelous, the magnificent corners of his own fecund imagination—may, in this benighted age, seem hopelessly anachronistic and square—those bell bottoms and Western vests, the blue of a Parrish sky, and the tongue-twisting oaths of Dr. Strange.

Yet the originality of his vision endures, regardless of what cretinous entrepreneurs were later to make of it. Even today, when every fern-decked, stained-glassed, and natural-wooded emporium of the Me Decade stands as a shameless denuding of the spirit of Hunter. George Hunter's world was simply fantastic, with its progenitor a rare original in the classic mold of the Dandy.

Scion of a well-to-do SoCal family, Hunter studied architecture at San Francisco State, where he discovered a coterie of like-minded proto-hippies like Jerry Garcia, Darby Slick, and the members of Hunter's own wigged-out idea of what a rock and roll band should be—the Charlatans. The name had more than a euphonious significance. Hunter had birthed the band more as a vehicle for his inspired visual constructs than as a musical entity. He himself could hardly play a note and usually occupied himself onstage banging a tambourine or strumming an inaudible autoharp. Before the band played a single rehearsal, Hunter had snapped hundreds of publicity stills, featuring the quintet in an inexhaustible variety of turn-of-the-century regalia salvaged from San Francisco thrift stores. They played their first gig in Virginia City, Nevada, and were right at home with the burg's weirdo population, who fancied themselves gunslingers and wore the sidearms to prove it. Returning to San Francisco, they found themselves certified culture stars and Hunter's ragtime pop art the standard for everything from dance posters to fashion to apartment decor.

The Summer of Love followed and the world beat a path to the Haight Ashbury, palms upturned to gather the manna of drug-addled truth. Hippies became homogeneous, but it was all over for Hunter, at precisely the moment it had begun for everyone else.

(In its seventh issue—that of March 1968—*Rolling Stone,* itself a newcomer, pronounced the Charlatans dead, and touted such fresh copy as Jimi Hendrix, Ravi Shankar, and the Maharishi Mahesh Yogi.) Hunter's private dream was public domain—it was time to move on.

After starting a graphic arts studio, a restaurant, and a family (featuring a son named Maxwell), Hunter currently languishes in relative obscurity in Marin County, operating a modest woodworking concern. Whatever his ultimate fate, his gilt-edged originality will forever transcend the sad demise of the time in which it was unveiled to a sleeping world.

(As of this writing, plans are afoot to release the Charlatans' LP, cut in 1966. It's uncertain whether the original ad copy will be used to announce its arrival: "Remedy for a Drugged Market.")

They soar. They spoof. Some freak. Some fly like turkeys. From beyond the Valley of the Ultravixens come

the fifty coolest movies ever made...

BEACH BALL (1965). Edd Byrnes was already showing crow's feet in this wet-suit wonderama about a hungry rock band ("the Wigglers"). To their credit, Kookie's dialogue writers feed him great lines. Kook to girl who interrupts him on dance floor: "Catch me later, baby, I'm in orbit!"

THE BEAT GENERATION (1959). What do you expect when the producer of **High School Confidential** and **LSD, I Hate You!** turns his savage eye on the Beatnik movement? Jive talk, a rape-crazy psycho, Mamie Van Doren and Vampira, and such beat jazz innovators as Louis Armstrong and Ray Anthony. Wail.

Hollywood Book and Poster Co.

DOLLS

BEYOND THE VALLEY OF THE DOLLS (1970). Some prefer **The Immoral Mr. Teas,** some get their kicks from **Faster Pussycat, Kill, Kill!** But all Russ Meyer fans know this is among the sleaze king's sleaziest. Member of feminist rock band (the Carrie Nations) to manager, after he's pulled a Myra Breckinridge and revealed himself as a transsexual: "Z-man, you're a chick!"

BRINGING UP BABY. Howard Hawks invents a prehistorical (1938) vision of cool as verbal thrust-and-parry between Cary Grant and Kate Hepburn. Breathless. See also **Holiday** (1938).

D.S.

CAGED MEN (1973). Wrestling great Abdullah the Butcher and his (real life) midget manager make screen debuts, playing desperate lifers trying to grow pot in a jail greenhouse. Hammerlocks and hopheads.

G.T.

CHE! (1969). Unwatchable, even within its genre (bogus "revolutionary" films of the late Sixties), but singularly brilliant for its perverse casting: Jack Palance as Fidel Castro. Arriba!

THE COOL AND THE CRAZY (1958). Scott Marlowe looks like Lou Reed, blows reefer, and walks on the jive side.

Seedy pushers, flaming car crashes, and dozens of ducktailed teens "hooked on smoke."

R.B.

THE COOL ONES (1967). Au go-go mania with Roddy McDowall as a flip Spector-type music mogul. Teens twist and shout from an aerial tramway, invent a dance sensation ("the Tantrum"), and bug grizzly TV exec Phil Harris. An underling catches embarrassed Harris perfecting his Tantrum, causing Philsy to stop mid-frug: "It's my underwear. My wife buys it too small and it itches." Gear.

DECOY FOR TERROR (1970). Beatnik artist murders his models ("They always **move!**") by freezing them. Cool climax: a power outage causes one, frozen posed with a bow and arrow, to release the arrow, killing artist who's just finished his masterpiece. Neil Sedaka sings "Do the Waterbug" ("Do the Cow/If you want it right now...").

CLINT brandishes
badge of cool
in *Dirty Harry.*

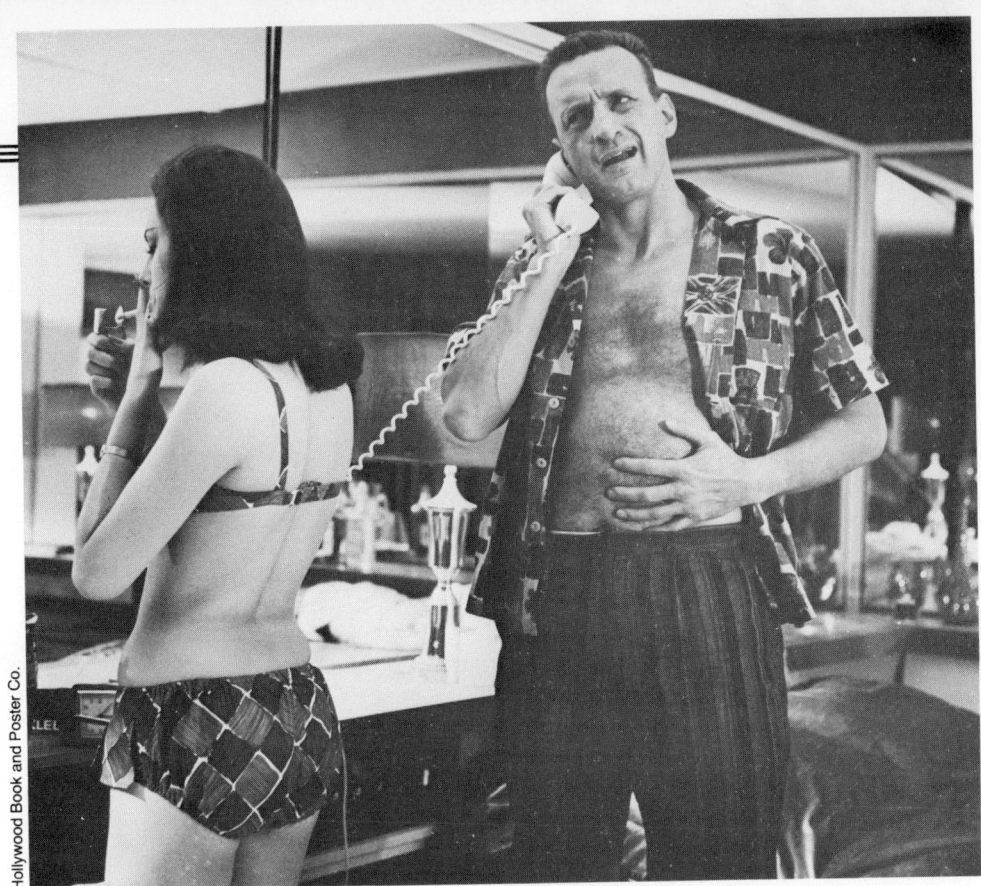

GEORGE C. SCOTT wails in the war room, in *Dr. Strangelove*.

Hollywood Book and Poster Co.

DIRTY HARRY (1971). Detective Clint Eastwood to cringing crook: "I know what you're thinking, punk. You're thinking did I fire six shots or only five? Now to tell you the truth, I've forgotten myself in all this excitement. But being this is a forty-four magnum, the most powerful handgun in the world and it'll blow your head clean off, you could ask yourself a question, 'Do I feel lucky?' ... Well, **do** you, **punk?**" R.S.

DOCTOR STRANGELOVE (1964). The more real the madness gets these days, the hipper Southern's script and Kubrick's shots become. The mineshaft gap, the precious-bodily-fluids drain, and General "Buck" Turgidson and Lieutenant Bat Guano said it all, to say nothing of Slim Pickens' bombsight soliloquy as Captain "King" Kong. Peter Sellers' silliest.

DUEL (1971). The absolute Big Daddy of anthropomorphic auto-horror movies, beating both the alien-powered **Killdozer** (1974) and the Satanic limo of **The Car** (1977). Dennis Weaver is inexplicably pursued through four Western states by a demonic diesel. A vehicle that could only be made for TV.

EATING RAOUL (1982). Squaresville couple with no bread (Mary Woronov, Paul Bartel) advertise for sex freaks, bop them with skillets, then sell freaks' cars. Supercool Raoul, chicano con man, spoils the party. A wiggy morality play with every "hip" attitude turned inside out.

GET CARTER (1971). Subzero cool Brit flick starring Michael Caine, who pisses off an entire railway pub by ordering his bitter "in a thin glass." After

47

MAMIE VAN DOREN
preps for her
part in
*High School
Confidential.*

balling an overripe hotel manageress in Newcastle, Caine, naked, faces down two other hoods with a shotgun and walks them outside into a kiddie parade, making deadpan wisecracks. R.B.

THE GIRL CAN'T HELP IT (1956). Bill Reed and David Ehrenstein said it best, in **Rock on Film** (Delilah Books, 1981). "Jayne Mansfield is a succulent A-Bomb just waiting to explode in this satire of record industry hucksterism. And the **look** of the film is just right! Cinemascope, stereophonic sound and Technicolor you can eat with a spoon." Music by Gene Vincent, Little Richard, Fats Domino, Eddie Cochran.

GLEN OR GLENDA (1952). Two separate narratives for this pic "about the serious question of sex change." Lyle Talbot as the shrink, with Bela Lugosi the doddering voice of God. Plot intercut with shots of a steel mill, living room lovemaking scene (with balalaika music), buffalo and lightning bolts. At one point the camera cuts to a radiator for no discernible reason. R.M.

GODFATHER II (1974). New heights in ethno-Cool, Mediterranean division: Dons Tessio and Fanucci, Johnny Five Angels (Michael Gazzo). Arkie cool: the investigating senator who calls the GF "Don **Core**-lay-oh-nay." B.M.

HIGH SCHOOL CONFIDENTIAL (1958). Quick! Cut from square biz jerk behind desk doing anti-weed rap to Jerry Lee Lewis screaming the title tune from a flatbed truck. Nonstop hepcat jargon, plus surreal plot and cast (Jackie Coogan as the heroin-peddling "Mr. A"). As undercover agent Russ Tamblyn's "aunt," Mamie Van Doren points her turrets at him next to the refrigerator — "Want some milk?" R.B.

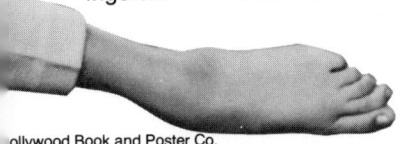

HIT LADY (1974). Women's lib comes knocking in sharp threads: Yvette Mimeux as a bikini-clad mob assassin. Groovy.

THE HORROR OF PARTY BEACH (1964). **Attack of the Crab Monsters** (1957) beat this one to the Three Mile Island riff (radiation as the root of all evil), but Stephen King celebrates the monster-and-surf pic for its supreme lack of a "context of reality." **Party Beach,** writes Steve, is "perhaps only topped by **Plan Nine from Outer Space** as the worst horror movie ever made." You bet.

JIGSAW (1968). Bizarro TV yarn starts with acid flashback, gets progressively weirder. **Blow Up** references, Hope Lange, Michael J. Pollard, and a fantabulous finale: Up on the roof, paint-covered baddies pass a heating duct, ignite, and jump twelve stories to fiery deaths. Real gone. T.V.

KITTEN WITH A WHIP (1964). Ann-Margret, as a delinquent-on-the-run, holes up with Senator John Forsythe and threatens to cry rape if he chucks her. Two Ivy League psychopaths (Skip Ward and Peter Brown) fall by. An argument ensues. Ward slashes Brown's arm with a blade then apologizes. Brown: "Hey buddy, no pain. No pain at all." Yeahhh. R.B.

LOLITA (1962). Unquestionably the choicest example of post-Beat, pre-hippie esthetics on film. Peter Sellers as Claire Quilty is the personification of hip erudition, while *Lolita*'s ultra theme is an early nod at pop trash from the intelligentsia (Kubrick). D.S.

LORD LOVE A DUCK (1965). Roddy McDowall again, in the finest satirical take on Southern California manners, mores, and architecture that an Easterner could ask for. Neal Hefti contributes inspired ersatz rock 'n' roll. Tuesday Weld gives the cinema's coolest

DeNiro, Keitel (on the left) prepare for imminent mook attack in *Mean Streets*.   Warner Bros.

portrayal of a teen wet dream as a starlet scoring a part in a film titled **Bikini Widow**.   R.S.

THE LOVES OF HERCULES (1964). Jayne Mansfield goes Greek just before her untimely demise. She wears a dark wig, undulates under a loincloth, and does lots of horseback riding in what is obviously the first "jiggly."   M.M.

THE MAN WITH THE X-RAY EYES (1963). Among Roger Corman's finest ninety minutes. A heavy theme decked out in triumphant B-movie ciphers. Who can forget Ray Milland ripping out his orbs at that tent revival? Old Testament sci-fi.   D.S.

MEAN STREETS (1973). DeNiro as the quintessential Cool Jerk "Johnny-boy" drops cherry bombs in mail-boxes, starts fights for Harvey Keitel to finish, acts goofy and gallant ("Give dese girls a seven-and-seven"). Best use of rock 'n' roll in a motion picture (pool hall scene, etc.). Film introduces word *mook* into contemporary lexicon.

MICKEY ONE (1965). Offbeat with a ten-point "0." The original **One from the Heart** and lots more: Caligari sets, schizoid cutting, and Warren Beatty as a Lenny Bruce-type comic on the brink of a big crack-up. This movie deserves a cult.

MONDO TRASHO (1969). The less

(much less) precious tunes-as-soundtrack version of **Scorpio Rising,** this early John Waters opus uses snippets of pop songs (and stuff like "Pomp and Circumstance" totally out of context) behind Divine killing Mary Vivian Pearce in her car and trying to revive her — first asking the aid of the Blessed Virgin, then seeking out the local mad scientist, who not only revives Pearce but gives her web feet. Rape scene features "Baby Let's Play House."　　R.M.

MOTEL HELL (1981). Texas Chainsaw meets Oscar Mayer. Rory Calhoun outstanding as "Farmer Vincent" who cures dead folks' organs into a special recipe for home-styled cold cuts. This is a tasty little sucker.　　G.T.

NOT OF THIS EARTH (1957). Alien visitor must wear wraparound shades to protect alien eyes from earth's bright sunlight (ha!). Blood is sucked from earthling victims via transfusion into **milk bottles!** Very "cool" performances by Beverly Garland and Corman vet Dick Miller (as a vacuum cleaner salesman).　　G.T.

OCEAN'S ELEVEN (1960). Sinatra's Rat Pack in its first screen fling. Dino, Sammy, Angie Dickinson, and the rest ("the hipster saints of the Booze Culture," said **High Times**) invade Vegas armed with in-jokes and swizzle sticks. Loose, juicy, it all leads to **Four for Texas, Robin and the Seven Hoods,** and the ultimate dry-out. Yuks on the rocks.

OUR MAN FLINT (1966). James Coburn began his continuing exposition of the Coolest Man Alive character with this spicy James Bond spoof involving lots of skin and an espionage agency called Z.O.W.I.E. See also **In Like Flint,** and **The President's Analyst.**

THE PARTY (1968). Peter Sellers, in between **Strangelove** and **Alice B. Toklas,** plays an Indian space case accidentally invited to a swingin' Hollywood soiree. Go-go boots, body paint, and a graffiti-covered elephant taking a bubble bath. "Birdy num nums."　　T.V.

PEEPING TOM (1959). Class director Michael Powell **(Red Shoes)** commits career-icide with a voyeuristic tale to end all voyeuristic tales. A weirdo films and tapes his victims' suffering just as his dad did to him. Character actor Miles Malleson enters a sweetshop-porno den, lips aquiver: "I understand you have some **views** for sale."　　R.B.

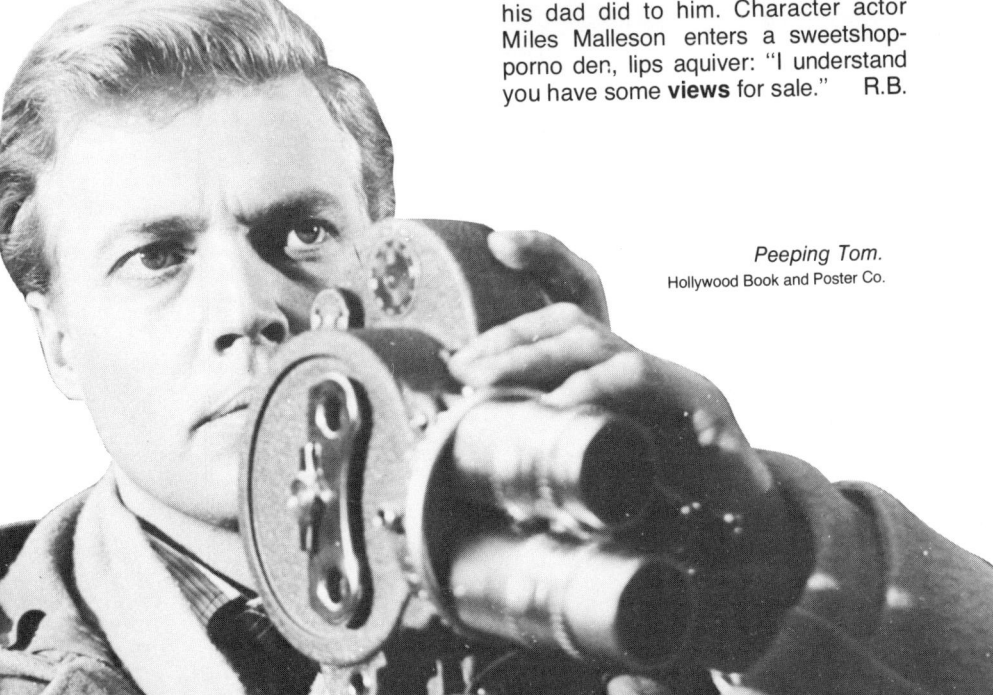

Peeping Tom.
Hollywood Book and Poster Co.

PETULIA (1968). Julie Christie at her sexy best in a saga of crumbling marriages and civilization set against the psyche-out world of Frisco '67. A young Grateful Dead grok and groove for swingers in a Telegraph Hill pad. Trip or freak.

PICKUP ON SOUTH STREET (1953). Sneering Richard Widmark ("Don't wave the flag at me!") accidentally cops some government secrets en route to the Commies, starts to feel the heat. Widmark lives in a shack in New York Harbor containing only a hammock and a rope, which he uses to haul cold beer out of the Hudson. Sexy Jean Peters bathes in bubbles with a smoke stuck in the corner of her mouth. Craazy. R.B.

PRIME CUT (1972). Totally flipsville! Gene Hackman eaten by pigs, a gangster's moll in a Louis Quinze houseboat on the Missouri, a pitchfork thrown into the side of a speeding Cadillac limo. A shotgun fight in a field of huge black-eyed Susans. A man pushed into a grinder, ground into hot dogs, and sent in a package to his wife. And more! R.B.

R.P.M. (1970). The only thing that could beat Ann-Margret playing a campus radical is Anthony Quinn as a left-leaning, motorcycle-riding professor named Taco. **R.P.M.** offers both.

SHACK OUT ON 101 (1955). Goofy gray paranoia from the Fifties. Lee Marvin plays Slob, a shambling short-order chef in Keenan Wynn's beachfront greasy spoon. While FBI agent Frank Lovejoy cops a cut-rate **From Here to Eternity** with Terry Moore on the sand (they look like cubes mating), Lee smuggles microfilm to the Reds. At one point the "story" stops dead for fifteen minutes while Marvin and Wynn hoist weights and compare lats and delts. Cheap thrills! R.B.

SHAKEDOWN (1950). Fuck-em-over news photographer Howard Duff tells a drowning man to raise his arms so it'll make a better picture, then booby-traps a mobster's car, popping his flash as the hood blows himself to bits. Editor: "How'd you get **this** shot?!" Duff (lighting a match with his fingernail): "Just happened to be passin' by..." R.B.

SKI PARTY (1965). Too cool: James Brown singing "I Feel Good" in a ski sweater on the slopes. T.V.

SLITHIS (1978). Not just another fish-man remake, this one takes place in Venice (California) canals and features the heaviest dose yet of high school science causality ("Louis Pasteur proved in 1872..."); great winos and riff-raff, including one guy with a real-looking burned-up face. Monsters so-so, but film's general shoddiness (at least five distinct types of bad acting incarnate) more than carries it. R.M.

SOLDIER IN THE RAIN (1963). Two decades have not made this existential Army pic any less strange, which is perfect. Sergeant Jackie Gleason drinks Cokes, philosophizes. Corporal Steve McQueen watches, listens. Tuesday Weld calls Gleason "Jellybelly."

SWEET SMELL OF SUCCESS (1957). Tony Curtis, a Brylcreemed weasel in a continental suit, and Burt Lancaster, a brush cut paranoiac in bifocals, trade hot riffs like Basie sidemen — "The cat's in the bag and the bag's in the river!" "Here's your head, what's your hurry?" "Who could love a man," asks Burt's sis (Susan Harrison), "who makes you jump through burning hoops like a trained poodle?" R.B.

THUNDER ROAD (1958). Flickdom's granddaddy of cool, bad Bob Mitchum in a barbiturate-soaked performance with equally zoned-out love interest Keely Smith. When some creep tries running moonshiner Mitch off the road, Mr. Heavylids coolly removes the old cig from his lip and flicks it across his car, out the window, and into the creep's car. It lands in his lap and he drives screaming to his death over an embankment.

WILD ANGELS (1966). The bikes start here in an epic cycle-drama starring Peter Fonda and his obsessively cool pals (Bruce Dern, Michael J. Pollard, and a leatherbound Nancy Sinatra). An idealized Blank Generation waltzes and wheelies to "Blues' Theme."

Mitchum never changes his expression!   R.B.

THE TREASURE OF SIERRA MADRE (1948). Not only does bandito Alfonso Bedoya "don't have to show you any stinkin' badges," he gets to reprimand Bogie himself — "Why don' you try to be a lettle more polite?"

WINCHESTER '73 (1950). Rock Hudson plays an Injun ("Young Calf"), and Dan Duryea gleefully upholds his reputation as the baddest bad-ass in the Old West, "Waco Johnny Dean." When a female admirer tells Duryea, "Waco Johnny, you're the meanest man in Texas," he replies, "Lady, don't limit me."   R.B.

the coolest movie of them all?

by Sal Zero

Between 1966 and 1967, James Coburn practically made a career of screen cool. His spy pics **Our Man Flint** and **In Like Flint** out-Bond Connery's Bond and trash Dean Martin's Matt Helm in a gale of demonic horselaughter. **Dead Heat On A Merry-Go-Round** (1967, with Camilla Sparv) is a nicely bent caper film, but it is **The President's Analyst,** released the same year, that yolks the Flint cool guy to the most extreme variety of mid-Sixties paranoia and ultimately pushes the gong-banging Coburn over the top and beyond the freaking pale.

Janitors and Russkies

The riff: Jim's a mild-mannered professional, a Washington shrink who answers his country's call by agreeing to become the President's personal analyst. Once he starts doing his duty, he's kidnapped … by unknown "enemies" who wrongly assume he's privy to the Prez's innermost thoughts and secrets. Coburn wrangles free, fleeing along a hellish escape route, collecting adversaries as he goes. By mid-film, he's pursued by Russkies, FBI, CIA, Pentagon, D.C. cops, and the White House janitorial staff. His girl, his best friend, and all acquaintances have either fled his side or stayed on as duplicitous double agents, faking him out in the most chilling evocation of over-the-shoulder paranoia since those pods started popping in **The Body Snatchers.**

Microbes and Ma Bell

He drops in and out of sight and scenes, including a brief stay with a band of flower children (led by Barry McGuire, fresh from "Eve of Destruction" duty), runs through a dozen jungles until he emerges as the Ultimate Paranoiac — hair-trigger nerves, rabbit reflexes, a bullshit detection system that bores through every come-on and setup thrown at him. Pressure molds Coburn's humble shrink into a bobbing and weaving paragon of cool that makes his Flint roles resemble a badly inked cartoon.

Ultimately, he gets to confront the root source of all this trouble — bigger than the CIA, more powerful than the FBI or the microbe-toting Russkies. In their futuristic subterranean headquarters, Mr. Jim faces the Enemy: faceless, multi-national corporate America. And the script doesn't pussyfoot. We're not talking some gray flannel **general** caricature of Big Business, all Babbitt-inspired and sitting like a duck. The enemy, the great subverter of faith and morals, says **The President's Analyst,** is … the phone company! It's the grand dame Ma Bell herself, with all her codes and hidden charges, unmanageable cords, dangling clauses disguising taxes within taxes, tolls, irritating tones, and sexless recorded voices. Go ahead and dial.

The scenario flips the wig and closes the film in short order, but the revelation — as tongue-in-cheek and chilling as it simultaneously manages to be — lingers, like Coburn's cool heroics, and earns **Analyst** enough extra chips to make it easily outstack the heartiest contenders.

Born Too Late

Too late and great to classify, two recent films deserve closer looks.

THE LOVELESS (1982). Obsessive cool fuels this too-tough tribute to Brando's **Wild One.** Black leather bikers, led by Robert Gordon and his pard with craggy Grand Canyon cheeks, breeze into hicksville. Grand Canyon deflowers an extremely wanton local whose hayseed pop gets on a revenge riff. Plot twists, surreal dialogue, plus Gordon's gothic Jack Scott variations and Lounge Lizard John Lurie's ultra-Beat theme music.

DIVA (1982). French techno-sensual thriller featuring a sci-fi punk killer, a moped chase in a subway, a shoplifting Oriental teenybopper, apartments decorated in Early Auto Wreckage. Bonus: a guy in a snorkel mask peeling onions. Whew!   R.B.

Most Sunglasses Worn in a Single Movie

The award goes to **Johnny Cool** (1963), starring Henry Silva as a hood (with Joey Bishop as a car salesman), and **The Comedians** (1967), which features Liz Taylor, Richard Burton, and Peter Ustinov, all at one point or another hiding behind Foster Grants.

A Discourse on Horror, Gore, Zombie Distinction and the 13 Schools of Dementia. For credit.

ghoul cool

by Gregg Turner

Scalpels glisten in the subterranean operating room, jungle servant apes surgeon barking out orders. Victim Number One, strapped to a slab table, screams for mercy but Dr. Butcher, M.D., will have none of it: **"Shaddup! I don't care about you. All I want is your brain."** This is a gruff Dr. Butcher! Blood-soaked brains awaiting transplant and a legion of obsequious zombies testify to the serious business at hand. No one's smiling. Everybody will die in a bloodbath of gratuitous gore and gorged gratuity! **Dr. B. M.D.** (1982) inherits a proud filmic tradition.

So-called **splatter movies** aim "not to scare or drive audiences to the edge of their seats in suspense, but to **morti-**

fy them with scenes of explicit gore," explains genre expert John McCarty in his book **Splatter Movies.** "Mutilation is the message — sometimes the only one."

But why stop there? Within even the so-called closed system of Splatter reside dozens of thus far unaccredited cool sub schools. The wide world of low-budget sleazy horror sends signals to dozens of message centers. These days, almost every new feature breeds a new subgenre, expanding previous parameters.

Take **The Hills Have Eyes,** for example, Wes Craven's camper-family-stranded - in - the - desert - and - surrounded-by-maniacs saga. It borrows heavily from Tobe Hooper's **Texas Chainsaw Massacre.** But **Hills'** expansive Splatter spirit adds new rules to the game. Craven's new dimensions pile up the fear factors like poker chips: rattlesnakes; kidnapped baby; missing daddy tied to a stake, bound, gagged and torched. An ear of bright yellow corn stops the old geezer's mouth from screaming; as the flames lick his clothes, Craven's disaffected camera rolls around the guy's head. There's a newfound, demented cleverness here that doesn't stop with wild characteriza-

Class-obsessed
Two-type (right)
embraces next
of kin in
Jerry Gross
Organization's
Zombie.

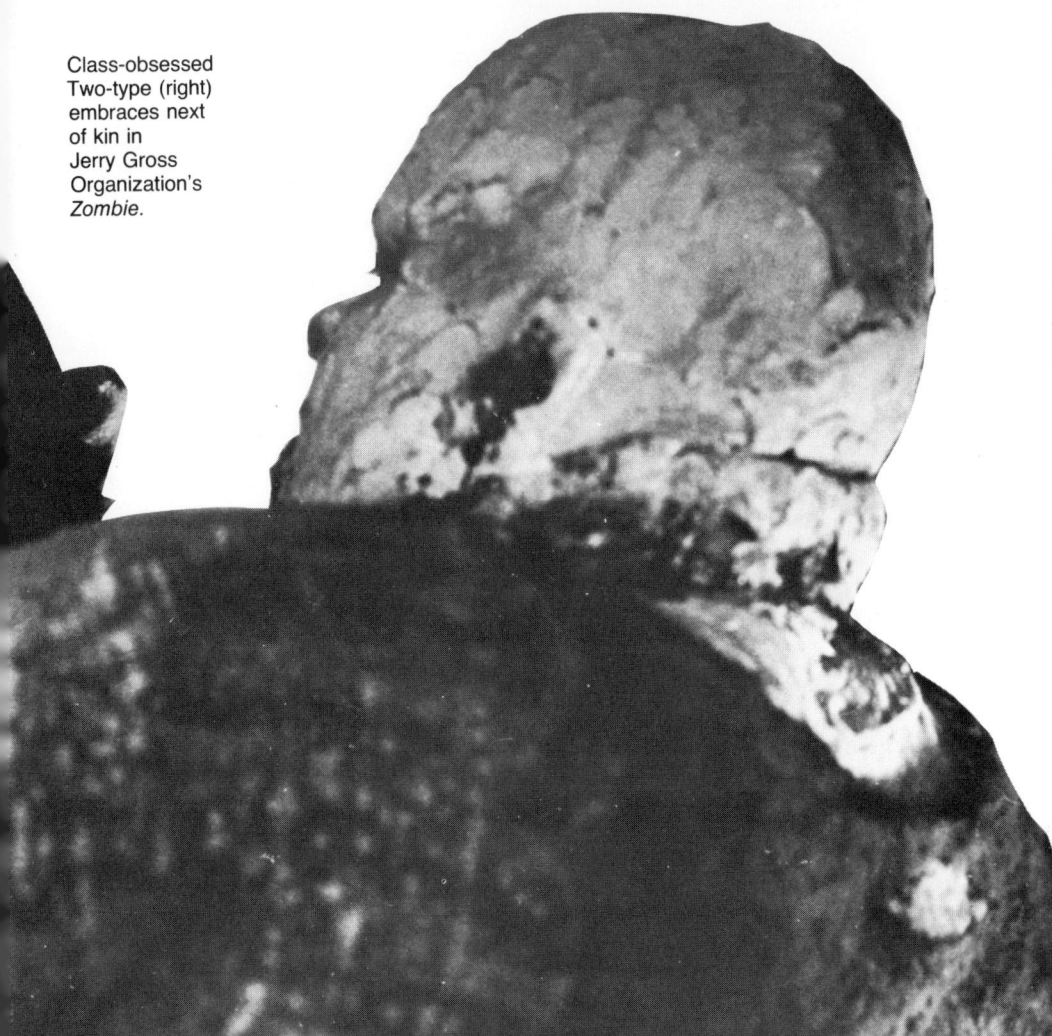

1980's **Doc Butcher** wears its cool on its plasma-drenched sleeve by not even bothering to apologize — for its incomprehensible plot and unintelligible dialogue (overdubbed and lip-synched in English!).

tion and taffylike plot twisting (shades of Edward Albee).

Or take old **Doc Butcher** himself. This weasely imitation of 1980's vastly superior **Zombie** wears its cool on its plasma-drenched sleeve by not even bothering to apologize for its incomprehensible plot and unintelligible dialogue (overdubbed and lip-synched in English!) The film's initial setting, N.Y.C., dissolves into tropical junglescape and a regular Gilligan's Island of blade-crazy headhunters and decaying zombies. Throats are slit, guts devoured, all in outlandish satanic rites whose sole purpose seems to be (many times mute's "the only message") propagation of the splatter species itself.

Some species. When did the crazy parenting start?

Theatre du Grand Guignol. The French theater "created initially in the late 1800s for the benefit of those with jaded tastes," says McCarty, gravitated even further toward "a more unsophisticated audience." Eventually they were portraying realistic eye-gougings and beheadings (leave it to those French). Claims McC: "Plots were openly derivative or nonexistent. In **Grand Guignol,** gore, not drama, was the thing. Like a ghoulish magic show." Hi mom, hi dad.

That's what the immortal Herschell Gordon Lewis must've said in 1963

when he began filming what experts agree was the very first of its kind — **Blood Feast,** a no-holds-barred barrage of violence and psychosis from start to finish. Lewis, a "one-time" prof of English at the University of Mississippi (M.A. in journalism, doctorate in psychology), tinkered uneventfully with "serious cinema" before making some modest attempts at sexploitation with **Daughters of the Sun** and **B-O-I-N-N-N-G.** Feast itself followed, with an unrepentant orgy of gore. Synopsis: a deranged head-case, on a crusade to replenish the "life force" of a long dead Egyptian princess, winds up tearing limbs and organs from well-endowed young women with lots to offer.

Even the Medveds, in their **Golden Turkey Awards** book (Putnam's, 1980), salute the film's most famous scene, which depicts "the youthful hero reaching into the mouth of one of his love victims and ripping out her tongue. To shoot the sequence, Lewis used a sheep's tongue. Sixty thousand dollars and nine days' filming in Miami were enough to complete the project." The tongue, not especially well refrigerated before its cinematic debut, required "a liberal dose of Pine-sol" before it was serviceable.

Full-scale leave-taking of one's senses was H.G.'s beat. (See also **2000 Maniacs, Gore Gore Girls,** and **She Devils On Wheels.**) Make no mistake. Such abandon is surely a credential of cool in the splatter realm. Not just brainless mummies or dim-bulb Franks and Dracs but the living dead (vampires, ghosts) — the whole senseless spectrum of human facsimiles charged with paranormal life force.

In the great **Not of This Earth** (1958), mindlessness is induced with an alien (Paul Birch) who comes from "somewhere else" (!). Birch becomes an icon of orthodox cool by donning a pair of '67 Lou Reed wraparound shades, then goes berserk. He gets hyperkinetic, hops around like an insurance salesman on acid, and begins speaking with this weird, maybe Armenian accent that makes zero sense. Birch is surely one of the coolest cats ever to script-speak horror flick dialogue. Once he snaps, his laconic drawl gives way to grunts, barks, and ranting commands not unlike Kevin McCarthy in the original **Invasion of the Body Snatchers.** (K.M. was last seen on the nighttime soap **Flamingo Road,** wearing a Southern accent that's about as convincing as a drugstore toupee.)

But Birch's mindless behavior (and the film's utter senselessness) is sublime. "Luke into my eyes! My eyes are **aa-lien!**" he bellows. After some friendly blood-siphoning (into milk bottles) and a vacuum cleaner demonstration by B-movie legend Dick Miller (Corman's **Bucket of Blood,** etc.), Birch pursues Beverly Garland in the most redundant chase scene ever shot — one series of roadway footage recycled six or seven times, end on end. "Luke at my eyes, you fool!" he yells from his car to Bev in hers. But she's too clever to "luke" into her rearview mirror, and shortly thereafter Birch cracks up on the highway.

Fear grips potential victim of Class I zombies in George Romero's *Night of the Living Dead.*

It's really not that far from irrationality to the blissfully witless. Absurdity and brilliant stupidity are just over the hill, and the place where they all collide — the veritable astral plane of cosmic horror show ridiculousness — is Zombieville. Since violence and grossness are common by-products of conventional monster movie insanity, zombs encompass **all** aspects of creep cool. It's a rare zomb epic that fails to incorporate all these strains. Bela Lugosi's **White Zombie** (1932) and **Revolt of the Zombies** (1936) bring you right up to the amazing **I Walked with a Zombie** (1945) and George Romero's workouts

Romero's zombies are all Class I's: grave-risen moms & grandma's merely answering the call of a higher command to get up and do the funky deathwalk around the streets of your town. They take orders.

in **Night of the Living Dead** and **Dawn of the Dead.**

Romero's zombies are all Class I's: grave-risen moms and grandmas merely answering the call of a higher command to get up and do the funky deathwalk around the streets of your town. They take orders. Class II zombies act on impulse and aren't nearly as predictable (or subservient). The creatures of 1981's **Zombie** are Class II's. Their path of orbit appears almost arbitrary, they're more self-propelled and pissed-off than the folks in **Last Man on Earth** (1964) or **Zombies of Mora-Tau** (1957).

Class II's can play night and day, but most Z-I's come to life when the sun sets. **Last Man**'s I's spend all eve chasing Vincent Price. They also share gene

secrets with their cousin Dracula — they don't like garlic, and it's suggested their condition is the result of "a rare blood disease," which links them to the swell **Dr. Butcher** once again, as well as to **They Came from Beyond Space** (1967) wherein an alien intelligence uses corpses to **spread the plague!** Class I zombies are rarely considered disease carriers. Zombie motivation leads to still more sub schools, such as the exotic robot z's of **Target Earth** (1954). Luke at them.

After zombies, we're left with little in the way of ghoul cool that hasn't been previously explored. There's the boring rational-parables-of-man's-demise routine — radiation, hothouse effects, marine life malaise in **Attack of the Crab Monsters, The Immortal Monster,** and **Caltiki** (malevolent jellyfish). **Creature from the Black Lagoon** in 1954 introduced actual fish-man monsters (nothing more than a gilled Class II zombie), which inspired **Slithis** and 1980's **Humanoids from the Deep.** Demon and devil-possession cool is well documented, and so's modern gothic **(Amityville Horror)** and the rube-fiend wing of Agri-horror (1981's **Motel Hell** and 1975's **Race with the Devil,** with Peter Fonda, Warren Oates, and their wives fleeing squads of hick devil-cultists).

For true creativity in a Hideously Underrated Semi-Splatter Work, the winner is **The Monster of Piedras Blancas** (1958). Unlike the **implied** violence that most ghoul films run on, **Piedras Blancas'** lead creatch goes for explicit decapitation. (This one'll never make it onto TV.) In the best tradition, stupidity and gross-out walk hand in hand here. In one mind-boggling scene, the monster strolls into the center of town, turns into a grocery store, makes it over to the produce section, and palms two freshly severed heads that have been tossed in with the romaine and iceberg.

Luke into my lettuce!

Once, the name of the movies'
swingin'-est spy was on everyone's lips.
Now, for all we know, he could be
losing it in Jamaica's Blue Mountains.

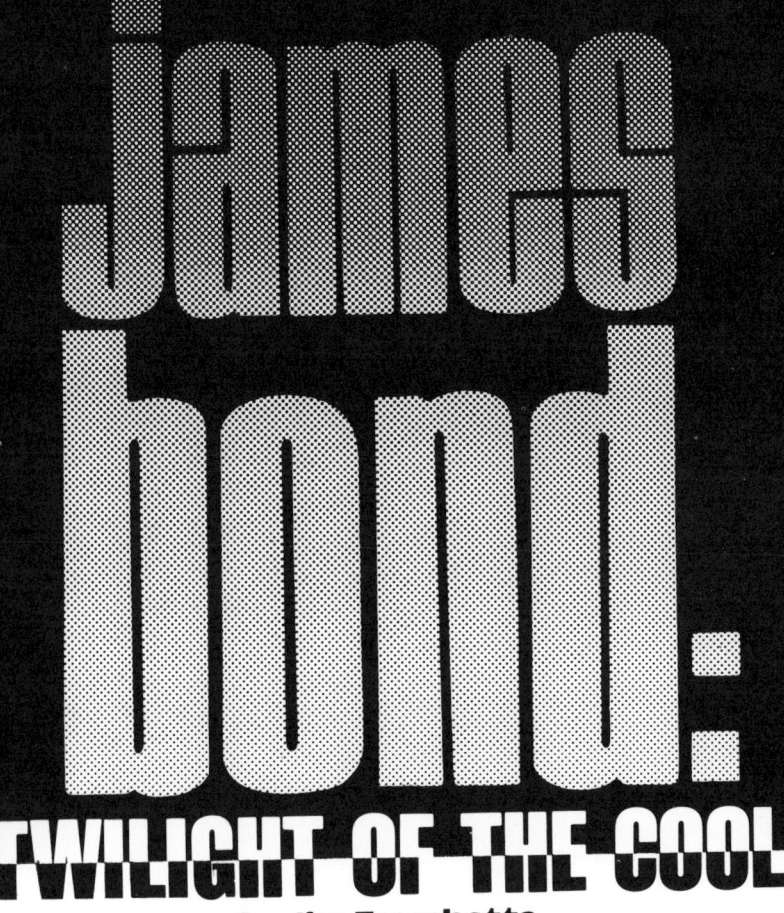

james bond:
TWILIGHT OF THE COOL

by Jim Trombetta

He was so cool he should have been
taken into the skies like a hero of classical myth and made into a constellation.
We would see him on clear nights in his
characteristic pose, upright yet relaxed,
one leg cocked, one hand holding up
the slender pistol so tastefully silenced.
Instead we see him on all the usual billboards. He has become one more
blue-chip property.

No doubt James Bond will be garner-
ing a healthy slice of our entertainment
dollar for fiscal years to come. Yet his
appeal is like light continuing to reach
us from a star that in reality faded long
ago. First he became camp, and now
he is nearly quaint. But once he was the
very form and model of cool.

Once his name was on everyone's
lips. Once his movies were events that

embodied the promise of wishes fulfilled. He was as big as the Beatles and merchandised just like them, in everything from tuxedoes to lingerie. "In today's world," a purveyor of 007 goods noted in the Sixties, "there are lots of people who think James Bond really existed. They even feel he is still operating somewhere." One of these people was a president of the United States who endorsed Bond and apparently identified with him — maybe a little too much.

Up there where the air is rare

Bond — his very name suggests the values that made him: sound currency, good whiskey, and a soupcon (at least) of actual integrity. Bond was the kind of whole man who, like the heroes of classical myth, was at home in every element of the world. He was at ease in underground caverns, beneath the sea, in the high snows, and in the air up to the verge of Space itself. In each realm he knew just what to do and just to how to handle himself. And while we might sometimes see a scene in which Bond, say, practiced his karate, there was no indication he'd ever struggled to learn anything. No, the skills he needed sprang immediately from his inborn being. What could be cooler than that?

Bond was surely a superman, but he was a superman in a suit and tie, and perhaps his coolest trait was that he was wonderful in such a middle-class

way. His world, rife with terror as it was, was also one of great convenience, stocked with usable objects. That he cheerfully relied on every handy device science could give him (from the briefcase packed with throwing knife and folding Armalite Survival Gun to the Aston-Martin with ejection seat) hardly made him seem less resourceful. Indeed, all these products were as much a part of him as his DNA and, moreover, made him one with his audience. Every time we recognized a quality brand, every time we put our hands on the steering wheel and our foot on the accelerator, every time we delicately lifted the tone arm of our belt-driven turntable, we shared in Bond's cool mastery.

And, of course, he always had the Best Girls. The Best Girls were perhaps more memorable for their promotional layouts in **Playboy** than for their actual participation in Bond's adventures (Diana Rigg we remember for more than either), but they were tantalizing in their essence. In a sense, they merge into one lithe torso, set off by bikini parts and packed with action. The Best Girls were noble savages in swimsuits, post-industrial Pocahontases, children of nature beholden to no one, yet in dire need, exotics whose kisses were unlike all others ... Bond got them just by showing up. In him, even lust was cool.

Sorry, Roger

Sean Connery is entitled to a lion's share of credit for the coolness of Bond. He had the earthiness without which coolness becomes too ethereal and the strength to support elegance and self-deprecating wit. In Connery's performances, Bond's subtle perception of style — like identifying a villain by the wine he orders — became more than the fetishistic nicety of a British Old Boy that it was in Fleming's books. It became something more universal — what

Americans used to call "class." (Those who felt a little jealous of Bond's cool perfection could console themselves that Sean was getting bald in front.)

Roger Moore seems like a hell of a nice guy — rather winning, really — but he's more tepid than cool. One thing he lacks is the streak of true menace.

In **Doctor No,** a Bond sidekick grasps the wrist of a suspect girl and asks, "James, should I break her arm?" Bond shrugs. "Another time, perhaps." A guy as cool as Bond needed a conscience like he needed a crutch. Not for him the neuroses of his hardboiled ancestors; not for him the melancholia of Philip Marlowe, the venom of Sam Spade. No, this most cultivated of men was also most natural, and though he presumably served the abstract interests of nation-states, his graceful and efficient violence really expressed a healthy personal dislike for its deserving targets. Bond was that enviable man who could give into his impulses because his impulses were always on the money. If he followed a grieving widow home after a funeral and suddenly bashed her, sure enough, it was a SPECTRE bastard in drag.

Top Cop in Town

It takes a civilized world to make a man as natural as Bond, and he had it. Bond's heyday was the future, the future which never quite came off: that sunny, electric, neotribal age we used to hear so much about, whose coming was announced when the astronauts took in the whole Earth at a glance. Bond was the sheriff of the Global Village, top cop of the whole strange but readily encompassed planet. In his world there was no wilderness so trackless it didn't conceal at least one secret fortress or superscientific installation. And the hybrid pedigrees of his antagonists — the blue-eyed Asiatic Doctor No or the Franco-Greco-Roman-Balkan Ernest Stavro Blofeld — came to embody not Ian Fleming's upper-class distrust of the half-caste, but bizarre cultural fusions popping up spontaneously, like new languages, as boundaries vanished in the imploding world.

As the Cold War got old, as detente came on, Bond's old Russian enemy SMERSH was retired in favor of SPECTRE, a consortium of free-lance bad-asses who transcended any nation. Bond's British identity was itself no more than a flag of convenience. At his best, he defended the consensus of Earth, the emerging global Utopia, against overweening outlaws.

Such conditions, it seems, no longer obtain. The world is once again too primitive, and too vast, to support a Bond.

He is no longer even affordable. There are new guys running the old intelligence agency now — for "M" has long since retired to his country house, where he sits, bleary-eyed, drink in hand, reminiscing for all comers — and these new guys bitch about what a prima donna Bond is. They query his expense reports, refuse to reimburse him for gas for the Aston-Martin. They try to get him to drive a Cortina; they try to give him assignments: "James, when you get down to [deleted], proceed to the village of [deleted] and terminate the mayor — he's helping the guerillas. On the way back, stop off at the capital and help herd the losers into the football stadium. Oh, by the way, here's our newest Field Torture Kit — see, it's no bigger than a cigarette lighter…"

007 balks. This job is not his style. So the new guys pull a political number, and Bond finds himself forcibly retired. He shrugs and buys a house in the Blue Mountains of Jamaica. There he toys with the idea of writing a book to expose his former employers, but one day someone comes along and offers him a spliff. He smokes them contentedly into his old age.

...Yet elsewhere, a much more secret and advanced agency has a sliver of skin from 007's fingertip. From cells therein they grow a New Cool Hero with all the genes of Bond. They bring him along and keep a close eye on him.

The New Cool Hero has forgotten all the standard brands, and in a world of name-droppers he cannot be impressed. He bides his time at a middle-class desk; he smokes cigarettes without really knowing why and thinks about giving them up; he pumps his own gas and hoards goods against a predicted earthquake. He dreams of leaping out of airplanes, given a parachute and one good reason. More than once he has glimpsed evil in the mirror, and at such times he sorely misses his old enemies, the old days when one man could juggle the Earth and a cool hero catch it in midair.

Surely his employers will have work for him soon. Surely they will say to him, "Do this for us and no more, James. No surprises, please." But he knows he will give them surprises.

His dream assignment arrives all at once with the flashing news: a string of assassinations in the Middle East, threatening to throw the whole region into chaos. Ayatollahs, sheiks, colonels, potentates of all stripes, left and right, go down like pins in an alley. The assassins do not flee; they stand and laugh; they bite down on the muzzles of their pistols and blow out the tops of their heads.

The man behind all this calls himself Hassan. He claims he is the reincarnation of Hassan-i-Sabbah, a.k.a. "The Old Man of the Mountain," the warlord who plagued the Crusaders, from whose names the words **assassin** and **hashish** are derived. Like his namesake, the new Hassan has a mountain fortress in Central Asia. There he brings his assassin recruits, whom he plies with the most sophisticated drugs. A master of illusions, he pretends to kill them... and then he wakes them up. In his pleasure gardens they taste all the delights of Eden, most especially the magnificent women, the **houris** of Islamic paradise, whose lithe loins mold men's hearts. Then Hassan appears to his recruits as a severed head impaled on a high stake and speaks: "You have already died and are immortal. Have you not known Paradise? Therefore fear nothing. Go forth and do evil in my name." And they do.

To reach Hassan it is necessary to cross mountains full of peril; zealot legions, roving Soviet gunships, Afghan cavalrymen who grew up playing polo with the body of a dead goat and would just as soon play it with the living body of an intruder. And who can encompass these dangers? Who can infiltrate the fortress, seduce the **houris,** quell the tyrant? Only one man...

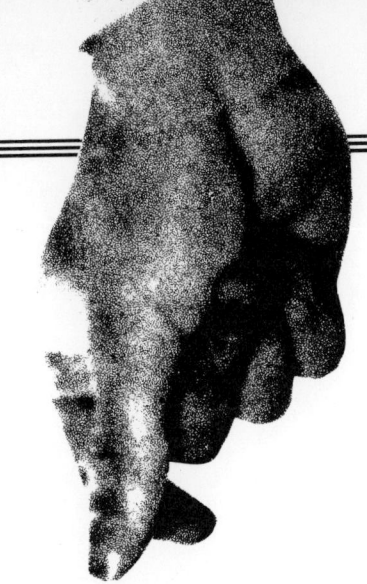

shop around...

OK. So now that you're hipped to the cool film cosmos, you're dying to see what Jack Palance looks like playing Fidel, and naturally you'd like to know where you can score a copy of, say, **Che!** for home viewing. Hold on.

Some measure of just how dire things are out there screen-wise is that of the thousands of movies now available for consumption in various video formats, barely half a dozen on our hit list show up in any manufacturer's catalog. We are happy to report that you can buy a copy of **Dirty Harry** or rent the immortal, mook-infested **Mean Streets** from Warner Home Video, and Paramount'll sell you **Godfather II**. Magic Carpet Video's got all the **Lolita**'s you want and Sound Video Unlimited can let loose **Slithis'** moldy fish-monsters in your living room tonight. Wizard Of Vid will happily put **Zombie** on your screen,

and RM Films International offers **Beyond the Valley of the Dolls** and other Russ Meyer masterpieces. (Write the old coot and tell him how anxious you are: RM Films International, P.O. Box 3748, Los Angeles, California 90028.)

But, by and large, it's real dark out there when it comes to cool classics procurement. A few bright ideas: scan your weekly **TV Guide** for advance viewing info on movies on TV, haunt your local video software store, and check the catalogs. (The major film studios now dump a hundred or so new titles into the VHS/Beta bins each month, and you never know when some studio whiz kid will realize the gold mine waiting to be struck when he exercises vid rights to **Kitten with a Whip** or **High School Confidential**.)

The monthly video mags are another source to keep tabs on, as they relay movie availability news fairly quickly. There's even **Video Swapper** ($12 for twelve issues to P.O. Box 309, Fraser, Michigan 48026), which boasts a small "Trading Post" classified section. (Sample ad: "HELP! I Need VHS copy of 'Zabriskie Point'! Will trade for 'Untouchables' episodes.")

Another convenient tool is Howard Polskin's **Mail Order Guide to Movies on Videotape** (Fireside Books), which lists movies in vid-release and offers convenient ordering information. As of presstime, Polskin's original 1980 version was still available at stores, though in dire need of updating. Watch for a new edition.

As a last resort, you could always go the American way — gather like-minded pals and petition your local "revival" movie theater with a request: Couldn't they chuck their regular midnight screenings of the **Rocky Horror Picture Show** and **The Song Remains the Same** just one night and throw on a triple bill of cool fare? Say, like maybe **The Beat Generation, Jigsaw,** and **Petulia**...

Buckley rolls on, in an extrapolation of black jazz-rap, to clue us in on Einstein's subsequent relocation to Switzerland: "Now, not digging the lick, you see, of these double-square kicks the cats were puttin' down, he saved his beans and finally he swung with a Swiss passport, *swooped* the scene and lit in the land of the Coool, to prove and groove with the Alpine-heads!"

Hipster Saint LORD BUCKLEY

Maybe we shouldn't be talking about Lord Buckley at all.

It's just that, having been a secret so long, could he stand the public acclaim? Besides, words were his axe, and when it comes to that instrument, nobody blew it better.

Richard "Lord" Buckley (1906-60) is in this *Catalog* because he was the embodiment of life lived coolly. If the coolest one can be is fashioning an accurate expression of what's inside, then Buckley was easily, to borrow a phrase from him, one of "the wildest, grooviest, hippest, swingin'-est, double-frantic, maddest, most exquisite" cats that ever breathed.

It also helps if what's inside is good to start with. Like maybe a huge heart. Tons of compassion. A mind that spontaneously generates material to entertain itself even when there are no audiences around. Or a conviction that language itself is the headiest brew and that staying drunk is divine.

Lord Buckley had all this inside. You'll know that when you hear his records. They're all that survive a life and a "career" that was by all accounts unpredictable and gloriously insane.

Much of the material on albums like *Way Out Humor* and *A Most Immaculately Hip Aristocrat* takes the form of parables. The best known may be his life of Christ "The Nazz" ("the sweetest far-out cat that ever stomped on this Sweet Green Sphere!"). There are also routines on Gandhi ("The Hip Gahn"), Jonah and the whale, Poe's "Raven," and Marc Antony's oration at Caesar's funeral.

The two that made a believer of me are Buckley's profile of the Spanish explorer Alvar Nuñez de Vaca and—best of all—his interpretation of the life of Einstein called "The Hip Einie."

On the multicandle brainpower of this most eminent "sphere-gasser" and his continual job-loot predicaments: "Now here was a cat who carried so much *wiggage*—he was gig-less! He *could* not find a wheel to turn! He sounded all the hubcaps within' reach but nathan shakin'. He could *not* connect." Buckley rolls on, in an extrapolation of black jazz-rap, to clue us in on Einstein's subsequent relocation to Switzerland: "Now, not digging the lick, you see, of these double-square kicks the cats were puttin' down, he saved his beans and finally he swung with a Swiss passport, *swooped* the scene and lit in the land of the Coool, to prove and groove with the Alpine-heads!"

Ultimately, the Hip Einie connects with a gig, a pad, a wife and kids. Writing down his scientific theories, he soon becomes "the king of all Space-heads," flips the physics-chemistry community on its ear, ascends to top dog status at the U of Zurich, and wows the world. Buckley shouts, whispers, wails like an evangelist wired to a generator, stomps through the tale (there is no way to repeat or paraphrase his explication of Einstein's theory—you have to be there) and finally winds down.

Buckley's personal (and sometimes highly public) life was a true trip itself. Born of Indian extraction in California's Mother Lode gold country in '06, he gravitated to Frisco, then to the Texas oil fields. He spent the Thirties doing standup in Capone-style Chicago speakeasies, made it to New York and married "Lady" Buckley. By the mid-Fifties he was reigning hepcat to a circle of admirers that included Sinatra, Robert Mitchum and Stuart Whitman. Ed Sullivan put him on TV; Jonathan Winters, Red Foxx, and every other comedian dug him. Ultimately, he suffered the Bruce-type fuzz busts—in New York City in '60, where he died in November.

Which is great and dramatic, and somebody should (and somebody else will) make a movie of it someday. But what really counts is first-person Buckley, his work. It goes like this . . .

Hipsters, Flipsters, and Finger-Poppin' Daddies

by Lord Richard Buckley

Now you see in Hip Talk, they call William Shakespeare "Willie the Shake"! You know why they call him "Willie the Shake"? Because HE SHOOK EVERYBODY!! They gave this Cat five cents' worth of ink and a nickel's worth of paper, and he sat down and wrote up such a breeze, WHAMMMMMM!!! Everybody got off! Period! He was a hard, tight, tough Cat. Pen in hand, he was a Mother Superior.

Now you remember when Mark and Cleo were swangin' up a storm on the velvet-lined Nile barge suckin' up a little Egyptian whiskey with that wild incense flyin' all over the place and that Buddha-headed moon pale Jazzmin colored flippin' the scene. It was Romance City! Caesar meantime had split to Rome, went over to that big Jam Session and they sliced the poo' Cat up all over the place. Naturally Mark has got to put Cleo down; this was a tight move for him 'cause this Cleo was an early day Elizabeth Taylor. This chick had more curves than the Sante Fe Railroad making the Grand Canyon. But he had to split 'cause Caesar was his Main-Day Buddy Cat and they were putting Caesar in the hole. "And you know every Fox has got his Box."

The Roman Senate is jumpin' salty all over the place so Mark the Spark showed on the scene, faced all the studs, wild and otherwise, and shook up the whole Scene! As he BLEW:

Hipsters, Flipsters, and Finger-Poppin'
    Daddies,
Knock me your lobes!
I came here to lay Caesar out,
Not to hip you to him.
The bad jazz a cat blows
Wails long after he's cut out.
The groovy is often stashed with their
    frames,
So don't put Caesar down.

The swinging Brutus had laid a story on you,
That Caesar was hooked for power.
If it were so, it was a sad drag
And sadly hath the Caesar cat answered it.
Here, with a pass from Brutus and the other brass,
For Brutus is a worthy stud.
Yea, so are they all worthy studs.

I come to wail at Caesar's wake,
He was my buddy-cat, and he leveled with me.
Yet Brutus digs that he has eyes for power,
And Brutus is a solid cat.
It is true he hath returned with many freaks in chains,
And brought them home to Rome!
Yea, the booty was looty and hipped the treasury well!

Dost thou dig that this was Caesar's groove for the push?
When the cats with the empty kicks have copped out,
Yeah—, Caesar hath copped out too, and cried up a storm!
To be a world grabber, a stiffer riff must be blown.

Without bread, a stud can't even rule an ant hill.

Yet Brutus was swinging for the moon,
And Yea, Brutus is a worthy stud.
And all you cats were gagged on the Lupercal,
When he came on like a King freak.
Three times I laid the Kingly wig on him,
And thrice did he put it down.
Was this the move of a greedy hipster?
Yet Brutus said he dug the lick,
And Yea, a hipper cat hath never blown.

Some claim that Brutus' story was a drag,
But I dug the story was solid!
I came here to blow, now stay cool while I blow!
You dug him all the way once because you were hip that he was solid.
How can you now come on so square?
Now that he has cut out of this world?
City Hall has flipped, and swung to a drunken zoo!
And all of you cats have goofed to wig city!
Dig me hard, my ticker is in the coffin there with Caesar,
And Yea, I must stay cool, 'Til it flippeth back to me.

Lord Buckley Bequeaths...

The Records

Euphoria (Vaya Records); *Way Out Humor* (World Pacific); *A Most Immaculately Hip Aristocrat* (Straight/Reprise); *Gettysburg Address & James Dean* (Hip); *Hipsters, Flipsters & Finger-Poppin' Daddies* (RCA); *Lord Buckley, Blowing His Mind (and Yours Too)* (World Pacific); *Lord Buckley in Concert* (WP). Sadly, the only one still in print is Elektra's *The Best of Lord Buckley*, which features "The Nazz," "Nero," "The Hip Gahn," and others.

The Book

City Lights Books still sells *Hiparama of the Classics,* transcriptions of seven of Buckley's best raps, including "The Bad Rapping of the Marquis de Sade" and "The Religious History Of Alvar Nuñez Cabaza de Vaca." Send $3 plus 75¢ postage to City Lights, 261 Columbus Avenue, San Francisco, California 94133.

What was that guy's name? The Canuck prof who blew his larynx out in the Sixties preaching the demise of print? We forget. But his message didn't really shake too many trees, since the Guttenberg galaxy keeps rolling along. We're of course talking novels, magazines, comics, special instruments of cool. They're all about to be covered right here, starting with the

great books
Forty Must-Haves, Hiply Writ

AGAINST NATURE—Joris-Karl Huysmans (Penguin paper). Decadent nobleman throws an all-black dinner party to celebrate his impotence; creates "taste symphonies" with liqueurs; gets horny over Dickens novels and pays for a street punk to go to the greatest whore for a month before cutting him off, hoping he'll turn to crime to keep balling. Like sick. R.B.

THE BEAT GENERATION AND THE ANGRY YOUNG MEN—edited by Gene Feldman and Max Gartenberg (Dell). "A product of the Age of Anxiety, this is the HIPSTER, a man without a country—who digs everything and is shocked by nothing." And that's just the opening blurb on this 1958 masterpiece that throws Mailer, Ginsberg, Kerouac, J. P. Donleavy, and Kingsley Amis into a pot and simmers. The essays are the best, with each writer trying like hell to tie down his part of the elephant. Howl on. P.L.

BEEN DOWN SO LONG IT LOOKS LIKE UP TO ME—Richard Fariña (Random House; Dell paper). The fact that he may inadvertently have invented Tom Robbins should not be held against this late great. This tale of a hopped-up dropout clashing with early Sixties college life is *the* missed link between the beatbooks of Kerouac,

Brossard, etc. and the great hippie novels that were never written. Maybe the flower kids took one look at *Been Down So Long* and gave up. Dig its dialogue, Fariña's wild prose dance, and characters like Gnossos and the malevolent hepcat Motherball. Pynchon called the book "hilarious, chilling, sexy." Fariña called it quits 4-30-66: Returning from a party celebrating *Been Down*'s publication, he was killed in a motorcycle accident. He was

twenty-nine. Somebody get this one back in print pronto. Sounds: his album with wife, Mimi, *Reflections in a Crystal Wind* (Vanguard, 1965). S.Z.

BRIGHTON ROCK—Graham Greene (various). A really cheap hood wreaks metaphysical havoc in Greene's best potboiler. Cool is here extrapolated as relentless evil and total alienation. Compared to "Pinky" here, James Dean, Elvis, *et al.* were a bunch of namby-pamby wimps. D.S.

CHOCOLATES FOR BREAKFAST— Pamela Moore (Holt, Rinehart and Winston; Bantam paper). This eighteen-year-old "answer to Francoise Sagan" penned the ultimate teen sophisticate fantasy in '56. Her fifteen-year-old heroine first balls a fag actor in H'wood, then makes it with some hermetic, filthy rich, hotel-bound Italian count in New York, where she's gone to swing at the Stork Club. At home, mom serves martinis at eleven, breakfast at noon. R.B.

COFFIN ED AND GRAVEDIGGER JONES series—Chester Himes (various paper). These two black plain-

A CONFEDERACY OF
B-474
$3.95

DUNCES

The Pulitzer Prize Novel
by
John Kennedy Toole

"A corker, an epic comedy, a rumbling, roaring avalanche of a book" —*Washington Post*

© 1980, Grove Press

clothesmen operate out of a Harlem full of drunks, ragpickers, religious nuts, street gangs, dykes, and sissies. Bizarre deadpan violence on every page, but Ed and Dig always keep their cool. *Cotton Comes to Harlem* was the (1970) movie version, starring Godfrey Cambridge. R.B.

A CONFEDERACY OF DUNCES— John Kennedy Toole (Grove Press). The coolest American hero of recent years wore earflaps, caroused with b-girls in a Bourbon Street dive called the Night of Joy, and contended with a mad world and a mother who feared he'd become "a communiss." They don't make 'em like this anymore.

CONFESSIONS OF A HOAXER— Alan Abel (Macmillan). OK, there've been odder political candidates than Yetta Bronstein, more ludicrous rock stars than Count Von Blitzstein, social protests every bit as ill-founded as the campaign to clothe nude animals. But they didn't all have a single mastermind behind them. Alan Abel got away with the above and more (including staging the debut of the world's first topless string quartet). *Confessions* makes it look easy, as well as eminently worthwhile. P.L.

DIALOGUES WITH MARCEL DUCHAMP—Pierre Cabanne (Viking Press). In which it is proved that there were great smart-asses even before our generation. The man who said "To be what people call anti-art is really to affirm art, in the same way that an atheist affirms God. The only way to be really anti-art is to be indifferent" says more still. R.S.

FLASH AND FILIGREE—Terry Southern (Dell paper). The brilliant comic

THE DOCUMENTS OF 20TH-CENTURY ART

Dialogues with Marcel Duchamp by Pierre Cabanne

© 1971, Viking Press

writer's first novel, containing the boss TV game show "What's My Disease," a seduction scene comprised solely of grappling maneuvers, and "Onononopleaeno's." Surpassed only by his short story "Blood of a Wig" (in *Red Dirt Marijuana and Other Tastes*). R.B.

FRANKENSTEIN—All-time cool ghoul profile. Inked by Mary Shelley. Ms. Mary, her goodman Percy Bysshe, and good friends Lord Byron and John Polidori were lounging in the land of Alpine-heads deep into spooky stories of Germanic origin, this being the year 1816 A.D. Out of the clear, Lord B. opined they should each and every get down to lucubration and quill their own. *Frankenstein* (subtitled *The Modern Prometheus*—proving this was one lady who knew her Greek) debuted in 1817 and in our own century has proven fodder of the finest degree for movie-landers, who have turned out such films as *Frankenstein, Bride of Frankenstein,* and *Frankenstein Meets the Wolfman.* M.M.

GORMENGHAST TRILOGY—Mervyn Peake (Ballantine paper). One critic described *Titus Groan, Gormenghast,* and *Titus Alone* as "Charles Dickens on opium." Psychologically rich, koo-koo characters live in a huge crumbling castle located somewhere in Peake's brain. The first two novels are great, the third isn't. A companion novella *Boy in Darkness* (which appeared only in Ballantine's sci-fi collection *Sometime, Never*) is even more unreal. Although Tolkien is full of epic sweep, he is arid in comparison. Plus, this poet-painter excludes all elves, fairies, and gnomes from his work. R.B.

A HALL OF MIRRORS—Robert Stone (Ballantine paper). His first and finest, set in a goofy, gone-to-seed French Quarter and starring a superhip DJ lush and a cast of weirdo squares who bug him. R.B.

HERACLITUS (collected fragments with a text by Philip Wheelright). This pre-Socratic son-of-a-gun "said it all" long before saying boss stuff succinctly was the topical vogue. No boho epigrammist ever said anything as on-the-money as "The way up and the way down are one and the same," or "You can't step in the same river twice" (and dig: "Nature loves to hide"). Why Western hipsters chose Lao-Tzu and Alan Watts over him is probably an accident of available pulp. R.M.

THE KILLER INSIDE ME—Jim Thompson (Lion paperback). The first appearance of a classic demented character: Sheriff Lew Ford, sadistic psychopath who comes on like a folksy cretin but is unequivocally unhinged. R.B.

THE LATE RISERS—Bernard Wolfe (Signet paper). Everybody's got a favorite; this is my "ultimate hip novel," first published in 1952. The guy who runs the *New York Times'* electric billboard on Times Square programs false messages in exchange for a small amount of marijuana. Cast includes "Movement" (a black pusher who's given to quoting Melville's *Confidence Man).* Sample interior monologue: "Do you realize a pickpocket who had only one finger could only steal Life Savers?" Wolfe also helped out on Mezz Mezzrow's jazz novel *Really the Blues.* J.G.

THE LONG GOODBYE—Raymond Chandler (various). The *actual* great American novel (so-called), this opus works its way into the woodwork of friendship debunked, marriage debunked, drunkenness as a way of life, etc., all with a touch of life-and-life-only that neither Dylan nor Melville (let alone Hemingway or Fitzgerald) can claim to hold a candle to. If Kerouac had taken Chandler seriously, he'd have been a *monster.* R.M.

LOS ANGELES—Reyner Banham (Harper & Row). Only a convert can write with such zeal. It took an English

Los Angeles
THE ARCHITECTURE OF FOUR ECOLOGIES

Reyner Banham

© 1971, Harper & Row

architectural critic to formulate a no-nonsense, non-snob appraisal of the Big Orange, but he did it so well, no one's bettered him (and this book is over a decade old). Banham's wide angle takes it all in, in one affectionate, informed sweep: freeways, surf, turf, everything from Brown Derbys and stucco Aztec eateries to the low-brow slop art of Jack In The Box. Good looks indeed.

LOVE IN THE RUINS—Walker Percy (Avon paper). Subtitled "The Adven-

Walker Percy

tures of a Bad Catholic at a Time Near the End of the World," Percy's too-real tale projects a fast-approaching future full of warring fellow Americans. Knot-heads, Bantus, Love People, and Catholics bearing lapsometers hole up in Ho-Jo's, sniping at each other with automatic weapons and Heavy Sodium rays. Doc, our hero, shacks with nurses in a gone-dead motel, prays, waiting "until the Campbell's soup and Early Times run out." *Que será será.* Equally great: *The Second Coming* (Farrar, Straus & Giroux). S.Z.

MINE ENEMY GROWS OLDER—Alexander King (Simon and Shuster; Signet paper). By 1958, the man Lenny Bruce christened "the junkie Mark Twain" had seen it all and done most of it twice. Long before he became a high-watt fixture on Jack Paar's TV show, Alex the Great had painted covers for Mencken's *Smart Set* mag, scrawled Chinese murals on the walls of kosher deli's, and been photo editor of *Life* (where he proudly published life-sized portraits of the Twenty-two Inch Man). He'd also been a morphine addict, submitted to bagel therapy at an asylum as batty as Kesey's cuckoo's nest, and played chess with A-bomb "spy" Alger Hiss. Bonus: King explains why, between the years 1917 and 1948, he only wore pink neckties.

ME AND BIG JOE—Michael Bloom-field with Scott Summerville (Re/Search). The eternal question "Hey, white boy, what you doin' uptown?" is answered directly: accompanying blues guitarist Big Joe Williams on an other-world tour between Chicago's South Side and St. Louis, navigating the funkiest streets imaginable. In Gary, Indiana, they find Lightnin' Hopkins entertaining in a roadhouse. Hopkins "had a real high conk on his head and

Farrar, Straus and Giroux Photo: Evelyn Hofer, courtesy *Esquire* magazine wore black, wraparound shades," recalls Bloomfield. "He had only a drummer behind him, and when the blue lights hit that conk—man, that was all she wrote."

MUMBO JUMBO—Ishmael Reed (Doubleday; Bantam paper). Fake history as the only after-the-fact cosmic vision. The Jazz Age in retrospect as the forces of voodoo versus Warren Harding (who was black anyway). St. Louis Woman as a cultural archetype realer than the stock market crash (a manipulation from on high to forestall the forces of jazz-boogie epidemic). Even as art criticism it has legs galore. R.M.

MY GUN IS QUICK—Mickey Spillane (various). Nobody ever took Hemingway more literally as a generatrix for banal dialogue and trigger-happy psychological rationalization. Still, Spillane had his head up his ass, and in this one he takes on the entire "call-girl establishment" of NYC, with a vengeance that in any less fucked-up writer would've ended him up in the toilet. (Give him points for being a proto-Scorsese buffoon without an inkling of irony or prevailing publishing-biz taste.) R.M.

NIGHTMARE IN PINK—John D. MacDonald (Fawcett paper) Any one of MacDonald's twenty-odd Travis McGee novels makes for a good rainy day read, but this is his finest 140 pages. A grown-up Hardy Boy, McGee enjoys racier scenes, real violence, and works out of the Florida Keys rather than Bayport. Here, helping a damsel in Manhattan, he unscrambles high finance shenanigans, hunts, hides, and gets dosed in what may be the first published account of the encounter between P.I. and LSD (1964). A color

freak whose prose always keeps on the right side of purple, MacDonald also turns in top Travis in *Darker Than Amber* and *The Long Lavender Look*. Surprise: two lame TV movies—*The Girl, the Gold Watch, and Everything* and *Condominium*—came from good MacDonald potboilers. S.Z.

NORTHANGER ABBEY—Jane Austen (various). Maybe it's better read *after* you've waded through a slough of authentic gothic novels. But Baby Jane's parody of eighteenth-century ghoul cool still comes on pen ablaze, standing dungeon-and-Drac style on its head. Despite heroine Catherine Morland's big eyes for the *Dark Shadows* scene, nothing happens. Frequently. S.Z.

ON THE ROAD—Jack Kerouac (various). Truman Capote dismissed this as mere "typing" and not quality literature. What he failed to realize was, this was really *cool* typing. R.S.

ONE FLEW OVER THE CUCKOO'S NEST—Ken Kesey (Viking Press; Signet paper). Like the Acid Test and those Zeitgeists, the Prankster moves on, having written up a storm those cold nights up on the ward. Cuckoo Randle Patrick McMurphy was surely Everyman, but he was also the metaphoric mystery tramp of the last new age that meant anything. Both facts make this one a must. P.L.

OZZIE—Ozzie Nelson (Prentice-Hall). Dedicated to Harriet. It takes 309 pages, but Daddy-O spills it all in this 1977 autobio: what he did for a living all those years on *Ozzie and Harriet*, his days on the road, that time at Rutgers when a young student presented him with a lit marijuana cigarette (Oz put it in his pocket. It burned).

THE PARKER SERIES—Richard Stark (Donald Westlake) (various). Pro heist-man Parker, living through stolen credit cards and aliases, has a steel heart and no room for small talk. Life as a series of calculated chess problems. If there's an obstacle blocking the goal, then remove the obstacle. If you can't survive at any cost.   R.B.

THE PHILOSOPHY OF ANDY WARHOL (FROM A TO B & BACK AGAIN) (Harcourt Brace Jovanovich). In which the Greatest Living Legend recalls almost dying (from the pistol attack by a member of the Society for Cutting Up Men), regrets not having invented blue jeans, and reveals the great unfulfilled ambition of his life: "my own regular TV show. I'm going to call it *Nothing Special.*"

PREJUDICES—H. L. Mencken (various). A great legacy. Every wiseguy living today has somehow been influenced by what H.L.M. wrote here, even if they haven't read it. R.S.

QUAKE—Rudolph Wurlitzer (E. P. Dutton). The hero is knocked out of his bed at Hollywood's seedy Tropicana Motel, and it's downhill from there on out. Some of the best end-of-the-world stuff ever. D.S.

RED DIRT MARIJUANA—Terry Southern (New American Library). Where to begin? In "Apartment for Exchange," Franz Kafka and mom place an ad to rent their flat; Freud answers the ad. In "Put-down," Boris and his boho friends get loaded and chase a ball of quicksilver along the floorboards. Fake cool gets its comeuppance in "You're Too Hip, Baby" and "The Night the Bird Blew for Doctor Warner," and—best of all—there's "The Road Out of Axotle," which reads like a wired-up Jazzbeaux Collins monologue and can scare the pants off you at twenty paces. Did we get to "The Blood of a Wig" or "Terry Southern Interviews a Faggot Male Nurse"?

THE SECRET LIFE OF SALVADOR DALI—(Dial Press). A Forties autobiography from the twentieth century's most profound comedian. Mind-boggling anecdotes, opinions, and self-

Ken Kesey

© Viking Penquin Inc.

analysis spill out over the page, filtered through Dali's aristo-punk attitude (he once shellacked his hair). Always outrageous, *never* dull. R.B.

SOMETIMES A GREAT NOTION— Ken Kesey (Viking Press; Bantam paper). "Second verse same as the first" was a line Kesey decided not to sing. As wide-skyed as *Cuckoo's Nest* is claustrophobic, this blood-and-tears story of life among lumberjack brothers

© 1958 Lippincott

reaches for more and often achieves it. Readers have been impatient for Novel #3 ever since. Be thankful for what you've got: a three-part search for ancient pyramids (*Rolling Stone,* 1974) and a still-smoking Neal Cassady obit ("The Day after Superman Died," *Esquire,* October 1979).

SOMEWHERE THERE'S MUSIC— George Lea (Lippincott paper). This 1957 Kerouacked jazz novel is a later version of *Who Walk in Darkness,* itself

spawned, as were most boho novels, by *The Sun Also Rises.* "What's my habit?" muses bopster guru Lucretius. "I don't know exactly. I switch around . . . I get bored with drugs an' chemicals an' pot, because the music takes me a way out farther. That's truth." R.B.

VEGAS—John Gregory Dunne (Warner paper). "In the summer of my nervous breakdown, I went to live in Las Vegas, Clark County, Nevada." So begins Dunne's masterpiece, published a scant three years before his *True Confessions* hit. This "memoir of a dark season" comes on like a *One from the Heart,* with all bulbs blown, power out, as Dunne's narrator swaps hard-luck sagas with P.I. Buster Mano, hooker Artha Ging, and lounge comic Jackie Casey. Have mercy.

THE WANDERERS—Richard Price (Houghton Mifflin; Avon paper). The coolest, craziest juvenile delinquent trip ever put down. Noo Yawk at its most fearsome, funniest. Irish Ducky Boys roam their gang turf like midget dinosaurs, Chinese Wongs take no shit, and everybody listens to Dion. Never to be forgotten: "Going Down with Murray the K," Price's priceless DJ obit, in *Rolling Stone* April 15, 1982.

WHO WALKS IN DARKNESS— Chandler Brossard (Harper & Row). First Beat novel with a cool (as opposed to frantic or fuzzy) style. Lots of reefer, jazz, boxing, and neurosis. R.B.

WRITE IF YOU GET WORK: THE BEST OF BOB & RAY (Random House). Worth hunting for if you remember their insane commercials, *Mad* articles, or the deadpan dada of their radio comedy. Reprints classic bits—"Spelling Bee," "Lightbulb Collector," and more. Bob & Ray's House of Toast is somewhere in here, too.

TOM WOLFE:
The Ruling Cool-Write King

Yyyyeeooowwww!!! So what you're saying is, not only has Tom Wolfe attained to the postultimate heights of journalism—as in not only reporting what *he* sees and hears, but what ever other lovin' subject of his nine masterpieces of modern reportage not only sees and hears, but thinks, feels, muses, understands, and misunderstands—not only has T.W. edged himself out on the trembling brink of blinking immortality, but he's also (and correct me if I'm wrong) the absolute last word in literary high fashion!?!! Hold on a minute ... slam on the brakes! Sssssskkkkeeecchhh!!!

Yeah, well, fashion's got nothing to do with it, really. It just means that for once, the public pack, the all-consuming disposable-assets horde caught up with, ran alongside, kept running, Jesus, *with* one of the greats. "(puffpuff) Hi (puff), Tom, how you (whuffwhuff) doin'? (Huffffffshwoo!) Make it up to the stoplight with you?" It means his profiles of Kesey, Ed "Big Daddy" Roth, Walt "Silver Prince" Gropius, Jackson Pollack, the Pump Housers, and astronauts will keep Wolfe in patent leather loafers and linen forever.

The ruling cool-write king on things cultural has written the following great books. All are worth your attention.

The Kandy-Kolored Tangerine-Flake Streamline Baby (1965)
The Pump House Gang (1968)
The Electric Kool-Aid Acid Test (1968)

Radical Chic & Mau-Mauing the Flak Catchers (1970)
The New Journalism (1973)
Mauve Gloves & Madmen, Clutter & Vine (1976)
The Right Stuff (1979)
In Our Time (1980)
From Bauhaus to Our House (1981)

(All hardbound editions: Farrar, Straus & Giroux. All Paperback editions: Bantam, Pocket.)
Too freaking much.   D.S.

TEN MINUTES WITH TERRY

He'd be a natural for one of those American Express commercials. His looks may be a secret, but not the fact that he's one of the world's coolest living writers. In 1964 the publication of *Candy* turned Terry Southern into a literary celeb. His new rep sent readers back to his earlier novels, *Flash and Filigree* and *The Magic Christian.* The former was subtler than *Candy,* and the latter was arguably funnier. He next conquered the screenplay when he teamed up with Stanley Kubrick to write *Dr. Strangelove;* soon audiences were in the aisles over "pre-verts" and "precious bodily fluids." His work on subsequent films was always easy to spot, but nothing topped *Strangelove* until *Easy Rider,* the Sixties' countercultural blah-blah-blah.

SOUTHERN
On Elvis, Strangelove, Barbeque, and Barbarella

In the meantime, a brilliant collection of short pieces had come out, *Red Dirt Marijuana and Other Tastes,* itself followed by the novel *Blue Movie* (1970), which chronicled the goings-on of a movie crew attempting to make the ultimate big-budget skinflick.

Southern still remains friends with such iconoclasts as William Burroughs, whose *Naked Lunch* he was instrumen-tal in getting published, and Dennis Hopper, who originally wanted the opening scene of *Easy Rider* to be shown upside down! Other buddies: actors Michael Parks and fellow Texan Rip Torn, with whom he hunts and fishes near his Connecticut home.

Southern's next novel, *Youngblood,* should be out soon.

The following talk took place in TS's

office at NBC in New York, where he's currently writing for *Saturday Night Live.* On one wall was a framed poster of a forgotten film which bore the legend "WOMEN COULD FEEL HIM ACROSS A ROOM!" In the background Randy Newman sang slyly of rednecks, teen-age girls, and Huey Long . . .

R.B.

CATALOG: *Where were you born?*
TERRY: Alvarado, Texas.
C: *Your early stories that were set in Texas are a little like Hemingway's Nick Adams stories. Were they an influence?*
T: No, those stories were based on stuff that happened—growing up there in rural Texas. They're part of a longer work, the novel called *Youngblood.*
C: *Do you carry an identity as a Texan?*
T: Well, yes, I guess I took the whole "Texas Uber Alles" thing for granted, right up through about the junior year in high school, when I hitch-hiked out to L.A. and then over to Chicago and I began to see things besides sagebrush.
C: *What writers influenced you when you were young?*
T: I liked Edgar Allan Poe and *Weird Tales*—H. P. Lovecraft . . . things in the weird vein. Nathanael West. The English writer Henry Green—very intricate style, and funny. Probably the way Evelyn Waugh would have written if he'd had more patience for rewriting.
C: *Did you ever read Huysmans, the French nineteenth-century guy?*
T: *Against the Grain* and *La Bas, Down There.* He was one of the first "surrealist" writers of interest to me. I recall a great scene in one of his books where he's making it with this lady ventriloquist who's required to project her voice outside the door of the room, pretending to be her angry husband. You know, "Hey! What the devil's going on in there!" He's highly contemporary and I've often thought it would be a very worthwhile project to update the transla-

tion of writers like that. Lautremont and Canetti might be others.
C: *How'd you manage to go from those Texas life stories to the wild satiric use of language and obscene farcical situations?*
T: Well, Poe wrote this sea adventure, "The Narrative of Arthur Gordon Pym," where a ship's rudder and masts are lost in a storm and it just drifts. The crew freaks into extreme weirdness. In one section the hero, forced into cannibalism by hunger, is eating a human liver, and a seagull swoops down, snatches it away, then drops it on the deck with a hideous SPLAT! The hero scrambles over, grabs it again, then gets into a terrible fight for it with one of the other survivors.

Well, the whole thing was so outlandish that I wanted to turn to my best friend—Big Herb—on to it. He said, "Gawd-damn, you mus' be crazy!" He couldn't even read it. But it was the *style* that put him off, so I decided to rewrite it, using classmates and teachers of ours in this very strange story. I did it in more of a Zane Grey style. *Then* he dug it.

It was my mother who had first read me a Poe story—"The Gold Bug" or something equally innocuous—so I thought about asking her to read mine. But now, in the Big Herb version, I figured it was too much.
C: *Was black culture an influence on your sense of humor?*
T: Oh yeah. I think most people from the South pick it up. The influence is extraordinary—sense of humor, taste in food, music, dope, everything . . . even speech. The whole "Southern accent" is an obvious derivation from black speech patterns.
C: *In one of your early stories you put in a reference to "Bullmoose" Jackson's R&B record "Big Ten Inch Record."*
T: Yeah. "My gal don't go for smokin'/ Liquor just makes her flinch/Seems she don't go for nothin'/'Ceptin' my big ten

inch!" (laughs). That was another nice thing about Texas: There was this whole body of music that existed called "race records," that were put out only for blacks. They weren't even distributed in music stores. You used to be able to go into "Niggertown," across what they called "the Central tracks," where they had all this great barbeque and ribs and the music, too. And it was surprisingly cool to go there. It wasn't antisocial then. I guess they needed the money. And I think they liked the idea that we dug the music and the food. It was really hot stuff, too—drenched in red pepper. Lots of people went to these places just to pick up barbeque. I went for the music, and there was always some interesting action . . . razor fights. When Elvis came out with that black pronunciation, a lot of those records became more acceptable to whites.

C: *You liked Elvis.*

T: Yeah. Elvis was somethin' else. He styled himself on Ray Charles. He did a version of "I Got a Woman (Way 'Cross Town)" that was even more jumpin' than Ray's. He made black music mainstream. I met Elvis once, when he was doing *Harum Scarum* and I was working on *Cincinnati Kid.* I went over to his set to visit this girl, and he had his whole high school football team throwing the ball around between takes. They'd hit on all the girls in the film. So Elvis saw me with this girl and asked, "Who is that? Is he some damn Yankee?"

And they said, "Naw, he's a Texas boy. A writer, Terry Southern." So it turned out that one of Elvis's guys came over, very formal, and said, "Mr. Southern, my name is Red West, and Elvis would like to meet you." So Elvis came up, said, "Mighty glad to meet you. Don't you know that your movie *Dr. Strangelove* is a great favorite? We've seen it about—what, Red?—thirteen times!" Well, I was surprised, and I said

that I was surprised it had even played that long in Memphis. He said, "No, no. At the house. We run it up at the house!" So he had this sense of humor, and he especially liked Slim Pickens' role.

C: *How was Slim Pickens on* Strangelove?

T: He was a joy to work with. You know, the financing for *Dr. Strangelove* came about because Peter Sellers was to play all these different roles, including the bomber pilot (Pickens' part). *But,* when it came time to shoot it, Sellers had sprained his ankle—out carousing, if memory serves—and had to be replaced for the pilot role because it meant moving around a lot. So Stanley said that you couldn't replace Sellers with an *actor.* You had to get someone authentic. The ideal choice, of course, was John Wayne, but I guess he thought it was part of a mad commie plot. So I suggested Dan Blocker from *Bonanza,* but his agent said it was definitely "pinko." So then Stanley said, "Get this guy Slim Pickens. He was great in *One Eyed Jacks.*" Well, Slim had never been out of the Southwest, except to do stunt work between rodeos, so he came over on the plane with his boots and cowboy hat, and when he arrived Stanley told me to talk to him, since I was from Texas. So I went down to the stage where Slim was standing with this la-de-dah production assistant, very Oxonian. I introduced myself, got us both three fingers of Wild Turkey in some water glasses, asked the assistant if he wanted any. "Bit early for me, heh heh!" So then Slim and I talked. And it later fell to me to introduce him to James Earl Jones when he arrived on the set. James Earl is always very dignified, very Shakespearean, and I had no idea how to find a common ground between them. Then it came to me how Slim had just been working in *One Eyed Jacks* with Marlon Brando, so I mentioned that and James Earl was impressed. "Brando's Mark Antony was superlative," he said. "It must be very satisfying to work with him." "Wal," said Slim, "ah worked with Bud Brando for ten months an' durin' that time ah never seen him do one single thing that wudn't all *man* an' all *white*," saying this, of course, without even thinking what he was saying, and just kept on talking. James Earl never cracked.

C: *I heard a story about how you were to be guest of honor at a party given by film critic Arthur Knight. You pulled up in a limo at four in the morning, when everybody remaining was barely conscious. There was a starlet making scrambled eggs, and you took a plate and started some endless spiel as you pushed the eggs onto the floor and ground them into the carpet in a kind of mosaic. Then you thanked everybody and split.*

T: Apocryphal. Never happened. And I never even *heard* of such an incident. You've mixed me up with Mailer or Vidal. Hmmm. Actually, though, a few times people have told me things like "There's this guy on Block Island, or Provincetown, or somewhere, pretending to be *you*." Running up tabs at bars and restaurants, renting limos, getting laid—all fabulous starlet and socialite poon, no doubt. Ha.

C: *There's a story about you and Dino De Laurentiis. He hired you to do some dumbbell musical version of* Roman Holiday, *and you farmed it out to a friend. You helped him only to the point of sending him your suggestion for the film's opening: a chorus of organ grinders singing "It's a Roman, Roman Holiday!" while their monkeys whack off into their cups.*

T: Well, yes, but I think it may have been a bit more imaginative than that. But anyway, that was during the time I was working on *Barbarella,* which he

produced, and he kept bugging me about doing this dopey musical. So, just to cool him out, I said, "Oh sure," then I told the agent to price me out of it—you know, ask so much money that he'd just drop it. And so he did, but Dino D. went for it. The agent got all excited and said we had a great deal, but I couldn't see what would be great about a musical version of *Roman Holiday,* so I gave it to this friend of mine, Fred Segal, who needed the money and who was very talented. I mean, even though he'd never worked on a film script, I knew he could do it.

C: *Didn't you once work on a script for William Burroughs' novel,* Junkie?

T: Yes, I collaborated with Bill Burroughs on it. Dennis Hopper was to direct and play the lead, Bill Lee. For the first few days everything seemed to be going well. We had a big suite at the Grammercy Park Hotel, all paid for by the film's producer, the legendary Jacques 'Count Rothchild' Stern, who zoomed about in this motorized wheelchair. Then suddenly, Dennis said, "Jesus Christ, I thought we were making *Naked Lunch!* I've never read *Junkie!*" So he reads it, gets very excited, shouts something about "An actor prepares! An actor prepares!" And he rushes out into the night to experience the junk-life for a week or so. Anyway, he sort of disappears, and we have to go looking for him in these shooting galleries. It was a mess . . . but it'll still make a great movie one day.

C: *Are you working on a new book?*

T: Yes, it's a novel called *Youngblood.* I mentioned it earlier. Putnam's should be publishing it next year, in the spring.

C: *What's it about?*

T: It's like those early stories of mine. Set in Texas . . . Say, I'm getting a little, uh, dehydrated. Why don't we . . .

C: *Get a drink?*

T: Sure . . . something like that.

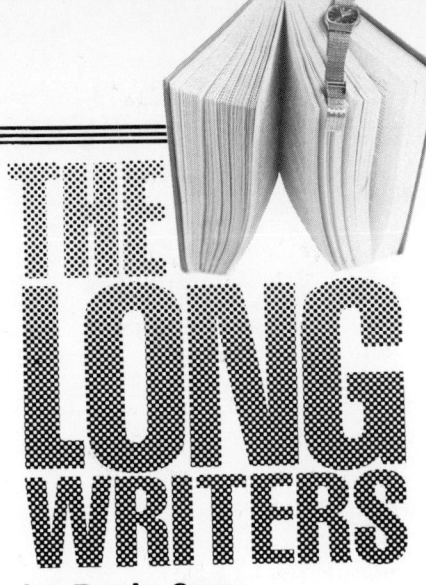

THE LONG WRITERS

by Davin Seay

Hey, no problem. Ten years from now the only thing we'll be interested in reading is our Pac Man scores, so why bother? Well, if you're one of the half dozen true believers in the Western Hemisphere hepped to the sanctified joys of, like, the pursuit of real *literature,* there's something you oughta know. It can still be had.

You've got to be careful, though. Set a few ground rules, or before you know it, you'll be booked at the Hotel New Hampshire overlooking Gorky Park and making choices for Sophie. The following should be carved in stone: Nothing on any bestseller list anywhere is worth reading. Period. Never touch anything with (a) an embossed and/or peekaboo cover, (b) a title that sounds even vaguely like *The Anthrax Hyperbola* (no Syndromes, Covenants, or Manifests). Ignore any book with its own display rack. Finally, and most important, never read anything less than 700 pages long.

Yeah, we've heard it all before—Dashiell Hammett, James M. Cain, and all those other exalted primitives who laid it out in 120 pages or less. Forget it. Ask yourself . . . you looking for something to do while the coffee cools or do you want to read a *book?!* Anyone who needs less than 700—minimum—

to say what he's gotta say isn't worth his sales tax.

This doesn't mean every fat tome's worth your attention. *Shogun* clocks in at 1200 plus—we wouldn't use it to wrap sushi. The key here is *density,* big, hulking slabs of dwarf-star-thick prose that takes as much out of the reader as it does the author. Staying power's what counts. There's no free lunch. You get out what you put in, and any writer who makes us work for our literary kicks, bucking the Book of the Month Club assembly line, is worth his weight in meaty metaphors. You want to be entertained? Watch Merv. You want some words that stick to your ribs? Sink your frontal lobes into these massive masterpieces:

1. **Gravity's Rainbow**—Thomas Pynchon (Viking Press). The best long read ever. Tyrone Slothrop takes on WW II, Black Nazis, Seaman Bodine, and I Ching Feet. A monster masterpiece, denser than a dwarf star and twice as bright. Do yourself a favor: Take a year and read it.

2. **The Recognitions**—William Gaddis (Alfred A. Knopf hardcover; Dell paper). The grandaddy of 'em all. Written in '52 and still light years ahead of the field.

3. **JR**—William Gaddis (Alfred A. Knopf). Ninety-eight percent unattributed dialogue. We think it's about business and moral decay. You tell us.

4. **The Flounder**—Günter Grass (Harcourt Brace Jovanovich). Immortal German fish witnesses rise and fall of Western Civ. Gulp

5. **Letters**—John Barth (Putnam's). Epistolary romp through American history. Postage due.

6. **D'Arconville's Cat**—Alexander Theroux (Doubleday). Guaranteed—twenty three-syllable words per paragraph. Good use of vocabulary.

And for you classics buffs . . . anything by Dickens, most of Tolstoy, and selected works by Melville and Hawthorne.

Burning Men, Byzantine Despots, and Godiva's Constrictor Thighs

the coolest sci-fi

by Jim Trombetta

Sci-Fi's Cool School has had little truck with hobbits, maidens on flying unicorns, iron-pumping sword jockeys, ideological preachments, or "simple" ideas suitable for synopsis in TV Guide. No, the Cool School was always for adults. It features ambiguous people you might know or even be, societies with histories that count, carefully documented realities—giving rise, in turn, to fabulous adventures, bizarre occasions, potential cerebral overload. The Cool School aspires to a pace approaching the speed of light. There's always an explanation on the way, though it may well arrive too late.

Finally, cool sci-fi is sexy—an illicit liaison between reason and madness is its very essence. Here's the best of it:

THE STARS MY DESTINATION— Alfred Bester (Signet, 1956). Buck Rogers would have had a nervous breakdown in this Twenty-fifth Century, "a fabulous century of freaks." Man's psychic abilities have been enhanced (teleportation is as common as a driver's license) but serve the same old masters: money, power, and lust. The freaks include an albino femme fatale who can only see radio waves, a radioactive genius physicist, a seventy-year-old mind reader who never passed puberty, disease junkies, commandos with souped-up nervous systems, and the terrifying Burning Man, who haunts our hero, Gully Foyle. A spaceman shipwrecked by war who seeks revenge on those who refused to rescue him, Foyle bullies, cons, seduces, and prays his way from *shlub* to superman, saving humanity in the process. The quest leads to ultimate trauma, which twists his senses —"sound registered as sight, motion registered as sound, colors became pain"—and sends him hurtling backward through his own story! The typographical effects created by Bester to convey the experience make this the first 3-D novel. Often imitated, never duplicated, *The Stars My Destination* is the great original cool sci-fi.

MARTIAN TIME-SLIP—Philip K. Dick (Ballantine, 1964). "Mr. Kott was a sack of bones, dirty and shiny-wet. His head was a skull that took in greens and bit them . . ." That's how Arnie Kott, a union big shot on colonial Mars, looks to Manfred Steiner, a schizophrenic little boy with a proven ability to see the future. Kott would like to use Manfred's gifts to make a bundle, but Manfred has more pressing concerns—he's been crazy since he had a vision of his own lingering death from old age. The boy would do anything to avoid this fate, including warping time for everyone who crosses his path. Several dwellers on boring suburban Mars—all beautifully drawn everyday people—begin to live crucial events over and over again, to the tune of Manfred's visions, as the boy struggles to literally *get his life in order*. Perhaps the best-realized novel by the late, irreplaceable Mr. Dick (who also wrote *Ubik* and *Three Stigmata of Palmer Eldritch*), *Martian Time-Slip* stays just this side of insanity and moves with the grace of an inspired

improvisation to one of the most bizarre happy endings in fiction.

MISTER JUSTICE—Doris Piserchia (Ace, 1974). Crammed into half of an Ace double and never reprinted, *Mister Justice* remains in a class by itself: hardboiled America, Sci-fi-style. Here the 2030s appear as a mutated 1930's, complete with an economic catastrophe that threatens evolution itself. The Shadow, the Green Hornet, the Untouchables—they never had what Mr. Justice has going for him. Sprung from humanity's threatened altruistic genes, this masked vigilante has the ability to travel into the past, where he can witness, but not prevent, murders. He then returns to the present, where he arranges "an eye for an eye" treatment for the slayers, including full-scale gangland rub-outs. But he can't easily dispose of one Arthur Bingle, global crime archon' who has the same powers as Mr. J. and then some. Bingle feels about the human race in general what Mr. Justice feels about criminals, and he plans to thin us out and "empty the world." With the help of his powers, his syndicates of henchman and corrupt cops, and his dreadful lady friend Godiva—she of the constrictor thighs—Bingle gets the drop on humanity. But justice is just a matter of time. Piserchia relates this furious folktale with Chandler soul, Hammett snap, and not a trace of camp.

MASTERS OF THE MAZE—Avram Davidson (Manor, 1965). Conspiracy paranoia will never be this much fun again. An order of mystical adepts, now based in upstate New York, has guarded the Maze since the seventeenth century. Their secret is coveted by John Joseph Horn, fanatical Sunbelt plutocrat of the Dog Eat Dog school. But Horn himself is no more than the unwitting pawn of the alien Chulpex, a swarm of elephantine, razor-mandibled insects who think of man as a potential food supply and the earth as a nice new hive. These bugs hope to infest us via the Maze, which "traverses space, transects time"; enter it and you're likely to end up anywhere: the past, the future, other planets, realms deemed mythical . . . But getting to a desirable place often involves crossing nasty ones. Someone must get to the center of the Maze and alert the legendary Masters, and this chore devolves upon Nate Gordon, a hack author of fake adventures for *Man's Man*-type magazines. There's nothing hack about *this* adventure, with its breakneck pace, historical detail, delight in occult esoterica, and jazzy style, which yields up the coolest last sentence in sci-fi—describing Horn's thuggish driver, marooned in prehistoric Australia, where "sometimes he smiled and babbled contentedly about cars as he stumbled across the achingly empty continent which had never seen a wheel."

THE BOOK OF THE NEW SUN—Gene Wolfe (Timescape Books):
VOLUME I: *THE SHADOW OF THE TORTURER* (1980)
VOLUME II: *THE CLAW OF THE CONCILIATOR* (1981)
VOLUME III: *THE SWORD OF THE LICTOR* (1982)
VOLUME IV: *THE CITADEL OF THE AUTARCH* (1982)
The last word in cool sci-fi—a mind-boggling cliffhanger, this tetralogy opens a future in which what we think of as "the future" is ancient history—where whole mountain ranges have been carved into statues of long-dead rulers, where the long-ago forested moon sheds a greenish light, where you can look directly at the sun at noon, so rapidly is it fading . . . Man's conquest of the stars is long past, and we have slipped back to byzantine despotism.

The hero Severian, trained since childhood as an official torturer, exiled for sins of compassion, goes forth into a world haunted by uncanny technologies and alien visitors: titanic intelligences imprisoned under the seas, the beast which speaks with the voices of its victims, the maimed machine-man patched with flesh, the mirrors that transport vision faster than light, and much, much more. The most adept of killers, Severian possesses a relic that enables him to heal the sick and raise the dead. Can he fix the sun itself? All this invention, and the literary juice which powers it, comes to us through the fingers of Gene Wolfe, in daily life an editor of *Plant Engineering* magazine. He lends even swords and sorceries a technical rigor, and faraway events the urgency of your secret dreams.

FIVE RUNNERS-UP

GLADIATOR-AT-LAW—Frederick Pohl and C. M. Kornbluth (Ballantine, 1955). Citizens fight for dream homes in real-life TV bloodbaths, while financial brains who have dispensed with their bodies keep score.
"WALL OF CRYSTAL, EYE OF NIGHT"—Algis Budrys (Berkley, 1961). Sollenar has the sweetheart contract on total sensory thrills sewed up, until an alien competitor changes all the rules. (A novel imploded into twenty pages, this is available in the author's collection *Blood and Burning,* Berkley, 1978.)
THE DEMOLISHED MAN—Alfred Bester (Signet, 1954). Killer outwits mind-reading cops and reaps Chaos itself.
AND CHAOS DIED—Joanna Russ (Ace, 1973). Coolest telepathic fuck scene.
THE FAIRY CHESSMEN—Lewis Padgett (Gnome Press, 1947). Coolest first sentence: "The doorknob opened a blue eye and looked at him."

The Coolest P.I.'s

"So you're a private detective. I didn't know they existed, except in books—or else they were greasy little men snooping around hotel corridors. My, you're a mess, aren't you?"

—Lauren Bacall to
Humphrey Bogart
in *The Big Sleep*

by Steven X. Rea

Private dick. Private eye. Private investigator. The operative word for these operatives is *private*. They keep to themselves. They call their own shots, make their own plans, keep their own hours. The rules they break are the ones they made up in the first place. Some of them are smart, some just smart-assed. Hard-boiled, flinty exteriors; sentimental mush-hearts underneath.

That's one kind. There are others: effete greenhouse dandies, cuddly, beshawled old ladies, well-heeled society sleuths, even a few strong-willed dames—the get-out-of-the-way- you-dumb-lug- I'll-take-care-of-this-myself variety.

Whatever and whoever, the P.I. in mystery fiction is a maverick hero. A nonconformist with an innate (and sometimes fatal) sense of honor and justice. A seeker of truth. Someone with a strong stomach who maybe doesn't understand why Joe Blow has offed his wife, embezzled his company's funds, and hightailed it to the Bahamas with his twenty-year-old secretary, but who knows there are Joe Blows all over the place and that they'll always be pulling this stuff.

Some of them are packing heat; some are packing steamer trunks for a global jaunt. Some drink too much (Marlowe), others mainline cocaine (Sherlock Holmes). They can wear fedoras or deerstalkers or no hat at all. They can charge a pair of C-notes a day plus expenses or render their services free of charge. The private detective is a puzzle solver, a newsmonger, a voyeur. They are "Sirs" and "Lords," flatfoots and gumshoes. They deal in questions and answers, missing persons and missing things. And corpses . . . lots of corpses.

The Nocturnal Ratiocinator And The World's First Consulting Detective

C. Auguste Dupin. A brainy Parisian who detested daylight, closeting himself up in his shuttered garret, Dupin—the creation of Edgar Allan Poe—is generally acknowledged to be the first fictional detective. Though he appeared in only three stories, "The Murders in the Rue Morgue," "The Mystery of Marie Rôget," and "The Purloined Letter," Dupin's m.o.—part armchair analysis (*ratiocination* is the term Poe coined for this cerebrum-flexing) and part scene-of-the-crime inquiry—became the model for all to follow.

Down These Mean Streets a Man Must Go

Philip Marlowe. Raymond Chandler's hard-boiled L.A. dick rarely used a gun but often quoted Flaubert. He kept a bottle of whiskey filed in his desk drawer, and women tried to sit on his lap while he was standing up. He got knocked around a lot by crooked cops and cheap hoods but (through bloody teeth) always spat back a cool bit of flip. Chandler penned seven Marlowe books—*The Big Sleep; Farewell, My Lovely; The High Window; The Lady in the Lake; The Little Sister; The Long Goodbye;* and the critically maligned *Playback*—all with plots as tangled as the wiring on a British sports car and characters as real as the ones walking the streets right now. (Ballantine Books)

Sam Spade. In Dashiell Hammett's *The Maltese Falcon,* the tall, tough-as-nails Frisco P.I. Sam Spade hunts down his partner's killer (even though Spade hated his guts and was making it with his wife), embroils himself with a leggy redhead named Brigid, and gets sapped over the head while he's looking for a little black bird. (Vintage)

Down These Mean Streets a Swarm Must Follow

Lew Archer. Author Ross MacDonald handily carries the Chandler/Hammett torch into the Sixties and Seventies with Archer, a quiet, questioning ex-cop whose cases seem to center around family breakups, missing sons and daughters, and smarmy secrets from the past that come back to haunt his clients. There are eighteen Archer novels, beginning with *The Moving Target* (1949). With *The Drowning Pool, The Zebra-Striped Hearse, The Goodbye Look* and *Sleeping Beauty,* MacDonald stepped from the shadow of his literary mentors, so much so that today Lew Archer is Lew Archer, not Marlowe or Spade in a different cut of suit. (Bantam)

Thomas Kyd. "You want to solve a crime, Granville? Why don't you go arrest your tailor?" That and many other snappy rejoinders run rampant through

Timothy Harris' two Kyd novels, *Kyd for Hire* (Dell) and *Good Night and Good-Bye* (Dell). A thirty-ish private eye with an office on the corner of Hollywood and Western, Kyd ambles his way through modern-day L.A., rubbing elbows with glamorous show biz types and sleazy porn kings, falling for a couple of beautiful broads in the process. Known to tote a high caliber Mauser when things turn ugly, he can also wax serious: "A gun is just a bad idea waiting for its time."

Spenser. A self-styled gourmet with enough machismo to arm a division of Marines, Robert B. Parker's Boston-based dick started off in a promising Chandleresque vein with *The Godwulf Manuscript* (set in the world of academia) and *Mortal Stakes* (professional baseball), but has since taken a nose dive of remarkable velocity. (Berkley Medallion)

Harry Stoner. Stoner calls Cincinnati home, which probably explains the death wish that got him into the gumshoe racket. Three books by writer Jonathan Valin—*The Lime Pit* (Avon), *Final Notice*, and *Dead Letter* (both Dodd, Mead)—feature Stoner, a soft touch and a bad judge of character, risking life and limb to smash a kiddie prostitution ring, hunt down a library vandal-psycho killer, and figure out who bumped off a college prof trading in government secrets.

Fletch. Irwin Maurice Fletcher, a crack newspaper reporter, goes undercover as a California beach bum to track a millionaire industrialist who wants to have himself offed. Gregory McDonald's *Fletch* ends with our hero on a plane to Rio, $3 million in unmarked bills under his seat. In *Confess, Fletch* and *Fletch's Fortune* the dialogue crackles with vim and vigor, but by the time McDonald gets to *Fletch and the Widow Bradley* another top sleuthhound has bitten the dust. (Avon)

Hard-boiled Yucks

Jack LeVine. "How was she to know that in a matter of hours I would be slugged, drugged, drawn into a warm bath with her hot body, and forced to kiss off my best intentions on the trail of her husband's cold-blooded killer?" That's just one of the queries New York P.I. LeVine puts to himself in Andrew Bergman's *Hollywood and LeVine,* a funny, loving send-up of the Chandler style and milieu, replete with cameos by Bogart and Bacall. Also: *The Big Kiss-Off of 1941.* (Ballantine)

Toby Peters. Writer Stuart Kaminsky's mysteries commingle the fictional life of Pepsi-swizzling flatfoot Toby Peters with the likes of Judy Garland, the Marx Brothers, Gary Cooper, William Faulkner, and Errol Flynn. In the best of them—*Murder on the Yellow Brick Road, Bullet for a Star, Never Cross a Vampire*—Kaminsky's uncanny knack for biographical detail and vivid rendering of L.A. in the Forties makes for more than just a quick, clever read. (Penguin)

A Couple of Poets Sitting Around Sucking Bullets

Charlie Bradshaw. In poet Stephen Dobyns' second novel, *Saratoga Longshot,* a shlumpy, sleepy-eyed upstate New York police detective makes for the Big Apple in search of a girl. In *Saratoga Swimmer,* Bradshaw has ankled the force and becomes the head security guard at a big Saratoga racing stable. In both books, Dobyns has crafted subtle, suspenseful thrillers and has created, in Bradshaw, a guy of such average dimensions that his sheer normalcy becomes heroic. (Atheneum)

Al Barnes. Nicknamed "Mush Heart" from his ten-year stint as a softy cop in the Seattle homicide division, Barnes moves to the backwater burg of Plains, Montana, ready for an easy job as a deputy sheriff. What this contemplative old coot gets in famed poet Richard Hugo's *Death and the Good Life* (St. Martin's) is a vicious axe murderer and more twists than a dance party at the Peppermint Lounge.

Death Wears a Union Jack

Cordelia Gray. In P.D. James' *An Unsuitable Job for a Woman* (Popular Library), a fledgling female P.I. inherits an agency from her (male) mentor-partner and goes about trying to prove to herself—and her client—that she's up to the task of detecting. A sordid mock suicide, a gaggle of strange Cambridge University students, and some truly lethal goings-on set the scene for this complex, richly character-ized book. Ms. Gray turns out to be a young, modern heroine with enough pluck and pride to get her through all the carnage—barely.

Sid Halley, Philip Nore. Halley is a moody, crippled former jockey who sets up a detective agency to smash a British racing scam in Dick Francis' *Odds Against* (Pocket Books). Nore, also a jockey, and an amateur photog-rapher, gets caught up in a blackmail racket (in Francis's *Reflex* Fawcett). In these and most of Welsh scribe and former jockey Francis' twenty-odd books, the backdrop is racing, the protagonist stoic, and the villains car-nivorous slime who will stop at nothing.

Strictly for Swells

Nick and Nora Charles. In *The Thin Man* (Vintage), Dashiell Hammett fash-ioned a husband-and-wife team so arch, so debonair, and so besotten with cocktails that their charm and wit virtually ooze off the pages. Wisecrack-ing Nick, an ex-detective, has married wisecracking millionairess Nora, and he has no plans beyond fixing them both a shaker of martinis. Of course, through Nora's nudging, Nick finds himself knee-deep in crime, hunting down a missing scientist (the Thin Man) while he slurps down a succession of alcoholic beverages.

Hooper Taliaferro and Dr. Mary Finney; In 1955, under the pseudonym Matthew Head, New York art critic John Canaday scribed *Murder at the Flea Club* (Perennial Library) a classic bit of classy detection set against the deca-dent demimonde of a Paris nightclub. Prostitutes (male and female), wealthy widows, languid foreigners and the Flea Club's singer-proprietress are among the characters that the raffish Hooper Taliaferro and his overweight African missionary friend Dr. Finney (the real brains of the team) must contend with if they're to solve the question of who killed . . . well, we won't get into that. Canaday/Head's first-person narrative is stylishly loop and rife with a sort of easygoing Continentalese.

Detective-Inspector Wilkins. The Brit-ish Stately Home mystery is resurrected in a pair of seductively silly whodunits by English writer James Anderson—*The Case of the Mutilated Mink Coat* and *The Affair of the Blood-Stained Egg Cosy* (Avon). Wilkins and sidekick Detective-Sergeant Leather don't even appear in these drawing room dramas until the thieving, cheating, and poison-ing have all been accomplished (about halfway through the books), but the coterie of earls, MPs, Texas million-aires, foreign spies, playboys, French baronesses, and mysterious strangers keep the reader amused, bemused, and totally at a loss as to what's going on.

(Those wishing to follow some of the aforementioned sleuths on their ap-pointed rounds are advised to investi-gate *The Armchair Detective* caper: $16 for four quarterly issues of mystery news and views to TAD, 129 West 56th Street, New York, New York 10019.)

The beauty of magazines is that they recreate themselves (and their best and worst aspects) every month. They've therefore got more chances to peak and decline than books, which, after all, may go on selling, gathering readers for years. But periodicals flash, crash, and burn, and each one's peculiar idiosyncrasies—what it is that makes it especially appealing or dull—blaze forth with every new issue. Those special qualities are what place the following unique publications on our list of...

THIRTEEN MAGS FOR MODERNS

"Vietnam: A Major Market Fades." That's how **ADVERTISING AGE,** the weekly read by *all* the hotshot ad guys and gals, announced the fall of Saigon a few years ago. And they weren't kidding, for *Ad Age,* the magazine of scientific hucksterism, is a chronicle of the forces that *really* run our lives. Cool here is, for the outsider, the vicarious thrill of eavesdropping on Madison Avenue. One issue in spring 1982 covered the Falklands Islands conflict by announcing that Argentina, in hopes of winning the islanders' allegiance, was beaming color TV propaganda commercials to that embattled archipelago. Several pages inward, it's announced that Pabst Brewing, "stalking the competitive beer jungle," has prepared a TV spot "which utilizes a 50-pound Siberian tiger and the theme 'It's gonna get you.'" Moving right along, an article entitled "Daring Strategic Move Keys Tic Tac Turnaround" provides a fascinating "corporate closeup."

But stop laughing and pay attention. Every now and then, the lay reader is spoon-fed a truly stunning fact in the guise of a routine marketing announcement. For instance, did you know that *Time, Inc.* makes more money on its cable television operations than on all its (extremely profitable) magazines combined? The boys down at the agencies do: They might not know the truth if it landed on their Burberrys—but for them, this magazine is the real thing. Read it and know the future. At newsstands. A.M.

AMERICAN SPLENDOR. This infrequent, indescribable "underground" comic is the brainchild of Cleveland scripter Harvey Pekar, who uses artists R. Crumb, Gary Dumm, and others to illustrate his "depressing stories from Harvey Pekar's hum-drum life." Never has nothing happened so spectacularly as in the zen-gray pages of *American Splendor.* Seven existential issues out, at comics collectors' stores.

Forget *Soldier Of Fortune.* **AVIATION WEEK & SPACE TECHNOLOGY** is the bible of the true, card-carrying honchos of the military-industrial complex. A trade weekly, it's put out for the guys who turn out bombers, missiles . . . you get the picture. All the latest developments in mass destruction: juicy articles (*way* before the popular press gets wind of anything) about killer

FROM OFF THE STREETS OF CLEVELAND COMES:

AMERICAN SPLENDOR

No. 2

HOW SMART IS SHE? I DUNNO, I GUESS SHE'S ABOUT AVERAGE.

AVERAGE? HEY, MAN, AVERAGE IS DUMB!

ALL STORIES BY HARVEY PEKAR ART BY GREG BUDGETT GARY DUMM BRIAN BRAM ROBERT CRUMB

MORE DEPRESSING STORIES FROM *HARVEY PEKAR'S* HUM-DRUM LIFE

MORE THAN **60** PAGES

BUDGETT DUMM/PEKAR

© 1977 by Harvey Pekar Photo: Mike Koehn

satellites, nuclear-tipped cruise missiles, and nasty "smart" bombs that parachute down into the boondocks and then lie in wait until a column of tanks passes, to spew "submunitions" at their infrared "signatures." For intelligence buffs, *AW&SP* is chock-full of grainy sightings of Soviet "Kiev-class" carriers and "Hormone" helicopters. But the biggest treats: lavish ads—aimed at God knows which tinhorn sheiks and dictators—for tanks, bombs, fighter planes, and missiles. These ads aren't the ones you see in

Life. "Shoots down everything that's up. Blows up everything that's down" was the head on a recent McDonnell-Douglas pitch for its F-15. Check your newsstand or drop thirty-nine big ones for a year's worth: 1221 Avenue of the Americas, New York, New York 10020. A.M.

BIG BEAUTIFUL WOMAN, the magazine for hefty babes everywhere, has *got* to be the greatest match of audience and editorial anywhere. Let's face it, folks: Most fat ladies live in split levels and tract houses; they don't follow Liza and Halston to Biarritz. So *BBW*—about the most wondrous collection of avoirdupois you'll see on slick paper—is an unabashed celebration of lower middle class fat fantasies. Lots of lovely Quiana creations worn by *really* fat models. Lots of perky recipes for tuna casseroles and such. "BBW Picture Parade," a collage of readers' photographs that looks like it was pasted up with Elmer's. Personal ads from men who yearn for sheer poundage. "Conversation With My Face," a loony, introspective column about nothing in particular. And best of all, a series of fawning celebrity profiles written without the (inevitably overweight) subject's participation. How'd you like yours, Dom DeLuise? Beverly Sills? Liz Taylor? A.M.

BIKINI GIRL. In earlier times ('79-80), this mimeo wonder might've been called a "fanzine" or an "art book." Thankfully, there are no easy terms at hand to describe what Lisa Baumgardner does in a variety of formats (usually *BG* comes in black-on-pink, measures 7"x 7" or 8"x 8"). In other words, an unsquare mag of many dimensions. A typical issue might feature reprints of Fifties lingerie ads, an appreciation of "cool fan clubs," "An Interview with a Boot," collages, flexi-disc records, or an article discussing the differences be-

tween grooved and oval lipstick containers. Non-coverage of William Burroughs' 1979 Mudd Club was a real gas. Each ish carries Baumgardner's disclaimer: "Because this is a book for everybody, we're going to leave nothing out. If, at any point, your intelligence is insulted, just remember that there are others perhaps not as knowledgeable as you, and the more basic material is meant for them." Write P.O. Box 319, Peter Stuyvesant Station, New York, New York 10009-0319. S.Z.

FEAR OF DARKNESS. In Bill Landis's long dark shadow (see *Sleazoid Express)* comes "the new magazine of unusual and bizarre aspects of the cinema!" A recent forty-page issue offered a John Waters interview, a survey of Godzilla movies, and an essay entitled "The *I Spit on Your Grave* Controversy Continued." Send $2 for a sample to P.O. Box 02252, Columbus, Ohio 43202.

HOLLYWOOD STAR. Not since the demise of *Confidential* magazine in 1958 has the tradition of American scandal sheets breathed so deeply. Bill Dakota's nasty newspaper hits the racks irregularly, but when it does, it brandishes headlines like "Natalie Wood's Autopsy Report Could Lead to 'Manslaughter' Charges!" and "Paul

Lynde Tricked with Rough Trade!" One recent ish published hundred-plus lists of "Hollywood Celebrities Who Have Used Cocaine!" and "Bi-Sexual Male Stars!" Sorry, no subscriptions, but Bill digs letters (P.O. Box 76356, Los Angeles, California 90020).

JONAH HEX. Who says the Western is dead? The hippest comic book on the stands just celebrated its tenth anniversary. Its hero, a mangy Confederate rebel with a misshapen face and a bad habit of drilling strangers with his anxious Colt .45, has been dodging varmints and poisoned waterholes since first popping up in DC's *All Star Western* (issue #10) in 1972. He vamoosed over to *Weird Western* (#12) then talked himself into his own book in '77. Sergio Leone spaghetti meets basic black humor. Still only 60¢ monthly at newsstands and supermarkets everywhere. (Early issues are best, and most are still available in collectors' shops.) This mag should be a movie.

LOW RIDER. *Hey loco!* Twenty-five years from now, slick Hollywood producers will be making "nostalgic" musicals about the cute Chicanos of the Eighties. But *Low Rider* is the real thing now, *vatos*—it's published right there in San Jose, *Califas,* where lots of the

homeboys hang out. Filled to the brim with ads for illegal hydraulics, it's got lots of news of *cuelludo* (important) car clubs like the Artistics, Epics, Street Life, and the Night Sensations; lots of *hijos* and *hijas* wearing mean threads from the Forties; and plenty of interviews with big shots like Ricardo Montalban and Erik Estrada. Best of all,

though, it's stuffed with photos of lots of b-a-a-d rides: all of them equipped with state-of-the-art tuck-and-roll, silver-dollar-sized chain steering wheels, and suspensions so much lowered from stock they bottom out if they run over a candy wrapper. *Mira lo!* Only $15 for twelve issues: A.T.M. Communications, Inc., 444 East William Street, San Jose, California 95112. A.M.

POPULAR SCIENCE. Your own personal styrofoam gyrocopter! A methane-powered stereo/heart pace-maker *you* can build! Since the dawn of the machine age, *Popular Science* has been the common man's utopian dream journal, the harbinger of a toil-free future that never quite arrives. Packed through and through with nifty show cars, laser cloud cover measurers, outboard motors so large you need a crane to lift them over the transom, it gives you all the cheap thrills you need without personal risk or pollution. And those nifty monthly features! True, the most anachronistic recurring column in American journalism —a highly stylized short story format called

"Gus and the Model Garage," which somehow incorporated a searching analysis of small-town mores along with a clever example of automotive trouble-shooting—expired sometime during the mid-Sixties. But still around is Smokey Yunick, "America's most famous mechanic," dispensing automotive advice and fulminating against small-block diesels. There's Roy Doty's "Wordless Workshop," in which with nary a word spoken or written—his pipe-smoking typical suburbanite builds a different unnecessary piece of furniture each month. And especially wonderful, and still tantalizing, are the semi-fraudulent classified ads appearing in the back of the magazine. Psst! All you sleep learners out there—wanna buy a jeep for . . . $35? A.M.

PREVUE. Marvel artist Jim Steranko (*Captain America, Nick Fury*) edits this "bi-monthly publication devoted to popular culture in multi-media." *Prevue* doesn't keep its bi-monthly pledge too well, but it walks the pop cult beat like few other mags, with book excerpts, articles on Disney animators and Debbie Harry, and (recently) a near-edible color spread on *One from the Heart* and Nastassia Kinski. One year's worth: $14 to P.O. Box 48, Reading, Pennsylvania 19603.

RAW. The only magazine currently offering two-issue subscriptions isn't a comic, isn't *National Lampoon.* "The Graphix Magazine for Your Bomb Shelter's Coffee Table" is a forty-page, 10½ by 14-inch brainbust of cartoons, offbeat commentary, and non-sequitur serials. Bruno Richard's "Autobiography" in *Raw* #4 uses forty stamp-size sketches to illustrate forty first personal film titles, all the way from *I Am a Camera* through *I Led Three Lives* and *I Married a Monster from Outer Space.* Gary Panter's perma-

nently bugged Jimbo character gigs regularly in *Raw.* Two annual issues for $11 to Raw Books & Graphics, Inc., 27 Greene Street, New York, New York 10013.

SLEAZOID EXPRESS. Editor Bill Landis calls himself a "sleaze civil service worker," and his monthly news-

letter enables him to perform his appointed tasks admirably. In-depth discussions of Russ Meyer films, kung-fu, softcore and "body-count" flicks delivered to your doorstep. Where else to get advance word on *Wizard of Gore, Africa Blood and Guts,* or *Revenge of the Shogun Women*? Eight bucks for a bloody year's worth to: Landis, P.O. Box 709, Peter Stuyvesant Station, New York, New York 10009.

Ahead of their time or behind on their rent, some swell mags have gone to the great newsstand in the sky. Trees died for these, too...

BACK ISSUES

CHEETAH (1967-68). The first and final fling of "Youthquake" publishing included some groovy glossies. *Cheetah* came on hip, then slipped and ultimately fell, but its covers were tasty in a junior *Esquire* kind of way. Inside: Tom Wolfe, Brian Wilson, Mama Cass nude, Van Dyke Parks, Peter Max, and an Owsley Stanley profile titled "The Henry Ford of Acid."

The showdown between Square and Underground took place on the over-sized pages of the Hearst Corp's **EYE** (1968-69). Trippy layout (op art color inserts, a *Spiderman* comic glued to the front of Volume 2, Number 2), and time warp contents: "Warren Beatty Raps," "Grooviest Unisex Fashions," "An Evening With Tim Leary." Even the ads tried to turn on. Simplicity dress patterns bragged of styles "as far-in or as far-out as you like . . . Sew your own thing."

More exotic Sixties fallout includes **TEENSET,** the official **SHINDIG!** and **HULLABALOO** magazines; also **AUM, STROBE,** and **FREAK OUT U.S.A.** The most amazing artifact may be the two issues of **BROTHER POWER, THE GEEK** (DC Comics, 1968), a mind-mangling comic designed to steer American youth away from "the Real-Life Scene of the Dangers of Hippie Land!" *The Geek*'s priceless appeal lies beyond camp, and comic collector

Koehn

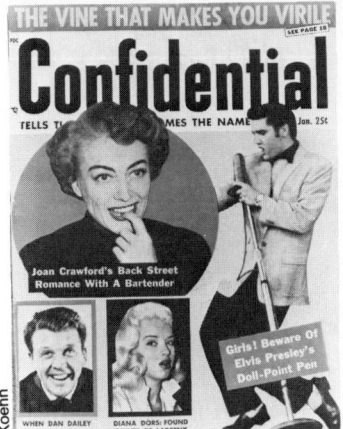

shops will charge you less than $3 apiece for issues, if you can find them.

CONFIDENTIAL (1952-58). The summit of sleaze, reached and held for six years. Never again such scandalous cover stories as "Proof Positive: Picasso Was an Opium Addict!" or "Anita Ekberg, the Smorgas-broad! Doctors Prove Anita's Bust Abnormal!" An anthology is way overdue.

ESQUIRE (1954-71). The old *Esquire*'s achievements were rarely dubious: caustic wit, issues observed from odd angles, and, perhaps best of all, George Lois' Sixties covers. Beyond cool: in the mid-Fifties, "Esquire's Lady Fair" featured clothed women!

EVERGREEN REVIEW (1957-73). For fifteen years, *the* playground in print for boho-beat-leftie America. Among those who made it great: Sontag, Borges, Behan, Kerouac, Dali, William Carlos Williams, and Ho Chi Minh. Grove Press recently published two or three volumes of *Evergreen Review Reader,* paperback anthologies now available (often remaindered) in bookstores everywhere.

HIDDEN WORLDS and **SEARCH** (1955-68). Before psychic phenomena came aboveground and became a talk show staple, publications like these were the main channel of communication between non-teleporting loons. Locked in the closet, things could get pretty wild—"The UFO That Changed My Life," "The Vampire Who Wanted to Be My Wife," and classifieds selling the secrets of zone therapy, theosophism, and "space television." Watch the skies. R.B.

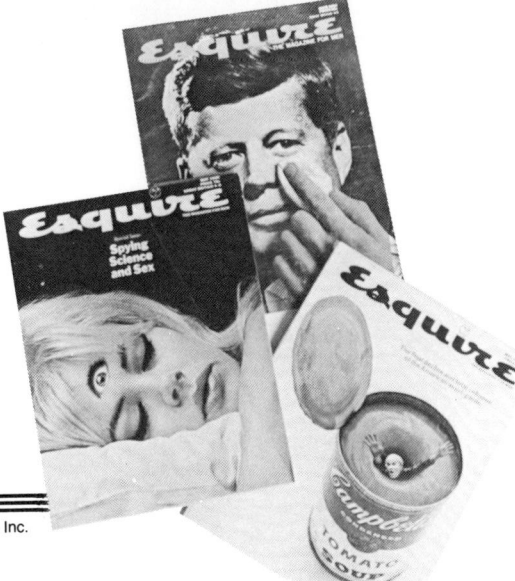

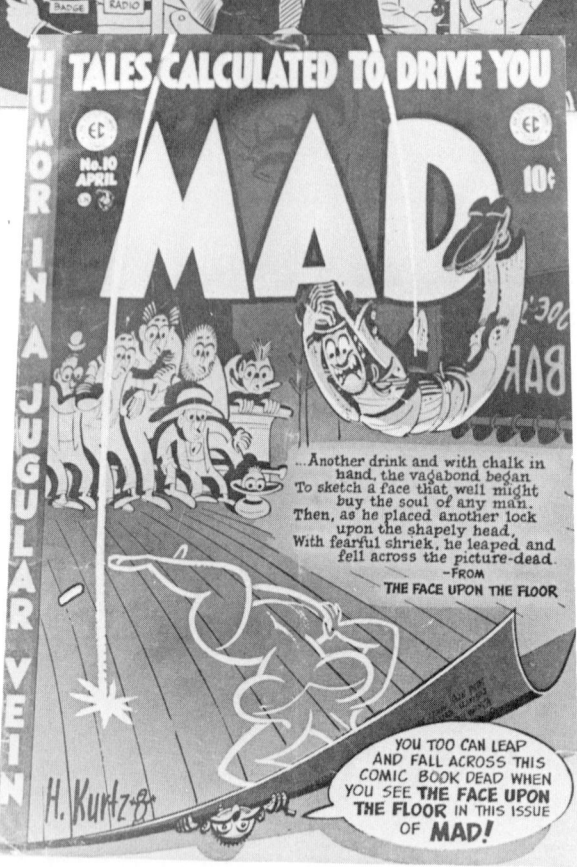

MAD (1954-63). Of course it's still around, but its glory resides on those dust-covered panels drawn by Wally Wood, Davis, Elder, and Woodbridge during the first decade. We'd run out of ribbon citing *Mad*'s accomplishments as the keenest twin-edge blade in postwar U.S. culture, so we won't try. Mainly, we'll just suggest that you pay whatever it costs to get your eyes on some early issues, like those edited by Harvey Kurtzman, namely #1 through #28.

Kurtzman? "He is to comic book art what Jackson Pollack was to spatter-painting," said *Look*. One critic credited him with inventing "the Muck School" of art and another cited *Mad*'s "hyperventilated maverick goofiness" during Harv's reign. Hell, he's probably a great bartender, too. Owner and operator of the coolest sense of humor in the continental United States (but there's this igloo manager in the Aleutians . . .), Kurtzman left *Mad* to found a trio of boss books: the lavishly lampooning **TRUMP** (1957), **HUMBUG** ('57-'58), and **HELP!** ('60-'65). The latter ran on wild ideas contributed by Gloria Steinem, R. Crumb, Woody Allen, and Terry Gilliam and John Cleese in their pre-Monty Python incarnations. Since 1962, Kurtzman's been writing and sketching *Playboy*'s "Little Annie Fanny." Hoo hah. Somebody give this man a magazine!

Less inspired but soundly wacky, the *Mad* imitations from the Fifties. They likewise burlesqued current fantasies (Elvis Pretzel, Cinerama, and Sputnik) with satire in a cut-rate vein. Know them by their names: **WILD, LOCO, NUTS, PANIC, CRAZY, FRENZY, FRANTIC, EH!, FLIP, BUGHOUSE** and **THIMK** (sic). Wherever.

PLASTIC MAN. Superheroes come and go like colds. Where are Doc Savage, Supergirl, Ragman, or Ms. Marvel now? Who cares? The most gone of all was a loopy apparition in wrestling togs and bulging wraparounds who, "accidentally doused with an experimental acid, was transformed into a human rubber band!" Introduced in 1943, Plas and his polka dot pal Woozy Winks did their things—battling zoot-suited hoods, beating Batman to cartoon camp by two decades—until '56 then left. D.C. Comics revived them in '66 and '77. In '81, the shape-shifting sleuth popped up in *All-Star Squadron,* wisecracked with Wonder Woman, and split.

PUNK MAGAZINE (1976-79) What the last revolution was supposed to look like. The best transposition into print of TV, trash, and the residue from a thousand previous pop explosions, all in one dense, chaotic tabloid slick. Reviews of records (on the Doors' *American Poem:* "Who said this was good?!?!!! THIS STINKS!!!") maga-

THIS IS NO UP-AND-DOWN MAGAZINE! THIS IS A SIDEWAYS...

HUMOR IN A VARICOSE VEIN

EC NO. 5 NOV. **PANIC** 10¢

★ E.C.'S ANSWER TO CINERAMASCOPE WIDE-SCREEN-TYPE MOVIES!

SHOP AROUND
Books

Like nature, cool loves to hide. The fact that half of *our* Great Books are currently out of print should be greeted as a challenge (or at least as an opportunity to get out of the house). Some of the books are easily found, while others may send you searching on safari. After your local (new book) retailer, the next stop is the used book shops. Every city worth its salt has a few, and they're usually true marvels—repositories of arcane knowledge, keepers of organizational secrets, and filing systems descended from the Rosicrucians and known only to their owners. They're also apt to be over-stocked with recent square-biz titles (*The Scarsdale Diet, Even Cowgirls Get the Blues*) and rather thin on their supply of *The Beat Generation and the Angry Young Men.* Don't be discouraged.

Thrift stores, rummages, and yard sales can yield treasures, too, though the percentages are spotty. (True ink nuts, like record collectors, have been known to saddle up and canvas the whole country for rare items.) If you strike out after a reasonable amount of time, you can turn to the mail-order book search services. It'll cost, but their dragnet's bigger than yours. Try these:

Book Tracers, P.O. Box 114, Fords, New Jersey 03863
Reliable Book Service, P.O. Box 2033, Paterson, New Jersey 07509
Frances Klenett Book Service, 13 Cranberry Street, Brooklyn Heights, New York 11201.

zines, and instant dinners. A "Mutant Monster Beach Party" *fumetto* starred Deborah Harry, Andy Warhol, and Joey Ramone. *Punk's* Playmate of the Bi-month (May-June '79) was Leonid Brezhnev. Gabba gabba.

(When going the search route, always ask for cost quotes up front, and give searchers a reasonable time schedule. Be specific. If you need to read *Been Down So Long It looks Like Up to Me* before bedtime tomorrow night, it'll cost you more than if you can wait five or six weeks.)

In addition to search services, many of the larger overstock houses and used-book emporiums regularly publish catalogs of bargain-priced out-of-print items. Ordering's as close as a stamp. Last time we looked, Nationwide Book Service's (Box 211, Williamsburg Station, Brooklyn, New York 11211) catalog was offering hardcover Austen, Wolfe, and Southern at paper prices. Other catalogs are available from the Strand Book Store (828 Broadway, New York, New York 10003), Hamilton's (98-05 Clapboard, Danbury, Connecticut 06810), and Editions (Desk T, Boiceville, New York 12412).

A national list of "hip" bookstores would make a whole tome itself, so we're not even going to try and assemble one. But we have our favorites of the places we've been, and they include City Lights and McDonald's (which deals in used, and also has back-dated mags) in San Francisco . . . Other Times and Cosmopolitan and Westwood Books in L.A. . . . Booked Up in Washington, D.C . . . Gotham and Gryphon, Mendoza's, Sylvan, and the Barnes & Noble Annex in New York . . .

Magazines and Comics

For past periodicals, used-book shops are where the action is. The most likely are the ones who make a point of advertising "back-dated magazines"—they're the ones who take the business seriously enough to keep indexes and price lists (and to take some care of their stock), as opposed to the stores who merely have a box of well-thumbed *Peoples* and *Playboys* by the door.

Surprisingly, the Fifties and Sixties *Esquires* we've touted can often be had for under $5 in such haunts. Rarer goodies like *Cheetah* and *Eye* (and *Confidential,* if you can find copies) go for slightly more. (Mail order ups the cost, but one operation we've dealt with that's got the goods and charges reasonably for a variety of back-date titles is Jay Bee Magazines, 143 West 29th Street, New York, New Yrok 10001. Send them a stamped, self-addressed envelope telling them what you're after, and they'll quote you prices.)

When it comes to *Plastic Man* and *Mad* and all those other "only 10¢" and "25¢—Cheap" mags, be prepared to spend. Vintage comic book shops have now sprouted everywhere (even in malls). On your first visit to one, buy the latest (#12) Overstreet *Comic Book Price Guide,* a fat volume that lists every comic ever made and tells you, with some accuracy, what they're going for these days.

Among recommended comics stores . . .

Los Angeles—American Comic Book Company (two locations) and The Golden Apple
Denver—Mile High Comics
Baltimore—Geppi's
San Francisco—The Comics and Comix Chain
Chicago—Moondog's
Dallas—Lone Star Comics & Science Fiction
Miami—A&M Comics & Books
New York City—the infamous Batcave and West Side Comics
Las Vegas—don't forget your Friendly Neighborhood Comic Book Store.
Boston—in Beantown, try The Million Dollar Picnic (actually in Cambridge, Massachusetts).

That's all, folks.

Martinis, Triumphs, Nabokov, and narrow lapels. When was the last time the American Intellectual had style? It was twenty years ago today.

1962
The Last Good Year

by Davin Seay

It's rare when an esthetic consensus—a movement or school or linkage of like-minded—simply ceases to exist. It's relatively certain, after all, that the cherished flame of any fashion or fancy, no matter how transitory, must somewhere still be lit. In the foothills of the Hindu Kush or the backstreets of Oakland, some cat with bare feet and Goulimine beads still blows on the ruddy embers of peace and love. Off a dank alley in Greenwich Village or North Beach, a bereted and goateed hepster still howls the beatnik mantra. But nowhere it seems is the breath of that last great year still fogging the windows of our collective memory. Nineteen sixty-two is gone forever. Goodbye and amen.

So why '62? Why not '56 or '68, or why not even '23? Sixty-two seems, in retrospect, a year when the singular naiveté of the spanking new decade was at its guileless height, with only the vaguest, most indistinct hints of the agonies and ecstasies to come marring the fresh-scrubbed, if slightly sallow complexion of the times. On the first day of that year, the Federal Reserve raised the maximum interest on savings accounts to 4 percent while "The Twist" was sweeping the nation. A month later "Duke of Earl" was topping the charts, and John Glenn was orbiting the good, green globe. That spring Wilt Chamberlain set the NBA record by scoring 100 points in a single game and *West Side Story* won the Oscar for Best Picture. The Seattle World's Fair opened, followed five weeks later by the deployment of five thousand U.S. troops in Thailand. Dick Van Dyke and *The Defenders* won Emmys, and Adolph Eichman got his neck stretched. By that summer, the Supreme Court had banned prayer in public school, Algeria went indy, and Marilyn Monroe died of an overdose. "Loco-Motion" was Number One, Sherry Finkbine was on her way to a Swedish abortion, Sonny Liston K-O'd Floyd Patterson in the first round, and *The Beverly Hillbillies* graced the airwaves. By the time the grass of '62 had withered and died, the discovery of DNA's double helix had garnered the Nobel Prize, Kennedy had ordered the blockade of

Remember, in '62, LSD was still a smudge on a Swiss chemist's lab coat, weathermen were guys who told you if it was going to rain tomorrow, and banning the bomb was the dotty preoccupation of aging pacifists like Bertie Russell.

Sixty-two's best preserved artifact: James Mason and Sue Lyon in *Lolita*.

Cuba, "He's A Rebel" topped playlists and eleven thousand military advisers were in South Vietnam.

So it goes. a year much like any other in that debacle of a decade, fraught with crisis, fuming with the stench of change. But it was not what arrived in '62 that made it a year above other years—it was what passed. And what passed was the last, glorious gasp of the Angry Young Men.

"They are scum," pronounced Somerset Maugham on the subject of the AYM, and from his effete and lofty post he was doubtless right. The Angry Young Men were the result of the great proto-socialist postwar British experiment, which took the sons and daughters of working class louts, saw to their care, feeding, and education and had its hand severely bitten for the effort. The ingratitude was expressed primarily through a series of scathing novels in the mid-Fifties by such malcontents as John Osborne, Kingsley Amis, John Braine, Thomas Hinde, and Colin Wilson. Their books—*Hurry on Down, Room at the Top, Happy as Larry, Lucky Jim*—were eloquent rants against the bleak prospects offered by the brave new British dream. In their heyday the AYM brewed a literary tempest, primarily because they persisted in retaining working class suspicions of the inbred upper classes, rejecting notions of high art and avowing a rude and barbaric disdain for their elders.

Sound familiar? It shouldn't really. The vaunted parallels between the AYM and the Beat Generation—Kerouac, Ginsberg, *et al.*—were more fanciful than real. And herein lies the crux of 1962.

Remember, in '62, LSD was still a smudge on a Swiss chemist's lab coat, weathermen were guys who told you if it was going to rain tomorrow, and banning the bomb was the dotty preoccupation of aging pacifists like Bertie Russell. Social protest and the individual's right to weirdness had yet to find suitable forms of mass expression, especially for young, hyper-educated Americans for whom the prospect of life in the Beat mold—cold water flats, heroin, and filthy dungarees—held about as much appeal as the dour and colorless world of the squares. The AYM's had created a prototype of cynicism and cant, but by the early Sixties had fairly well shot their bolt. The bankruptcy of the AYM values was brilliantly satirized in an old Dudley Moore–Peter Cook *Beyond the Fringe* bit in which a gaggle of the former firebrands find themselves in the employ of Fleet Street magnate Lord Beaverbrook. Amongst besotted avowals to commence work on a "really accurate novel" that will "rip the lid off the whole filthy mess," they describe how they are working from within to bring down the system. "We drink and drink and drink," says one, ". . . and then we snigger quite openly behind our hands."

Sniggering may have been all that was left to some, but for others, the erudite, urbane, articulate, and wisely disaffected image of the Angry Young Man blended with a startling creative drive and a heightening sense of the potential of pop culture to create a brief, fanciful flowering that reached its apex in and around magical 1962.

In every field, it seemed, the best was being brought to bear. *Esquire,* everyone's favorite late lamented periodical, was championing a new kind of smart, discursive journalism and was, as much as any organ, the voice of the freshly hip. The stunning arrival and swift passage of Huntington Hartford's *Show* created a kind of fancy spread alternative to the plodding regularity of

Ties and vermouth-soaked olives and cool detachment were out— strobe lights and reefer oblivion and indiscriminate screwing in sleeping bags was the order of the day.

the *Life/Look* hegemony. Even such highbrow exercises as the hardbound *Horizon* or the absurdly continental *Realities* had a certain undeniable class that matched this new mini-renaissance. Conversely, Ralph Ginzburg's *Eros* stands, as did all his efforts, as a crass exploitation of the spirit of the times. The coffee table eroticism of its first issue—in the spring of '62—dared to feature grainy black-and-white snaps of people smooching in the subway, as well as an invaluable glossary of vulgar terms circa 1785.

The epitomizing fashion of '62 was unquestionably male. It was also a marvelous representation of the calculated arrogance and deep insularity of the insiders. Narrow lapels, narrow ties, narrow haircuts accentuating narrow, boney foreheads, blacks and whites and muted greys, martinis and carefully cocked cigs, Miltown tranqs by prescription. Cocktail parties were the common ground of the new elite; sex was a casual afterthought between fascinatingly preoccupied individuals. English sports cars—Triumphs and MG's—flitted them from place to place, and classical music in equal proportions to jazz served as uninvolved background sounds.

Television was the new frontier. The so-called Golden Age—a time when producers like Fred Coe could command talent like Reginald Rose, Robert Allen Arthur, and Paddy Chayefsky for shows like *Philco* and *Goodyear Playhouse*—had come and gone. But the new breed of TV scribes were intent on creating their own gilded era from such series as *Naked City* and *Route 66.* To the degree that they succeeded in crossing high- and lowbrow while simultaneously avoiding middlebrow, writers like Howard Rodman and Sterling Silliphant could be said to have molded a sort of brittle new art form. Don't forget, millions were weekly tuning in episodes of the above-mentioned programs with titles such as "Ever Ride the Waves to Oklahoma?" and "Today the Man Who Kills the Ants Is Coming." Rodman, who evidently took the task of recreating television very seriously indeed, once found fault with a studio editing job on one of his scripts. The show's producer received the next day a large package wrapped in black crepe. Inside was a pair of scissors. Such were the times.

Art was literally exploding. Painters and graphic experimenters (including Robert Rauschenberg, James Rosenquist, Robert Indiana, Roy Lichtenstein, Tom Wesselmann, and Claes Oldenburg) were upending possibilities by ignoring history and rediscovering primary reality. Rosenquist referred to what they were up to collectively as "loud, very magnified and disquieting. Many people," he later recalled, "hated what we were doing, and the name 'pop art' was quickly tacked onto it. People wanted it to be like 'popular' music, 'popular' psychology. They wanted to get rid of it, and if it was 'popular' they thought it wouldn't last. But it continued, continued, continued."

Indeed it did, unlike 1962. Although the form of hip erudition lingered on for a few more years, the crushing juggernaut of hippiedom—that final triumph of the Beat esthetic over the AYM's—was soon to swallow all traces of this brief flickering moment into the Dark Night of Patchouli. Ties and vermouth-soaked olives and cool detachment were out—strobe lights and reefer oblivion and indiscriminate screwing in sleeping bags was the order of the day.

Yet before 1962 vanished beneath the shifting sands without a trace, it left one enduring monument to its ineffable, enigmatic qualities, as well as an ominous symbolic talisman of its own doom. Nineteen sixty-two was the year Stanley Kubrick released his film version of Vladimir Nabokov's masterpiece *Lolita*. The flick—in the beautiful symmetry of its black-and-white photography, awesomely perfect performances, and lucid evocation of the tragi-comic pantomime at the core of the American dream—is without question the best preserved artifact remaining of that tiny enlightenment. But it is much more besides. In its characters we see the inescapable fate of the cultural vanguard of 1962. Claire Quilty personifies all that the spiritual descendants of the Angry Young Men had be-

Huntington Hartford's fancy alternative: *Show* magazine.

come: ephemeral, flighty, defined only by the circumstance of the moment. Humbert Humbert was the ham-fisted knock of reality, of encroaching age and a fearsome loss of detachment. And Lolita . . . Lolita was the dawning age— the hippie, the runaway, the crass, gum-popping, utterly seductive arrival of a strange, new generation fitted with nothing more than the flower of youth.

"Fashion is obsolescence," goes the old saw. Meaning that the real business of the fashion biz is planning this afternoon's demise of this morning's vogue, all in the name of style. The implication is, of course, that nobody wants to be caught dead in last year's threads. Who wants yesterday's paper dresses?

Cool fashion twists the old saw to read something like "Who cares for fashion? Obsolescence is cool." Meaning, as often as not, that what's cool is what's "out"—what's missing or omitted from prevailing mainstream tastes. Not that "retro" is where it's at. It's just that (a) nothing is new, and (b) sometimes only the discarded or the forgotten stands any chance of making a fresh impact or of tossing the first shovelful at the next big dig.

So don't be surprised at what plays on the following pages. You'll find no urban cowperson ensembles, no New Wave or New Romantic rigs, no looks utilizing headbands or jogging tops.

What is represented here are a few of the more colorful lengths to which women and men have gone in recent times to express that sense of whatever we've decided to call cool. Some of these clothes may be ripe for rediscovery, and some may not. Look close. Look sharp.

Ladies first.

GALS
Mini, Sack, Toreadors, and More
by Marsha Meyer

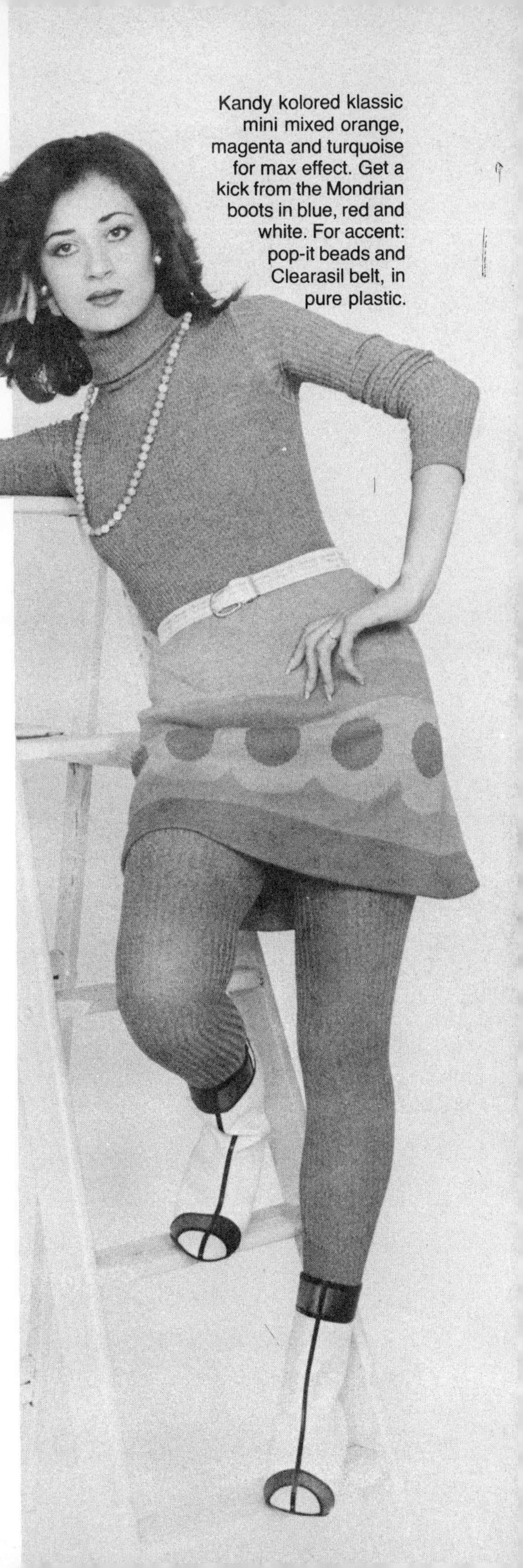

Kandy kolored klassic mini mixed orange, magenta and turquoise for max effect. Get a kick from the Mondrian boots in blue, red and white. For accent: pop-it beads and Clearasil belt, in pure plastic.

MINIS. The high gear of the high-go Sixties. Minis legged it onto center stage mid-decade, and thereafter their swing factor was never in doubt. The fashion squirearchy generally agree on the tog's parentage: a Ma Mini in England's Mary Quant (the hand behind the Chelsea look and the Mod look) and a Da Mini in France's André Courrèges, the architect of the Space Age look.

Measuring in at 6 to 8 inches pre-knee, the mini was followed by the bold micro-mini, skirting in at 11 inches above. Everybody who was anybody wore 'em, from Julie Christie to Jane Fonda to Q.E. 2's only girl child. And if some oldsters were drip-dropping on the splendiferous, spendiferous parade with syllabs of "If she were mine, I'd lock her up," others of the oatmeal thigh set were hitching up hems in timid stitches to heights 2 inches and even 4 inches above kneeline.

In short, everybody was squiffy on the mini. And on the neo rigging it required. Neonic body stockings and ribbed poor boys took it from the top. Plastic baby boots, preferably stark white or carrying the Mondrian motif, and baby heels of 1 inch, 1½ inches and 2 inches toed it off. In between, patterned hose, colored hose, and tights of all spots and stripes took up the slack, especially after a rumor went round that girls with minied knees would develop fatty deposits on said areas in cold weather. Faces went pale. Eyes went big. Lips shone in mahogany and burgundy hues. Hair fell down à la Jean Shrimpton (tips were available on how to iron for that straight, straighter, straightest look) or into geometrics, courtesy Vidal Sassoon.

From London, Loudon Wainwright mused in *Life* on the etiquette of the mini-ogle, while in the land of sounds one Brenton Wood assured all orblings that it was A-OK in the notes of "Oogum Boogum." In the U.S. of A., Rudi Gernreich intro'd the look, then busied himself with cutouts and the see-through blou and the topless bathing suit, and Betsy Johnson came up with a clear vinyl minidress featuring stars, numbers, fishes, and such in a paste-on kit.

The original minis—the boxy skirts and tending toward A-lines, Empires, and Victoriana dresses—aren't too difficult to locate today. But a Biba (ah, a Biba), from the London boutique that churned out less than a thousand of each style, priced at small change . . . to find a Biba would bring joy to the dedicated swinging hip.

TOREADOR PANTS—a.k.a. Capris. Originally named for those shapely gents on horseback, these trou should more probably be called toreros after those who fight the bull on foot. We're not talking Galligaskins here. We're not talking pedal pushers. We're not talking clam-diggers or gauchos. These two-legged waist-to-ankle outer garments should fit as snug as the body is sound. They're slick leggings. And they've boasted such top billings as Mamie Van Doren in *High School Confidential,* as well as poster fame in *Riot on Sunset Strip* ("Meet the . . . Teenyboppers with their too tight capris!") in their mid-Fifties, early Sixties prime. Toreadors can be worn with stiletto heels or with flats, toes both pointed and round. Toreadors are fine in all colors and

Soup's on. The all-paper Campbell's dress. Label reads: "The Souper Dress. No cleaning, no washing. It's carefree, fire resistant unless washed or cleaned. To refreshen, press lightly with warm iron. Eighty per cent cellulose, twenty per cent cotton."

prints. Toreadors must be ankle length or just above. Toreadors must be tight. But, per chance, should a pair be found festooned with the names of America's super Prez's in bold horizontals, even that quest for the second-skin fit can be foregone in the name of true fashion cool.

PAPER DRESSES. The ultimate in our fashion equation: fashion=obsolescence=fashion. A mere squib in the annals of garbdom, these (usually) cellulose wrappings floated onto the front lines in 66 and vaporized a scant 365 later. Not even a postcard since.

But while the new breed of paperwrights plied their trade, the media did the same. Mags from *Seventeen* to *Time* to *Good Housekeeping* chased paper items. *Business Week,* too, thought it all of import and in the week of July 22, 1967, reported on the phenomenon. The development of rustle-free paper in early '66 had opened the gate; sixty-plus manufacturers took to the track in a single year. When Scott Paper Company offered a premium dress, "The Paper Caper," at $1.25, around a half million earth-dwellers responded. And in Cal-by-the-sea Judith Brewer was designing "fur" coats of paper and selling them for $200 ('66 coinage) in her boutique.

Quite a spin for a non-woven fabric, but its utile side was not to be denied. Upkeep was at a min. It couldn't be washed, and it couldn't be dry cleaned or it would spill its fire retardants. Too long? Snip it up. Too short? Buy two and splice. And the truly enterprising needn't buy off the rack. For a minute or two the paper fabric itself was available. That and a Vogue pattern would mark you as in.

Prez pants, toreador style.

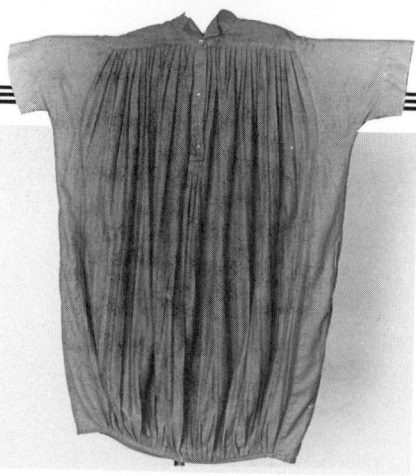

Even gourmet gowns were possible for the silver-quilted Mylar bunch. Bridal gear a given. A hostess could don a dress (print by Hallmark Cards, Inc.) and follow her theme right down to like-printed disposable napkins.

In April of '68, *Life* focused on graphic artist Harry Gordon, whose design of the moment was the "Poster Dress." These oh-so-cool sleeveless minis were to come off the presses in a quintet of prints—a rose, a cat, a rocket, an eye, and, the finest of the fine, a hand engaged in the Buddhist gesture of peace, on its palm "Uptown N.Y.", a poem by Allen Ginsberg appearing in its first American edition.

"You got a crazy shape/But I can't see it in that drape" sang the Beavers, whose 1958 record "Sack Dress" no one remembers. Shown here: a later modification of the song's subject. Who could forget it?

The word prepped us for a tomorrow filled with bedspreads, rugs, curtains, and . . . well, anything that was woven today could be unwoven in the future tense. But something unmentionable must have wrinkled the works. Today the lone survivors reposing on the recycled chic racks are few and far between.

It was as if Eisenhower himself had appeared in public in Louis XIV's high heels.

SACK DRESS a.k.a. the Chemise a.k.a. the Cocoon a.k.a. the Bag a.k.a. the only trim to skim the territorial imperatives of the fem form and come up on the hip side. A quick whiz through fashion tomes reveals that the basics of sack stitchery were practiced in Greek chiton days. Closer to our own era, the Twenties swagged with the tube dress in fine style. No matter, in Leotime of '57, Givenchy re-hipped the raiment biz on the frock that put the curves under wraps and shook the sphere to its very underpinnings. The hue and cry went up from all corners as this collarless rectangle fell square from the shoulders

to knees. It was as if Eisenhower himself had appeared in public in Louis XIV's high heels.

Still, chemiserie reigned from the need of neo-girdles to the need of neo-hose. The teens and younger wise ones went for it on the dime, and it trickled up into the upper numbers. There was even a greeting card offering a real "sack" inside.

The chemise also won positive nods from the nabobs in Moscow in '58. In a *Newsweek* piece that May, it was reported that a grocery clerk of feminine persuasion wrote the trade union paper *Trud* asking what the well-garbed lass should wear to a May Day celebration. An editor replied that the great advantage of the chemise was that one could purchase it readymade from the factory "without worrying about its not fitting well."

Alas, by the winter of '58-'59, the sack was an also-ran rack. But before it fell, it offered up a cluster of new fashion ABC's in such offspring as the Trapeze, the Empire Trapeze, the Balloon Bottom, the Bubble Bottom (and top), the Banded Bubble Bottom (and top), the chemise of the flounced hem, the sack skirt with the flounced hem, the barrel silhouette, *et cetera, et cetera, et cetera.*

And when fate's fickle scissors called a halt to sackomania, the protean attributes of this little beauty turned it into somebody's tunic and somebody's skirt and somebody's windshield wiper. But, like all things so hep they're hip, so hot they're cool, so swinging they're swag, a well-earned "Eureka!" will bring the seeker sheer spiritual bliss. After all, though the cries of "Sack the sack" and "The sack is slack" are but memory, what could be hipper than a martyred dress?

Creatures on the loose: Furry critter ties.

Boots of plastic "leather" in the mid and lower altitude range are good gear, but should be in white or of a Mondrian stripe.

POP-IT BEADS AND OTHER MUSTS DE COOL. Pop-it beads are a true fashion must for the discriminating lassie. First discovered by the late-Fifties kid culture, these soft plastic rounds won the pocket cents of America's first authorized preteen set. Turned out in colors not found in most

Pop-it beads. Today they hang around in toy stores.

rainbows, these semiprecious pearls were vari-sized, and the fashion sophisticate possessed a collection complete with the highly prized pearlized editions. Nowadays the honest item is nearly impossible to locate, but the basic shape and pizazz live on in an Eighties model found in most toy stores.

Way out front: rhinestone sweater guard.

OTHER JEWELS to keep a fine eye for: sweater guards, earrings that come in clumps and clusters, large hoops of nearly gold, clunky bracelets in vivids and lucite, charm bracelets someone else has collected, necklaces of fruit, furry critter ties, anklets. Among **BELTS,** a few truly odd items: the belt of copper, the one-time product offer, reversibles in plasticized colors, and (but for sure!) the cinch. A **GLOVE** can go far, wrist-length or opera, solid, polka dot, or striped (usually reserved for high go's and such). The **COAT** or **SWEA-TER** can be a problem. If you haven't found that perfect number in hamster fur, try a pea coat or a maxi; mix it with a mini. If you're going sweater, go beaded on the neckline, or don't go at all. **HATS:** a beret is the perfect funneltop for casual, but as for the rest, as always, let your own antenna set you free.

SHOES. Something it can oft be cool to be without. The shiny pearlized plastics of the Sixties were and are hot, and a clip-on earring will do in a pinch for the snap-on bows and buckles of years

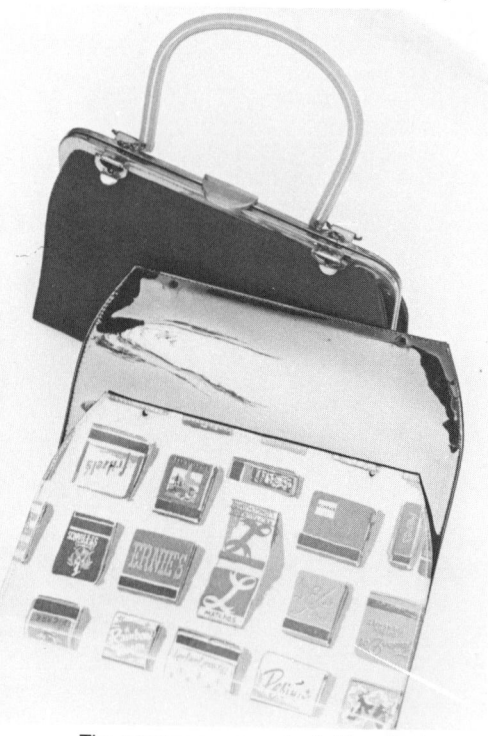

The reverse purse: we're talking Posh.

gone by. Flats of rounded toes and flats of pointy toes are just fine. Stilettos of the obviously tawdry sort and French heels of almost any sort are A-OK. Boots of plastic "leather" in the mid and lower altitude range are good gear, but should be in white or of a Mondrian stripe. The key to the cool shoe is in its odd ocelot vamp or stray polka dot. It's got to have *esprit*!

Obligato Garmenture ...of utmost importance to those who've got it and to those who don't...

PURSES. Carried by or for swankers for ages, the purse to lay down coin to put your coin in is probably the purse of the plastic panache. No antique bead-work, no ritzy handworked leathers, no, nay, never initials flaring. Plastic is cool and the purse of the showbox shape with the juicy fruit or imprisoned butterfly motif on the lid is among the coolest. Woven metal plate of geo-metric lines is also state-of-the-art. A rare and outstanding example of the use of natural material in a swinging bag is the 100 percent armadillo, shell intact (snout, claws, and all). A tactile, visual delight. If weird shapes are in your neversphere, something akin to the Three Faces of Eve (see photo) might be your bag. A real stunner, this little unit comes with a reversible second layer. So, should the appeal of its basic blue body wane, it's easy enough to change that face into the sleek shimmer of sophisticated black. Reverse again and a collection of matchbook covers from poshdom around the world emerges on a field of white. After all, why change your purse when your purse can almost change itself?

Plastic is cool and the purse of the showbox shape with the juicy fruit or imprisoned butterfly motif on its lid is among the coolest.

GUYS

Ties, Trou, Zoots, and Nehrus

by Perry Lane

THE BOW TIE. What could be squarer than the jolly little neckpiece popularized by Garry Moore, Bud Collyer, and Fred MacMurray in all those *Absent-Minded Professor* movies? They've been a standing symbol of nerd-dom for years, sort of the clothes world's Corvair. Hopelessly cubist, right?

Wrong, rayon breath. Constant abuse of the "skinny" neck tie by New Wave rock combos and uncool movie directors (especially Paul Shrader) has all but ruined that traditionally hip garment. But the bow's unspoiled. (Didn't Buddy Holly wear one?) Hand-tied or clip-on (the thinner the better), the bow proclaims its wearer's independence and announces the arrival of a true cool cat: "I'm here now." Wow.

THE CROSSOVER TIE. The bow's crazy continental cousin, cut for action and sayin' a taste. Wear one with a collarless coat and spring into swing—suddenly you're Darin at the Copa, Sammy on the Strip, Joey Dee commanding big boss lines inside the Peppermint Lounge. It's always 1962 when you're in your crossover, and that's a smart place to stay.

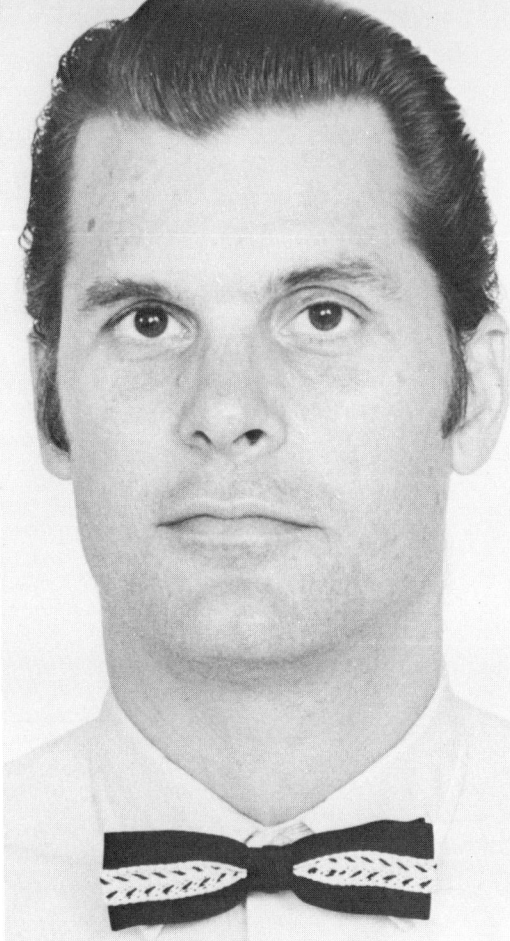

Like Monza, baby! The clip-on bow tie.

We can't mention the crossover without a word from its sponsor, the quintessentially hip **CONTINENTAL SUIT.** While it's true that trendies have

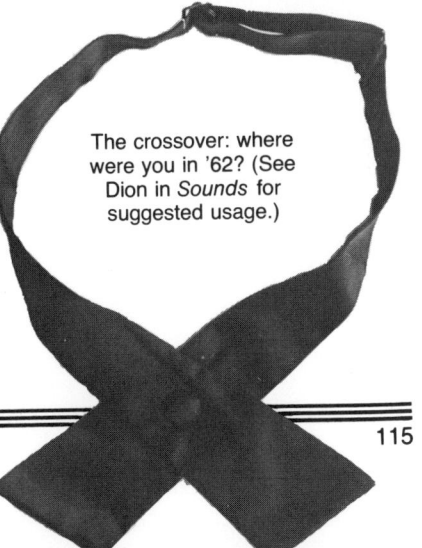

The crossover: where were you in '62? (See Dion in *Sounds* for suggested usage.)

115

lately soiled its standard skinny center-piece, the early Sixties connie suit still spells "class" in capital letters when done right. Tailoring's the thing, and it's the thing most New Wavers (and others who buy their duds off thrift-store racks and think the work's done) get wrong. Real continental styling emphasizes straight, downcut lines and helps the wearer of such a suit or sportjacket achieve the much desired look of a freshly cut shark fin.

PANTS. Lean's the word, too, when you're talking trou. It goes without saying that only cowboys and sailors would wear flared or bell-bottomed pants . . . or someone bullied about by the mainstream fashion industry for the last fifteen years. Which is precisely what's happened. Misguided attempts at commercializing Mod and flower power fashions have kept American men in ballooned out "flares" since '67 or '68. The belated recognition of "punk" has finally put straight-legs back in stores. Maybe in five or ten years they'll make tapered slacks available again.

The golden age of tapering or contour "pegging" of men's pants was the Fifties, which ended around 1964. Back then, fellas as well as gals knew a well-turned leg enhanced one's cool quotient mightily, and they thought nothing of hacking away excess fabric and stripping those trou's down, as the H-I-S jean commercials ran, "to a mean thirteen." These (and the skintight twelve-inch versions) were further high-lighted at various periods by being worn cuffless at "high water" levels, exposing considerable expanses of sock (often white) between shoe top and pant bottom.

Do-it-yourself pant-work is now a lost American art. But a few craftsmen linger on, goal-oriented, aiming toward the ultimate reinstatement of denim righteousness. Check the following account.

Custom Levis
by Byron Laursen

The relationship of jeans to cool has been widely misconstrued in our time. Designer jeans, for example, are perpetually nowhere. The practice of combining jeans with a sport coat, tweed or otherwise, is false hipness at its most pitiful. The only cool jeans are custom levis.

Levi Strauss's legal department wouldn't approve, but for cool people levis are thought of in lower case, no capital, strictly generic. Because who would wear something else? Pat Boone?

Custom levis have a perfect corollary in a chopped, nosed, and decked 1949 Mercury with frenched headlights. Detailing is reduced, not tarted up, as in the case of hippie multiple-patch paisley buns outfits. Custom levis are sleek and tough.

Always start with a new pair. Soak them overnight in cold water. The natives believe this will help set the dye. Custom levis should always look mighty close to brand new, yet almost able to stand in a corner by themselves. They aren't ever ironed. Roll the still-damp cuffs *under* to a generous length. (Cuffs turned up outward are for farm kids on flood alert.) Using a hand-held single-edge razor blade (or a regular seam ripper, if secretly a coward), begin removing one of the lines of stitching from the back pockets—those double curved lines that look like the top half of a cartoon heart. Step back and consider the result, because you need to decide: should one line go, or should two? The difference is subtle but powerful, even though each alternative is equally cool. The one-line look is more stylish, like Elvis; the no-line look is badder, like Jerry Lee. You'll probably want a pair of each.

The last step is crucial. Pull each of the belt loops away from the waistband and slice out the threads within the fold of the loop. (Cutting right by the pants themselves—a frequent mistake of novices—is almost bound to leave unwanted divots.) Finally, roll the stripped waistband over in half. That ain't the Jordache look, brother.

Pick up the pegged trou at these places:

California: Los Angeles—The May Company; San Francisco—Macy's of California

The Midwest—The Merry-Go-Round Stores

New York City—various outlets

Texas—try Joske's.

R.B.

Pleat All Reet!

You can walk into a thrift store and grab an easy approximation of the outfit pictured here for very little bread. The jacket might set you back two to seven bucks, the shirt a dollar or so, and ditto with the tie. With the shoes you have to be lucky, the real problem is the pants. Either they never seem to fit or, if they do, you wish they wouldn't.

The pants shown here weren't bought in a thrift store, but they really pull together all the other articles of clothing into one gone Fifties look. Sixteen years ago Cotler Pants had an exclusively black clientele. Now the pegged, pleated look (or "relaxed fit," as they call it) has crossed all ethnic boundaries. The pants retail for something under forty bills and come in all kinds of fabrics. When Cotler introduced them a few years back, sales weren't as red-hot as expected. The pants were modified—less full at the knee, less tight at the cuff—and sales went dead. Cotler realized then that those who want to swing with the vootie zoot look won't accept a compromise! The pants are now "correct" once again.

Cotler's latest wrinkle is the "Jazz Look"—a chalk stripe drape jacket with high-waisted pleated pants to match. By the time you read this, they may or may not be available, since Cotler is unsure of its marketing potential. But take it from us: this rig is zero-cool. Like *the* most.

Standing on the threshold of Zero-cool: pegged, pleated pants.

THE ZOOT SUIT. Pegged, pleated pants form the basis for one of the first "total look" uniforms, the zoots of the Forties. According to *Esquire's Encyclopedia of 20th Century Men's Fashion,* the long coat, peg-top, twirling-watch-chain outfit debuted in February 1939 and quickly became "the badge of the hoodlums." By the mid-Forties everyone from Latin *pachucos* to smart-ass white boys were brandishing the badge. Nowadays, zoots are seen mostly in movies like *1941* and *Zoot Suit,* though increasing numbers of Chicanos are getting hep to the jive.

The first one's free, man, and while you're up, douse the Edisons. The incomparable wood-grain Nehru.

The cool jazzman's **"BOP CLOTHES"** utilize zoot elements, but, true to their cerebral leanings, drop much of the zoot's heat in favor of subtlety. Like understatement.

THE NEHRU JACKET. The last full costume approach in U.S. men's fashion burst on the scene in '66 and was gone two years later. Despite its hot curry origins, the standing-collar Nehru jacket looked bogus and mannered from the word *go.* It was mainly seen being worn by regulars on *Laugh In.* Nehrus came in plain white flannel, paisley, even wood-grain, as shown in the Sears model depicted here. So hopelessly out of it, the Nehru might stand for something approaching camp-cool were it worn in public today. Try one and see.

Zoot's bop cousin, maybe from Kronfeld's.

Chuck Krall

Tab collars: buttoned,

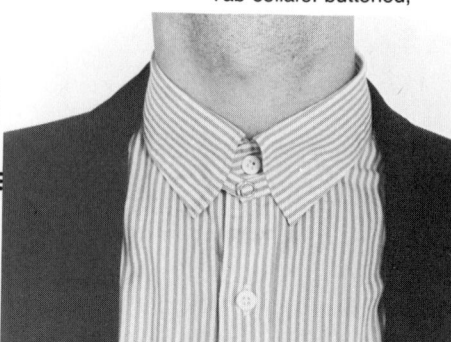

THE TAB-COLLAR SHIRT. For a few months (mid-1965), it signified, along with the black turtleneck t-shirt, the absolute zenith of disaffected rock-cool. Buttoned or unbuttoned, always tieless, it countered the popular blue workshirt with an air of white collar worldliness. See for yourself—Jagger on the back of *12 X 5*, Dylan on the front of his *Tarantula* book.

Shirt wise, there's not a lot to say that hasn't been said. Button-downs never look uncool, and the bossest use they've ever been put to may have been in the Pacific Northwest in the early Sixties. In 1964, Pendleton, makers of the 100 percent wool shirts made famous by the Beach Boys on the covers of *Surfin' Safari* and *Surfer Girl* and recently defiled by outdoorsy clods, made button-down wool shirts! These came in the usual subdued plaids (blue and black, brown and black), were of the same renowned quality and, when worn *over* a standard-issue Brooks Brothers button-down *white* shirt, made real waves, casual yet tack-sharp.

THE REST. We've said nothing about Ivy League sports caps, stingy-brim porkpies (DeNiro's Johnny-boy in *Mean Streets),* standard-issue boho turtle-neck-and-fatigue ensembles, or ID bracelets with extra links (any pictures of Phil Spector, and who's hipper?). Nor have we mentioned those three-quarter-length iridescent belted trench coats favored by the Sonics and Napoleon Solo, but we don't have to. These items have all contributed to sharp wardrobe maintenance and continue to serve the style well. They'll be back.

We've also said nothing about metals worn around the neck, plunging neck-lines, camouflage, LED watches that give you time, date, and presidents' birthdates, or what is now referred to as "men's activewear" but used to go by the handle sweat pants. It seems obvious that these accessories are

The Fleshtones revive the tab, 1982.

yards off the mark and require no discussion.

There is, however, a basic element—a color—associated more than any other with dressing cool. It's black. The fact that Lenny Bruce, Queen Victoria, Paladin, and Harvey Lembeck wore it is ample evidence of its eternal rightness.

unbuttoned.

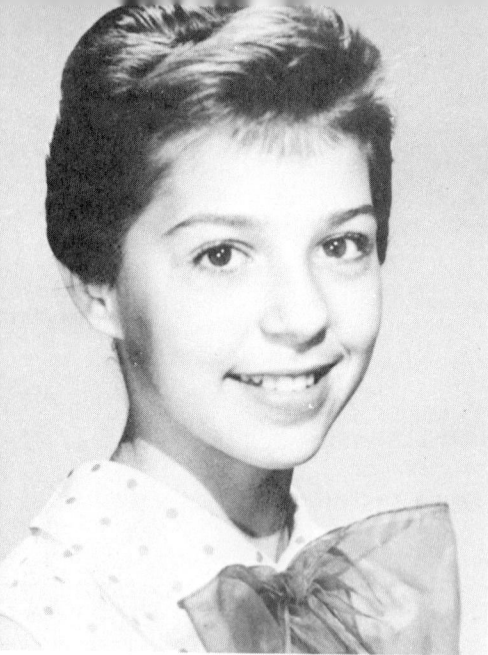

"Dodie then,"

"A Polka Dot Vest and Man Oh Man"

record were given lifetime memberships in Vic Tanny's Gym), and "Pink Shoe Laces" shot to Number Two on the national pop charts.

The record also made history as the biggest clothes-horse hit since "Blue Suede Shoes." Dodie sings of a dandy named Dooley whose obsession leads him to a deathbed declaration: He wants it in writing how cool he dressed when he was alive, and it's all dutifully catalogued: tan shoes, pink laces, a panama hat with a purple hat band, polka dot vest, and other sharp vines. A far better singer than her one hit would indicate, Dodie now sings backup for various name acts and has recently hit the rock revival circuit with her daughter and friend Wanda. Although she still sings "Pink Shoe Laces," Dodie's opinion of it hasn't changed. "I thought it was the dumbest song I ever heard."

R.B.

and "Dodie now."

Early in 1958, her parents drove twelve-year-old Dodie Stevens (real name Geraldine Pasquale) into Hollywood from Temple City, California. In a small studio, Dodie cut a song called "Pink Shoe Laces" for Crystalette Records. When the side was released, kids heard and dug, the label's owner handed out favors (DJ's who spun the

MADE IN THE SHADES
The Dark History of Sunglasses

Jackie O wowed 'em in wraparounds. Roy Orbison never took his off. When Sue Lyon slipped hers on, she gave James Mason heart failure in *Lolita*. They have symbolized cool for everyone from Garbo, James Dean, and Mastroianni to the Blues Brothers and the cheesiest starlets and would-be playboys.

The first sunglasses were made in 1885 in Philadelphia. Seeking an alternative to costly amber and mica-lensed glasses, a glazier simply put small circles of window glass out in the sun, exposing them to several summers' rays, thus inventing the modern shade. By the turn of the century, hundreds of Americans were hiding out behind hip Ben Frank specs tinted green and bottle blue.

While horn-rims enjoyed a brief vogue after World War I, it wasn't until the late Twenties that exotic "cheaters" actually became stylish. In the central France village of Oyonaux, a small firm manufacturing plastic combs and ac-

cessories went bust when women's hair fashion changed abruptly from long tresses to short, bobbed styles.

Switching to the production of shades, the Oyonaux factory began turning out fad glasses featuring an assortment of bizarre frames that would make Elton John blush—shaped like butterflies, peacocks, pistols, Kandinsky forms, wings, masks, etc. These were gobbled up by the international pre-jet set of the Thirties and soon became true "trinkets of the bourgeoisie." With the help of Paris Optical, Lumar, American Optical, and others, neighborhood optometrists dispensed thousands to style-conscious women all over the world.

March of the Mood Frames

Throughout the later Thirties and the Forties, despite a few fads (sun goggles were chic at one point), sunglass styles kept to the sensible middle of the road.

From Marcello to Jake and Elwood: Bausch & Lomb's trend-setting Wayfarers.

Then came the Fifties and all hell broke loose.

A new generation of consumers, with wads of cash and wacky tastes, demanded fulfillment of all its fantasies. Vampish dames went bananas for jeweled "harlequin" shades, made by France's Lumar and New York's Tura designers. "Mood frames" were suddenly everywhere—in pecan, espresso, and "wild mink" colors, sporting names like Tango, Florentine, and Madame X.

Inspired by the movies' suave new gigolos, men sprang into action, donning Polaroid's cheap Cool-Rays and Bausch & Lomb's trend-setting Wayfarers and Baloramas.

B & L virtually invented male cool the day they designed the Balorama or basic "wraparound." Impenetrable, mysterious, Balorama touched an untapped market, connecting instantly with the new wave of beatniks, jazzbos, potheads and proto-punks. No movie purporting to deal with juvenile delinquency or rock 'n' roll during the years 1955-65 did so without depicting dozens of leering hoods in Balorama wraps.

Mommy Dearest

Less mysterious but just as mystique-inspiring, the Wayfarer originated as medically prescribed sunglasses for Florida and California lifeguards. Best known today as "Blues Brothers" glasses, Wayfarers were adopted by a more respectable brand of culture hero: astronauts, high-powered execs, and secret agents. Righteous upscale stuff.

In 1961, Audrey Hepburn's appearance in *Breakfast At Tiffany's* kicked off the boom in huge lollipop frames. Jackie Kennedy popularized women's wraparounds her first year in the house on the Hill, and Marcello Mastroianni expressed the languor of the Continent's idle rich, wearing modified Wayfarers in *La Dolce Vita*. Three years later, on a stylish episode of *Route 66,* Joan Crawford closed the show by placing a pair of shades on her late hubby's dead body. Epitaph for cool, courtesy of Mommy Dearest.

By 1964, sales of cheaters topped 134 million (1960 sales: 60 million). The Harlequin was dead, replaced now by Pixies, Pookies, Sophias, Pucks, Geishas, Matadors, and Martianettes. Men could wear Seven-O-Sevens (patterned, as the ads said, "after the sweptback wings of their jetliner namesake") or Mustangs, made available in the same colors as Ford's new sports car of the same name.

By the mid-Sixties, everyone seemed to be heeding the American Optical Association's slogan, "Add a pair for outdoor wear." The industry had come of age; people were buying more shades than ever. But the bloom was beginning to fade. England's Mods were wearing Union Jack frames, while here the hippies flirted with rose-colored "granny glasses" and the Silva Thins man broadcast confidence with mirrored wraps. But the peak of style had passed.

The decline of cool specs began with

SHADES SHOP

Ladies' modified Harlequins in tortoise shell mood.

the Seventies, as a depressing army of non-styles (stark metal frames, aviators, and autographed "designer sunglasses") marched in and took over the action. Only lately, in the wake of punk's frantic search for usable icons, has there been a revival of interest in the item's diggable Fifties-Sixties roots. Now, more than ever, classic styles— both vintage and faithful recreations— are plentiful. In boutiques and collectors' shops, Harlequins, Lolitas, and Baloramas are changing hands once again, as a new crop of customers cruises for cool in the ruins of ages past.

Perfectly average, normal, regular guy type shows off B & L Baloramas minutes before jazzbo's and pot-heads usurp the style.

There aren't too many stores around the country like L.A. Eyeworks (7407 Melrose Avenue), who make it their business to find and keep in stock a healthy selection of hip lookers. There are, however, other routes if you're not frequently Coastbound. Most opticians can probably lay their hands on some antique frames if you specify what you're after. The problem is getting *your* hands on some examples to show the optician. Without a complete set of *Vogue* back issues (for gals) or a vid-cassette of *La Dolce Vita* (guys), it could be a drag.

Fortunately, the low end once again presents the cool-seeker with the best alternatives. Salvation Army stores and junk shops are liable to turn up some designs you wouldn't have fantasized in your wildest dreams. (Just think: shades that were too wiggy even back in '56 and '65, collecting dust in those counter boxes, right next to the pop-it beads and plastic jewelry nobody wants. Seize the time.) Like we said, the recent revival of interest has put reproductions back on the market, and many are available—cheap—by mail.

A place called *Motivator* (P.O. Box 301, Lovingston, Virginia 22949) advertises such exotic designs as "Spectrums," "Hearth Throbs," and "Window Wraps" ("plus twenty-six more"). One buck gets you a catalog. New York's infamous *Trash and Vaudeville* (4 St. Mark's Place, New York 10003) offers "Fifties full-wraps" in black, green, red, or blue, and they'll wing a catalog to you for a mere quarter. And *Incognitos* (P.O. Box 14086, Chicago, Illinois 60614) for a dollar will do the same. Their catalog has 'em all: "Slick," "Secret Agent," "Lolita," "Coolwave" and something called "Batman." Leapin' lenses!

DON'T MESS WITH THE DUCKTAIL!

"I think everyone should look like Elvis," says hair stylist Connie Clark of Hollywood. "Every time I read a magazine that said something like 'The wet look is dead, long live the Dry Look,' I'd tear it up!"

When rock 'n' roll pompadours were first introduced (by Little Richard and other blacks—see Esquerita's monstrous conk in the Haywire Hall of Fame, in Ink), impressionable white boys like Presley picked them up fast. In England, Teddy Boys and aging Rockers have kept their forehead waterfalls flowing for two decades. The recent "rockabilly revival" has sent a new wave of would-be hepcats scurrying to their neighborhood barber for pomps.

Unfortunately, when they get there, their neighborhood barber is more interested in sculpting their noggins into androgynous air-dried puffballs. That's why Connie's Santa Monica & Vine style station is doing big business. It's the place you go when you're looking for something a little bit different.

Go for the Grease

Connie, whose customers range from twelve-year-old surf nuts ("Gimme a real gnarly rockabilly cut!") to nostalgic boppers in their forties, claims that even if she gave everyone the standard Fifties cut, they'd all come out different. Her most requested versions are the James Dean and the Elvis. Also popular: the British Quiff (loose curls on the forehead, a large front pompadour wave), the Buzz Cut or Short Pomp (shorter conk, combed back). There's the Flattop Quiff, the Drainpipe, New Yorker (a flattop with long side "fenders"), and the upstanding Woodpecker (with a front that funnels straight into the air).

First Connie cuts the hair. She dries it, shapes it with a brush, sprays it with Aquanet, combs it, then goes for the grease. Vintage pomades do the job best: Excellente, Black & White, and Bud's Butch Wax, though the more readily available Dixie Peach or Three Flowers will do. Contrary to prevailing preferences for "natural" groomers—itself yet another aspect of the hippie revisionism that seems to taint everything these days—Connie insists these gooey products actually protect and nurture the hair. (To remove them, she recommends spraying with Aquanet before shampooing.)

Angelfish, Blondies

Women clients often ask for the same cuts as Connie's male customers but in general go for even more adventuresome looks. The Avenger is a woman's flattop with long hanging wings that point outward. Angelfish Strands are wispy, training tendrils that descend from around the ears and are often lighter in color than the rest of the hair.

Connie keeps her distance from most other hairdressers, finding them tacky and effete. "I only went to one hairdressers' convention," she says. "There was hardly anybody doing Fifties styles. And the ones who were, were just grotesque, all wrong."

While her clients include notorious L.A. punkers, she's coiffed and snipped members of Blondie, the Blasters, Madness, the Go Go's, Specials, Plimsouls, and others. She'll open her new shop ("I'm thinking of calling it Connie's Cuts and Do's") early in '83. The following photos come from her forthcoming book (with Gabrielle Raumberger), *Cuts and Do's of Who's Who*. Need a comb?

R.B.

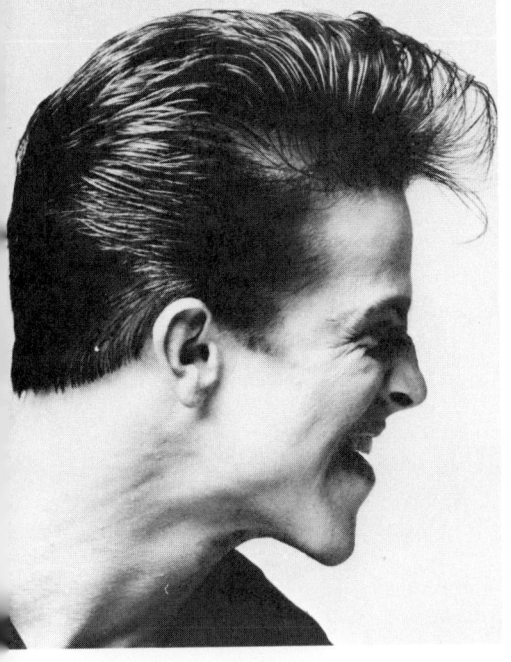

Ship-shape Cochran coif practically shouts "C'mon Everybody!"

Rockabilly Romeo Keith Joe Dick models two views of the infamous "Blockhead Flat-top."

The classic "Surfabilly Pomp."

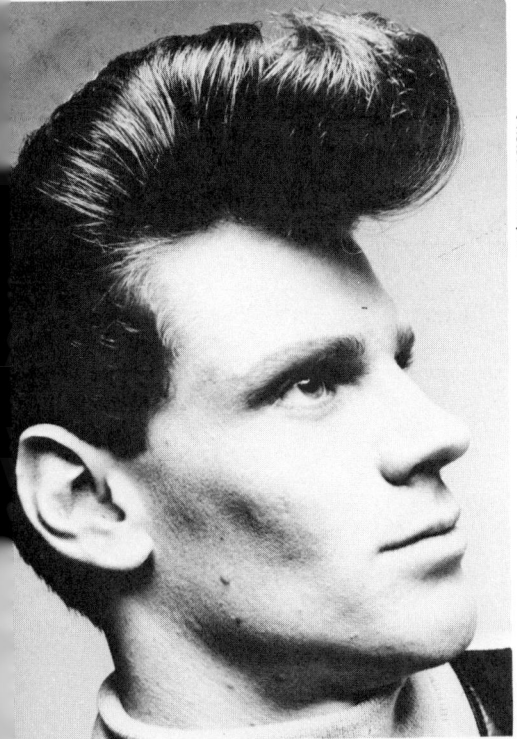

Photos: Bret Lopez

John Doe marks the spot with full flat-top, with fenders.

125

Freelance drummer Rae Von faces off competition with her "Fabian Fluff." Ear dagger optional.

Connie handles her own "Really don't care" cut.

The "Woodpecker" cut or "Psycho-Quiff."

Tito Larriva of L.A.'s Plugz gives side view of modified "JD" cut.

shop around....

The finest of cool finery, these recessive genes of coolsville garb won't likely be found on the racks of fashiondom's major consumer-oriented concerns. But wherever you call home, a little Dick Tracery will turn up orphanages for threadery where the coin of the realm is time and spare change and benefits include shoes that are already broken in and the opportunity to mix and match decades with your own special brand of hip.

If you don't already know where The Shops to shop are: ASK AROUND—a friend or a friend of a friend might be cool; READ AROUND—newsy journals such as Frisco's *Frisco* or NY's *Village Voice* frequently harbor ads for these special kind of stores. Or take up the telephone directory wherein lie treasures far beyond the Salvation Army and Goodwill Industries thrift marts; and, if all else fails, WALK AROUND—the streets of your city may not be lined with cool threads, but it's there somewhere, if you look.

And if you can find one for your area, regional guidebooks are a good way to locate fashion stores. But if you live in or plan to visit the L.A.—Orange County hub, look no further for your info than *Glad Rags II* (Chronicle Books), a veritable who's who of the where and what of Big O discount and recycled fashion. Its authors, Leigh Charlton and Annette Swanberg, are also about to be responsible for a book on the how-tos of putting it all together, *Chic on a Shoestring,* due in '83 (Doubleday).

Meanwhile, for starters, if you live in:
the San Francisco Bay Area—try a visit or two to Look Sharp, Hot Stuff, Waves and Upstairs, Downstairs and in Oakland, Bizarre Bazaar.

Chicago—Rocket 69, Divine Idea, and Flashy Trash.

New York—Trash and Vaudeville, Hollywood Legend, Fonda's, the Good Old Days, Cheap Jack's, and Star Struck.

Los Angeles—hotspots include the multi-loci Aardvark's Odd Ark, Bingo, Paleeze, Choux, Cowboys and Poodles, Let It Rock, and two of special note—Flip and Strait Jacket.

Flip is one of the few of its kind to have sibling stores in New York and London; it's also the home of the neckwear and square-collared shirt worn by our male model.

Strait Jacket, a friendly Third Street emporium, was kind enough to lend us the minis and soles, toreadors, and paper dress seen on our fem mannequin, as well as the reversible bag and Nehru jacket that stand by themselves. A cool kind of place, Strait Jacket stocks unadulterated originals, updates classics, and alters whatever you stroll in with that you want altered. (Elvis Costello and Carlene Carter are among ST's loyal customers.)

There are few things more satisfying than draping your shell, and few things more sublime than doing so in the mode of modern hep: with retread threads.

M.M.

ROBERT MITCHUM

by Jim Trombetta

Robert Mitchum's is the cool with a fourth dimension, the cool that conquers time as well as space. The man may age (though you'd hardly know it), but he just doesn't date. It's not just that his face, with its heavy lids and cherub mouth contained in an inverted triangle climaxing at the cleft chin, seems as primordial as the heads the space gods reportedly left on Easter Island. It's that Mitchum is always contemporary. Just when you've forgotten all about him, he turns up again, right on time, or a little ahead, with the perfect attitude. This has been going on for forty years.

Loyal dogface in 1945 (The Story of G.I. Joe), big city hard guy in 1947 (Out of the Past), he was already an urban cowboy in 1952 (The Lusty Men), had defined the essential all-American automotive desperado by 1958 (Thunder Road), and embodied the ultraviolent psycho who trashes every last family value by 1962 (Cape Fear). In 1973 (The Friends of Eddie Coyle) he had the balls to demonstrate just how tragically an average-Joe all-American hustler could run out of gas.

He was a good twenty years ahead of his time in 1948 when he became the first celebrity to get himself busted for pot. Unlike those who followed in his footsteps, Mitchum actually did time, sixty days on the L.A. sheriff's honor farm. "It was just like Palm Springs," he said on release, "but without the riffraff."

Unlike many movie stars too fastidious to dirty their images, Mitchum has never cared whether he was an unsympathetic character. He's not the kind of guy to look at a script and whimper, "I didn't like the people." Like the mad reverend in Night of the Hunter (1955), he's got LOVE tattooed on one hand and HATE on the other. Take your pick. He doesn't need you to root for him. At his lowest ebb, he's still too real for that.

Born in 1917, Mitchum formed his character a long time ago, before everybody was famous for fifteen minutes, before artists had to win the approval of vast publicity engines to know that they were real. Mitchum was a fourteen-year-old poet ("No love beckons me save that which I've forsaken") when he ran away from home in Bridgeport and hit the road in

the Depression. He rode the rails, shipped out, dug coal in Pennsylvania, and rolled drunks on the beach in Santa Monica. He was conversant with jail long before he was nailed with a joint in his mouth, having served at the age of fifteen thirty days of an indeterminate sentence for vagrancy on a chain gang in Chatham County, Georgia. "To this day," the Saturday Evening Post reported in 1962, "he refers to [policemen] derisively as 'the fuzz,' an uncomplimentary slang term."

Yet his film career, inaugurated by his appearance as a foil to Hopalong Cassidy's virtue in Hoppy Serves a Writ (1943), seems to have been inevitable. Not only a natural actor, but a powerful story-teller and gifted (though largely unpublished) author of plays, poems, and stories, Mitchum could probably have made it as an artist in any era. He would have regaled his Cro-Magnon mates 'round the first campfire, plucked the lyre among the Greeks, or done Shakespeare when it was the going language. He was born too soon to be Bob Dylan, but he *did* go calypso—his sleepy visage decorates a Caribbean barroom scene on the cover of his Capitol LP Calypso . . . Is Like So, still available at select outlets, on which he performs tunes the likes of "Mama Looka Boo Boo."

No doubt Mitchum can be an asshole with the best of them. In the "booze and broads" sweeps, big Bob is a well-advertised second-to-none. Why, one time (he told Rolling Stone) he found himself so drunk in the office of "wetlipped, sybaritic" David O. Selznick, that after "David's last conquest or victim was shown out . . . I finally just hunkered myself off to the side and pissed on the rug." Babes? A million have lined up to garner the precious bodily fluids of this prime stud. Has the Mitchum fist floored heavyweight fighters, soldiers, sailors, Shore Patrols? You betcha. Kirk Douglas himself only

narrowly escaped Mitchum's wrath after taunting him on the set of The Way West (1967). The duel of the cleft chins never came off because, Bob asserted, "as far as Douglas is concerned, all I have to do is whack him one between the horns and it'd be over."

Yet Mitchum's movie characters never seem designed to promote assholism. Mitchum's evil side is clearly marked as such. He doesn't sanctify bullies or wrap them in the American flag, as "Duke" Wayne was wont to do. Mitchum turned down the role of Dirty Harry—a "Thrifty Drug" conception, he called it. He took the role of the victimized Eddie Coyle in preference to that of the hit man who does Eddie in. And when he played the studio boss of The Last Tycoon (1975), generously supporting Robert DeNiro, none of his contempt for the breed infected the part itself.

Mitchum's loyalty is to the characters he creates, never to the film he's in. He's more like a mercenary than a patriot . . . the kind of revolutionary who quietly skips town as his comrades set up the Politburo. "When I look at a script I try to see how many days I'll get off," he says.

In fact, Mitchum has never dominated an era or a mood the way superstars generally do. He's never been that central. He is much more elusive, with something radically uncommitted in his nature, especially when it comes to the grand schemes of others.

And maybe this has been a shrewd way to go. The great superstars become extinct when the climate changes. You saw everything they were or were going to be. Not Mitchum. He keeps a portion of his charisma to himself. Behind the reams of blarney he spouts there are still secrets. There are still characters he hasn't played. At retirement age, the kid's still got potential. He's so cool time can't get his number.

The history of cool expression has been written at least as much in images as in words. We hold it to be self-evident that a streak of eccentric cool runs through such images as Oldenburg's ice packs and lipsticks, Mr. Peanut's mechanical pencil, and Japanese robots like Raideen. It's "the look," and the following eye gallery celebrates a few of the visualists who've had it and used it well. Some of their work hangs in galleries. Some you can eat, visit, climb, and dismantle, and some you can simply bring back home.

Fanta-fins do it Texas-style on the Cadillac Ranch, Amarillo. © 1974 Marquez, Michels, Lord

THE CADILLAC RANCH. In 1974, Texas millionaire Stanley Marsh commissioned Hudson Marquez and his Ant Farm buddies to do a work on Marsh's ten thousand-acre spread. They did, planting ten fish-finned Caddies (years '48-'60) right in Stan's Panhandle sod. These beauties are still there, making fine found-art eight miles west of Amarillo on Route 66. Don't tailgate.

Q: Who has the license plate "313" and lives at 1313 Webfoot Walk, Duckburg, Calisota?
A: Donald Duck.
Q: Who moved his five billion, quintuplatillion, umptaplatillion dollars to a money bin on Killmotor Hill?
A: Uncle Scrooge.
Q: When the former loses his temper and the latter loses a penny, what do they say?
A: WAK!! From 1942 to 1966, **Carl**

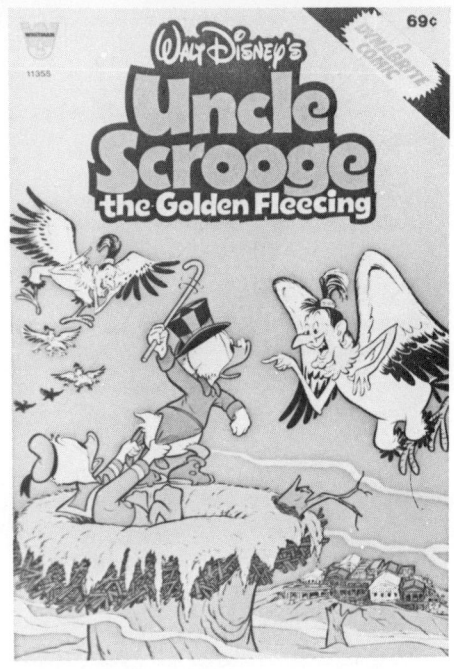

Barks literally wrote (and drew) the book on Walt Disney's wackiest ducks. Don's great, but Unc's where the surreal action is: cubistic Peruvian tribes, goofy gumdrop men ("Terry Fermies") after his dough in "Land Beneath the Ground." Money everywhere . . . plus Huey, Dewey and Louie, the Beagle Boys, and Gyro Gearloose, crazed inventor who hopped up and down on a pogo stick while clutching a bottle of cream in an attempt to find a new way of making butter. Barks' ducks are once again quacking loudly, thanks to Bill Cole Enterprises. With full Disney sanction, Cole sells everything from full-color comic books ($1 and up) to a limited edition *Informal Biography of Scrooge McDuck* ($10). Get in touch: P.O. Box 60, Dept. V-441, Wollaston, Massachusetts. 02170-0060. Telephone toll free: 1-800-225-8249. Wak! R.B.

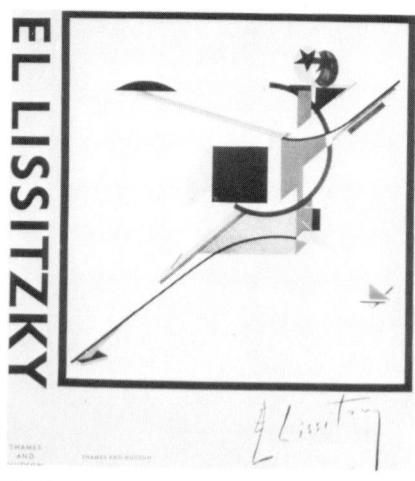

The Russkies' wildest wrinkles: Thames & Hudson's El Lissitzky collection.

RUSSIAN AVANT-GARDE ART 1910-30

Forget the lumpenproles charging through the streets of Petrograd on their way to the glorious socialist utopia. The real revolution in Mother Russia was, for two wonderful, willful (and, woefully, over) decades, in the hands of a handful of artists, designers, architects, photographers, poets, actors, set designers, fashion illustrators, and other oddballs-in-arms collectively known as the Russian Avant Garde. In the marvelous chaos that followed the overthrow of the czar, Russian art took a turn towards the utterly unexpected, throwing off new schools of thoughts, trans-medium synthesis, and loony philosophies of art like sparks from the bonfire of the old order. It didn't last for long—Joe Stalin was quick to assert the immutable maxim that apples had to look like apples and bare breasts were beacons of bourgeois decadence—but in its halcyon heyday, artists like the beatific El Lissitzky, Konstantin Malevich, Liubov Popova, Alexandr Rodchenko, Marc Chagall, Vladimir Tatlin, and a score of others created paintings, theater, costumes, buildings, cups and saucers, books, and strange ideas that set art spinning into some entirely other sphere.

They had a name for each new wrinkle in their wigged endeavors, from Rayonism to Futurism to Cubism to Suprematism to Cubo-Futurismo-Suprematism. Their manifestos were as much fun as their art. It was a great, naive, energetic, important time. Its precious artifacts can still be seen in the excellent *Rodchenko* and *El Lissitzky* editions published by Thames & Hudson. Also the *Russian Avant Garde Art (The George Costakis Collection)* by Abrams and the *New Perspectives* traveling exhibition funded by the National Endowment for the Humanities, the Schubert Foundation, and the Federal Council on the Arts and Humanities, visiting in various cities from time to time.   D.S.

MR. PEANUT. A groovy little guy, never a drag, always welcome whether he shows up as a toothbrush, mechanical pencil, sports sock or bank. Planters' "Mr. Peanut Premiums on Parade" brochure offers sixteen incarnations, ranging in price from 75¢ (a set of two straws) up to $4.95 (beach towel). Write: Planters Peanuts, PC-4, Wilkes-Barre, Pennsylvania 18762.

Cool little guy: Mr. Peanut, as coin bank (left) or peanut-butter maker. ® Planters Peanuts

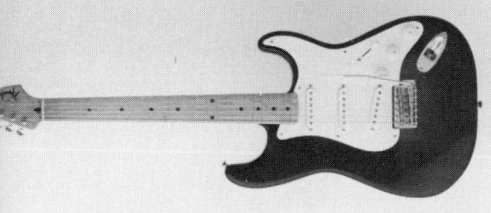 

Candy-apple Strats: '57, '62. Fender ®

FENDER STRATOCASTER ELEC- TRIC GUITAR. Part of the cool accoutrements of Buddy Holly and Bob Dylan, the gleaming '57 and '62 Strats are now being painstakingly reproduced in Fender's Fullerton, California, plant. In black, candy apple red, cherry sunburst, and Lake Placid Blue. Buy one and look at it — $945, at musical instrument stores everywhere.

Edible industrial design: Hostess' chocolate cakes.

CHOCOLATE HOSTESS CUP- CAKES. Design perfection in an American foodstuff. Not created by Raymond Loewy, but an icon every bit as venerable as the Coca Cola bottle. Buy two and watch them radiate chemical goodness.

E.C. COMICS (the Fifties). The graphic bullgoose loony of comic art, everything the genre should be, is no longer and may never be again. Lurid, scary, sexy, each panel packed with flash, each shadow filled in with black humor. Through such E.C. portals as *Tales from the Crypt, Weird Fantasy,* and *Mad* (see Ink) passed genius talent: Jack Davis, Bill Elder, Harvey Kurtzman, Wally Wood. The comics accused of melting the finest minds of a generation. Original issues could cost you the price of a new suit. Ross Cochran offers an alternative. He's midway through a publishing schedule that'll eventually reprint the entire E.C. library—with full color covers on 100-lb. coated stock, b&w insides, boxed in sets. His books are availabe in bookshops and by mail. For info: Russ Cochran, Publisher, P.O. Box 469, West Plains, Missouri 65775-0469.

Spine-tingling and splashy: E.C. Comics

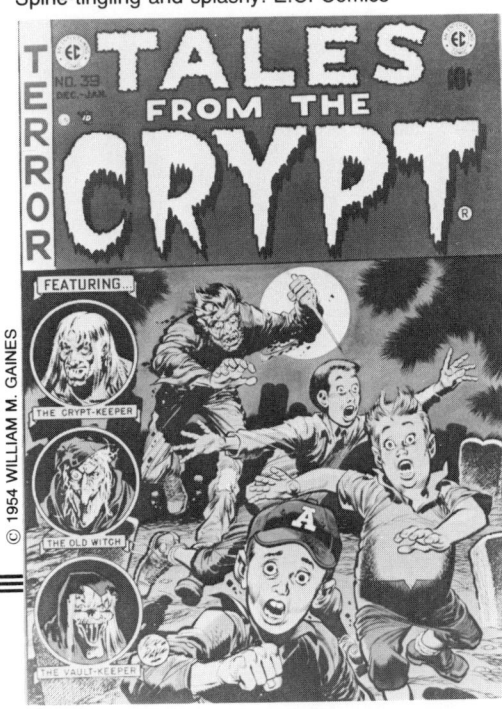

The late **WALLY WOOD** continues to be E.C.'s most celebrated alumnus. Best known for his *Mad* work, he worked for every major comic book company and produced a bizarre (and subsequently heavily edited) Alka Seltzer ad depicting hotdogs, peas, and tomatoes stabbing, tap-dancing, and jack-hammering a stomach into submission. Crazy-eight dynamics and detail were Wood's beat: every virgin voluptuous, every castle crumbling like bleu cheese, every rocket ship blinding the eye with monstrous hardware. Even his grotesques look heroic. In the Seventies, Nuance (P.O. Box 9076, Van Nuys, California 91409) published Wood's hardcover epics *Odkin* and *The Wizard King.* By the time you read this, they will have put out Wood's last complete work, *Lunar Tunes.*

RICK GRIFFIN. His legacy starts back in '62, when Griffin's "Murphy" strip began in *Surfer* magazine. But it's his San Francisco psychedelic work ('65-69) that draws gasps: great acid-gothic! Festooned dance posters, electro-shock five-color handbills hawking strange first trips, the Grateful Dead's *Aoxomoxoa* cover, bellicose animated eyeballs in *Zap Comix* ('68-69), the collosal non sequitur strips of his *Man from Utopia* book. Griff's latest stroke: rich, lacquery religious art, as in his illustrations to *The Gospel of John.*

Wood's beat: cover and interior detail from the forthcoming *Lunar Tunes.*

© 1982 Nuance Publishing

(Write Maranatha Music, P.O. Box 1396, Costa Meas, California 92626.) Comic shops still stock *Zap* and Perigee Books' *Rick Griffin*, which compiles representative work from '62 to '80 in a handsome trade paperback that features lots of color.

S.I.T.E. ARCHITECTURE. Once upon a time, Gaudi and Horta and the Art Nouveau weirdos stomped the terra in style. But their trance-inducing churches and apartment buildings always tilted toward Gone-for-the-Sake-of-Gone.

In the here and now, the torch of pop-arch is held by SITE, the New York-based firm whose delightfully deranged designs for the Best Products showrooms put the *Twilight Zone* as close as your local shopping center (if you happen to live in Miami, Sacramento, or Henrico, Virginia). SITE's Best store in Virginia has a giant notch cut out of one wall which allows trees and vegetation to march onto the showroom floor. The Sacramento, California, store is missing a bottom corner; customers calmly pass into a building whose brick facade looks recently quake-ridden. The best Best: Miami's South Dixie Highway store, where the

Alchemical patriotism: Griffin's turned-on Fourth of July ('67) handbill for a Family Dog dance.

showroom's front is segmented into four successive reductions of itself. The surreal effect, claims SITE, recalls De Chirico or Magritte. They're not kidding.

T-zone showrooms: SITE's Best Products stores, in Miami and (below) Henrico, Virginia.

THE CABAZON DINOSAURS. Semi-distant relatives of the Caddy Ranch dinosaurs, except that this is pure *unintentional* pop. Dinny the Bronto-saurus and a *Tyrannosaurus rex* are the lifesized creations of octogenarian Claude K. Bell. Dinny has a crummy souvenir shop and the world's worst museum in its belly, while the *T. rex* features a play slide for the kiddies on its tail. Both of Mr. Bell's unintentional pop masterworks can be seen from Highway 10 towering over the truckstop next door, fifteen miles west of Palm Springs, California. Easy-on, easy-off.

R.S.

ONE FROM THE HEART. *Film Comment* called it Theatrical Realism. Coppola may call it quits as a result of the film's less than boffo b.o. Why worry? Francis Ford, designer Dean Tavoularis, & co. fashioned the great-est-*looking* flick since who knows when. A Day-glo *Caligari,* off kilter and out of bleedin' sight.

P.L.

Unintentional Pop blooms in the California desert: Cabazon dinosaur under construction, 1981. Photo: Ronn Spencer

Two from the Heart: cat-like Kinski and neon jungle from Coppola's masterpiece. © Zoetrope Studios 1982

Hipster Saint

JACK KEROUAC

by Davin Seay

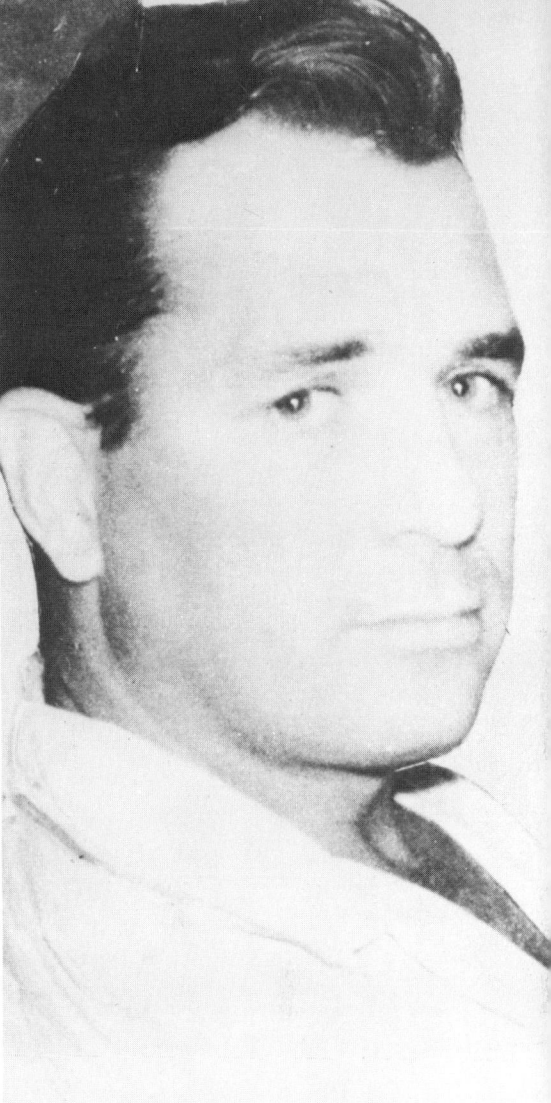
World Wide Photos

The indefatigable hepness of Kerouacian prose spurts from two close-kinned but contradictory founts. First, and most blindingly brilliant, was the hipster saint's heedless and headlong use of language—a rushing journalistic stream of consciousness that has and will forever be compared to the white hot sax runs of the hard-blowing black jazzbos with whom he claimed eternal spiritual camaraderie. Little wonder, as the legend has it, that Jack—in the thrall of his supercharged muse—couldn't be bothered changing sheets of paper in the old Underwood. He fed in a roll of butcher paper instead, pecking furiously one long, hysterical crescendo of verbiage, loath to stop lest some precious trilling riff of words escape in the pause.

The second, sadder circumstance of Jack's genius lay in his separation from the very wildness he celebrated, from the very same high karmic boho utopia he immortalized. Dour, taciturn, cautious, and—one can't help feeling—a bit suspicious, Kerouac could only stand aside to record the cascading craziness of Dean Moriarty and all the other beatnik madmen of his momentous novels, burning themselves out in a blaze of orgiastic dada Zeitgeist glory. Jack's craziness was in his words—he wailed on the keys while all around him life sputtered and fused and sparked. In the end, Jack—dissolute and bitter—was not at all sure it had been worth the ride. We can only be grateful that this sad-eyed lumberjack had been along to leave that trail of furious, glowing butcher paper.

Kerouac's masterpiece is, naturally, *On the Road,* but the man wrote reams—or rolls—and some of the best include *Doctor Sax, The Dharma Bums,* and *The Subterraneans.*

139

by Davin Seay

Far be it from us to suggest that there is more to leisure-time fun than pitting your wits against some infernal Oriental circuitry in the back room of a 7-11. If the bleeps, squonks, and deadly radiation of Pac Man, Space Invaders, *ad nauseam* is your idea of a swell evening, read no further. If, on the other hand, video gimcrackery leaves you cold, we thought you'd like to know ... true gaming thrills may still be had.

We're talking, of course, about board games, the peculiarly American variety with resemblances to such medieval mind-benders as chess and backgammon merely passing. A plethora of playtime delights are still available to the coolly discerning gamesman; what follows is a guide to the best and some of the rest, all available at any self-respecting toy store or hobby shop.

A word of caution: not everything with spinners, dice, and paper money is worth a berth on the dining room table. The aforementioned backgammon, for instance, has sunk so far into the Slough of Trendy it's been rendered beneath contempt. "Topical" games inviting you to be a rock star, deal drugs, or take off your clothes should likewise be scorned. Marbles-in-the-holes games like Milton Bradley's *Inner Circle* and *Stay Alive,* Schaper's *Stadium Checkers,* or the perennial *Chinese Checkers* are strictly from hunger — the same neck of the woods where TV

game show and sit-com one-offs such as Parker Brothers' *Mork & Mindy* and Ideal's *CHiPS* are hatched. There is, we admit, a perverse delight in taking a spin around the *Barbie Game* board by Whitman, a mindless diversion that invites you to "Take a Personal Appearance Tour with Barbie," but most of this ilk falls in the category of TSR's *Escape from New York* — a bad fantasy transformed into a worse game.

There's no question but that *Monopoly* (Parker Brothers) — the granddaddy of American board games — still embodies all that is true and right and real about this pastime.

Invented during the Great Depression, when TV was just another of Hugo Gernsback's bad dreams, *Monopoly* brings into play the full gamut of human emotions during the course of its endless, cyclical contest involving big money, Jersey beachfront speculation, and the omnipresent threat of prison time. Avarice and mercy, purpose and paranoia, epic struggles and calamitous reversals — this is gaming on the grand scale. Little wonder *Monopoly* has survived the test of time. It's the first and best example of the heights and depths to which a good board game can take its players. Little wonder as well that it has spawned dozens of lesser lights, including Selchow & Righter's *Go For Broke,* Milton Bradley's *Life,* and Parker Brothers' own *Payday* and *Careers.*

The aforementioned backgammon, for instance, has sunk so far into the Slough of Trendy it's been rendered beneath contempt. "Topical" games inviting you to be a rock star, deal drugs, or take off your clothes should likewise be scorned.

The latter trio are noteworthy for their decidedly middle class aspirations and rewards. One does not strive for a string of hotels on Boardwalk; one hopes only for a salary raise or unexpected insurance policy premiums. *Careers,* a long-time Parker Brothers fave, has recently been updated to include such job openings as "female politician" and "astronaut," proof that original editions should be sought for most games wherever possible.

For raw thrills, *Risk,* another Parker Brothers masterpiece, must be listed beside *Monopoly* as an all-time great board game. The object here is nothing less than conquest of the entire world, and the game is so designed as to catch up its players in the breathless sweep of large-scale military conquest. Like *Monopoly, Risk* can be played literally forever, the tide of battle ebbing and flowing as whole continents change hands again and again in uncanny approximation of real global roulette. As a combat contest, *Risk* is light years beyond the competition, represented primarily by Milton Bradley's *Battleship* and *Stratego,* lame search-and-destroy missions with unwieldy stand-up game boards. Avalon Hill's simulation battle

games do, however, deserve a mention: *Stalingrad, Gettysburg, Waterloo,* and a host of others boast agonizingly accurate detail concerning division strength, troop placement, and weather conditions of the actual battles, all explained in fifty-page instruction manuals. A must for the Napoleon Complex on your Christmas list.

While Selchow & Righter's *Scrabble* continues to offer its pedestrian pleasures, other word games, particularly those with lettered dice, have recently come into their own. While not strictly board games, such fast paced vocabulary swellers as Parker Brothers' *Punch Line* and *Razzle* as well as *Spill & Spell* (Parker Brothers) and *Quip Qubes* (Selchow & Righter) deserve your attention.

Considerably less appealing are the maddeningly frustrating variety of board game of which *Sorry* (Parker Brothers) is the lamentable prototype. A snotty, deliberating, unpleasant gaming experience, *Sorry* — along with such knock-offs as Lakeside's *Aggravation* and Milton Bradley's *Rack-O* — asks at every turn to be upended in a fit of justifiable rage. The same may be said for Parker Brothers' *Ruffhouse,* with a pitch that warns, "There's No Such Thing as a Friendly Game of Ruffhouse."

No compendium of board games would be complete without a nod to Parker Brothers' *Clue,* a not particularly well conceived game, but one with such a charming premise and such delightful accoutrements as to be well nigh irresistible. And finally, *Candyland* (Milton Bradley), far and away the most popular children's board game ever created. Transcendentally simplistic, *Candyland,* with its color-coded cards, gingerbread playing pieces, and sweet tooth stopovers, penetrates somehow to the very heart of board gaming — the ineffable joy of life and death in two dimensions.

3-D OR NOT 3-D

The Joys of View-master

Anyone who's sat through fifteen minutes of any Hollywood-issue 3-D pix knows too well the migraine-inducing effect of wearing paper glasses and trying to justify images floating in a thick fog of photographic emulsion. The same may be said for those Japanese vintage 3-D postcards festooning every tourist haunt in Times Square and featuring a lurid Christ, eyeballs rolling as blood spurts from his thorn-pricked brow. Let's face it: three dimensional art has so far stymied the techno whiz kids — spatial illusions elude everyone's best efforts.

Everyone, that is, but the fabulous GAF Corporation of Portland, Oregon, manufacturers of the amazing View-master. For nigh on thirty years, View-master has been evoking the same response from kids and parents alike — "How do they get all that stuff in that tiny little box?" The answer lies in the deep secret of the View-master discs, which, when inserted in the View-master viewer and held up to any handy light source, reveal veritable worlds of depth and dimension. Based on the venerable

stereoscopic viewers — a popular parlor diversion around the turn of the century — View-master's color, clarity and depth have never been matched. And at $1.75 each, who can pass up such alluring 3-D adventures as *Bible Stories, World of Science* (highlighting the breathtaking "Wonders of the Deep"), *Showtime* (including the 3-D version of "The Poseidon Adventure"), *United States Picture Tours* ("Monkey Jungle of Miami," "Palm Springs" and the heartstopping "Houston and Galveston")? And how about such perennial 3-D View-masterpieces as "The World of Liddle Kiddles," "Barbie's Great American Photo Race," and "Superman Meets Computer Crook"? The real world never looked this good. View-master three-reel packets, Talking View-master three-reel packets, View-master Standard Viewer, View-master Lighted Viewer, 30-watt Entertainer Projector, and over three hundred 3-D adventures can be ordered from GAF Corporation Consumer Photo Division, P.O. Box 444, Portland, Oregon 97207. D.S.

The Invasion of the Giant Japanese Robots

"This is no stroll down Sesame Street..."

by
Ronn Spencer

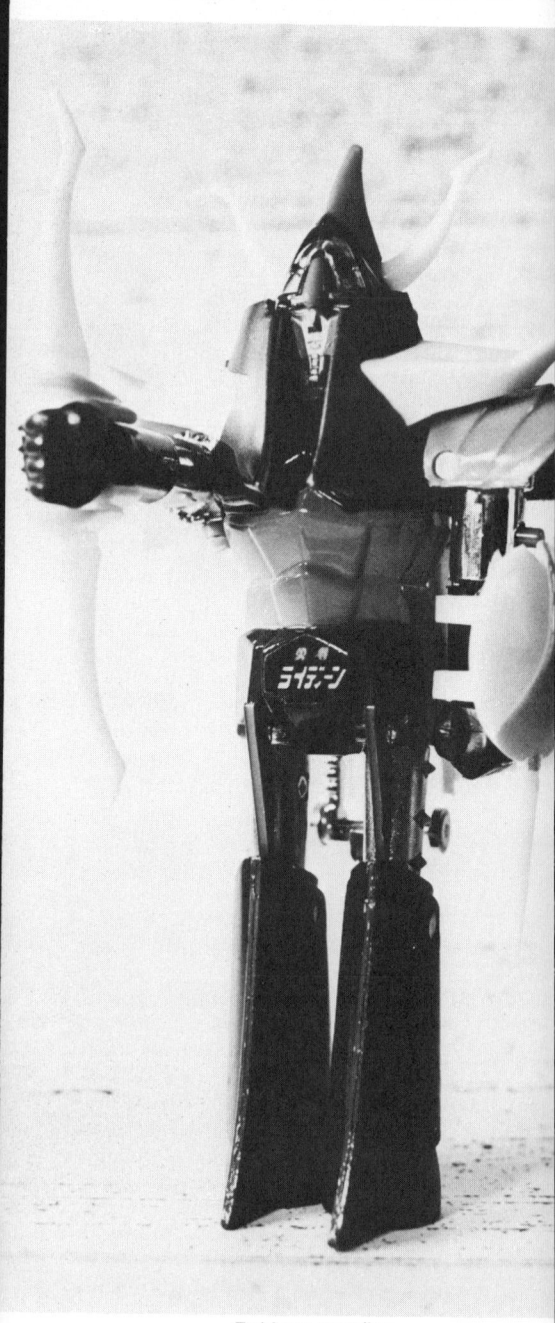

Raideen standing.

Raideen prepares for flight.

Ronn Spencer

I don't know about you, but I've had it up to here with pressure groups that have effectively neutered the cartoons in this country. To me, cartoons mean *action,* and I'd sooner eat Shredded Wheat dry than watch the moralizing and excessively nonviolent pap on Saturday morning television. If, like myself, you're a fan of die-hard mayhem, you've probably sated yourself with "Looney Tunes" reruns or, if you're lucky enough to have a Japanese language channel in your area, you might be a devotee of the giant robot shows. These programs, immensely popular in Japan during the Seventies, featured two-fisted mechanical contraptions with exotic names like Raideen, UFO Epsilon, Mekanda Robo, Getta-Robot-G, and the Great Mazinger, twenty-story instruments of chaos and destruction

that are best described in one word — *violent.*

How did the Japanese get away with depicting the kind of brute force that, in this country, would incur the wrath of everyone from sanctimonious P.T.A. types to Mr. and Ms. Phil Donahue? The answer is simple: technology. The Japanese are not only outstripping us in actual technology, but in its *imaginary* application as well. They have circumvented the entire kiddie-show violence issue by replacing "living" animal violence with robotic punch-outs and power-driven brawls. For example, in an old American cartoon a cute anthropomorphic duckie might, let's say, flatten a tomcat's head with a manhole cover. Not so in a Japanese robot program, where human characters use proxies — mechanical good guys and bad guys — who bash each other's bolts in with their sophisticated arsenal of buzz-saws, lasers, jet-powered hatchets, and heat-seeking missiles. (O.K. So maybe an occasional flesh-and-blood human is placed in jeopardy, but the primary emphasis is always on their technological substitutes jousting it out with the kind of futuristic weaponry that would make Alex Haig's entire body grow tumescent with lust.)

Eunuch Elvis Presley

Back around 1975 I was hooked on a large samurai warrior robot that could transform itself, if the situation warranted, into a birdlike jet plane. Its name was Raideen, and it was controlled by Akira, a Japanese teenager who looked like a eunuch Elvis Presley. Week after week I was glued to the box, marveling at the seemingly endless display of decapitations, limb removals, and shrapnelizations as Raideen demolished one villainous robot and mechanical dinosaur after the next. The animation style sucked me in; I felt as if I were in the very center of the maelstrom.

The sound effects were superb, some so powerful that I was certain they could induce involuntary vomiting or swelling of the brain. In fact, the average Raideen episode encompassed the full spectrum of audio irritation, from armor-piercing whistles to a low-frequency crunch that sounded like a madman attempting to shove a station wagon through an office paper-shredder. This was no stroll down Sesame Street.

At the same time that I jonesed out on Raideen, I discovered a toy shop in Los Angeles' Little Tokyo district selling miniature replicas of the big fellow, as well as dozens of other figures all based on cartoon robots. Like their TV counterparts, these toys are powerful manifestations of the esthetics of violence. Just place one of these babies next to some anemic American "educational" plaything or Star Bores knock-off, and you'll see why Japanese tykes are having a better time than their Yank cousins.

No Math Help

Japanese robot toys are dynamic; they look dangerous. The better ones are constructed largely of metal, not plastic. The proportions are so distorted, the colors primary and splashy, that they naturally appeal to a kid's love of the fantastic and the exaggerated. Like their cartoon brethren, they are capable of ingenious transformations (robot to plane, robot to car, etc.). Some are so complicated they require a Ph.D. in engineering just to operate. And we haven't even discussed secret compartments, missiles, and reconaissance devices. In short, there's nothing cutesy-poo about the majority of these toys; they're tough and merciless, and not one of them will help you or your kid learn to count to ten.

Japanese robot toys were in vogue among the trendies a few years back (you might remember Blondie's Debbie Harry cavorting with a few in an early promotional videotape), but have now faded in popularity. They can still be found, however, in our larger cities. Be prepared to pay anywhere from eight to thirty-five bucks, depending on the size of the toy and the amount of metal used in its construction. Beware of cheesy American imitations called "Shogun Warriors," with inferior detailing and fewer moving parts.

One final note: if you live in Truth Or Consequences, New Mexico, or International Falls, Minnesota, and you can't find one of these toys in your local store, try writing or calling the distributor: Marukai Trading Co., 17910 South Adria Maru Lane, Carson, California 90746. Telephone (213) 538-4025.

MARVELOUS MOUTHS

Among cool diversions, listening to music has always placed high on the list. In our Sounds section we ran down the rap on music, but we didn't say the last word on *records.* That might be reserved for two categories we now address: non-music records of the comedy type, and the people who spin records for the public — disk jockeys.

First, the laugh-getters.

Back in the late Fifties, the buzz in showbiz was "hip comics." Every club larger than a phone booth booked them, and every record label worth its innersleeve put out records by them. Some deserved the name, some didn't. There were an awful lot of cats who assumed a two-button suit, a smoke in one hand and a fast delivery of third-rate Lenny Bruce lines made them hip. They weren't.

There were, however, a handful of good stand-ups whose original styles marked them cool on their own terms. By the early Sixties, the best of these were represented in Jonathan Winters, Mort Sahl, and a few others. Sahl's still around and has lately sounded as sharp as ever. (On *Saturday Night Live:* "I'm tired of these smart kids. They've never fought anything seriously beyond acne.") In the old days, Sahl's forte was topical comedy, but, listening to the old albums now, his references to U-2's and McGeorge Bundy fall flat. What does connect on LPs like *At The hungry i* and *The Next President* (and others on Verve) is his savagery and the spontaneous edge of his attack. Onstage, he shot from the hip and scored a high percentage of humorous hits.

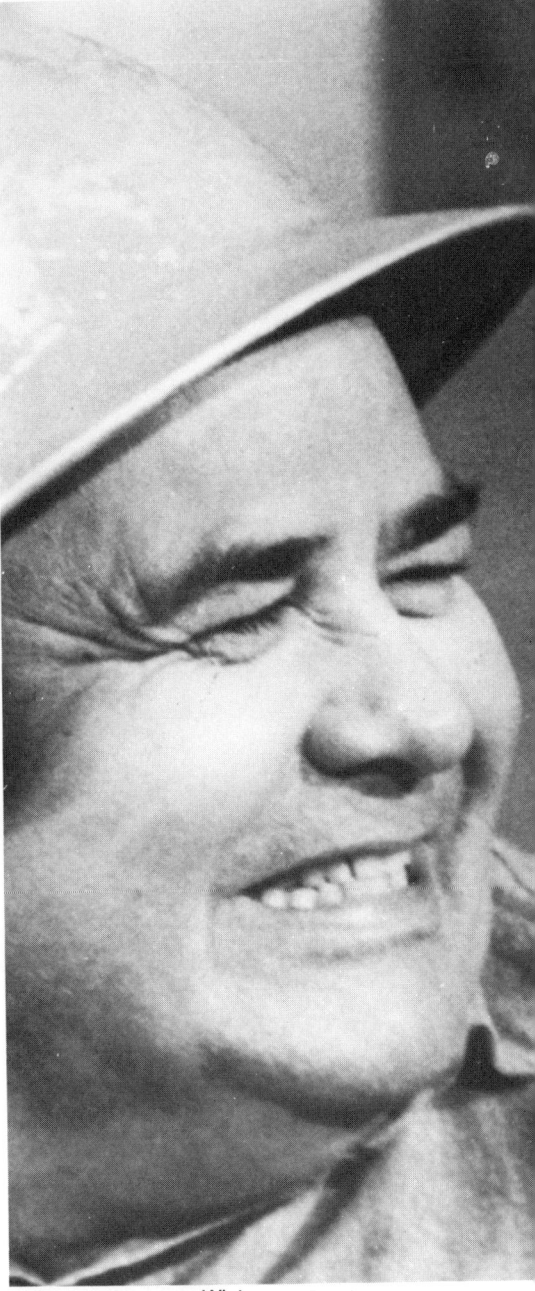

Wildest in the coop: Winters. © Showtime

In the beginning, Jonathan Winters presented himself as a barrel-chested Bruce, doing horror movie and prison-yard parodies and a "Hip Robin Hood" bit that just didn't fly. But eventually Winters let loose the Maudie Frickert stewardesses, the screaming fairy astronauts, and marble-mouthed Okies (Elwood P. Suggins) and proved to be the wildest cat in the whole coop. Check *Down to Earth; Mad, Mad, Mad, Mad, Mad World;* and other (out-of-print) Verve LPs.

There were also Bob Newhart, whose *Button Down Mind* series of Warners albums (some still available) defined the urban neurotic in classic "cool" fashion, and Brother Dave Gardner, a Southern sensation who handled Dixie dialect humor but came on like Jimmy Dean on diet pills. *Kick Thy Own Self, Rejoice, Dear Hearts!,* and other RCA LPs.

Working from a sensibility somewhere between Sahl's topical turf and Newhart's Madison Avenue man, Stan Freberg can probably lay claim to being the most creative audio-satirist America's produced. Freberg now does commercials exclusively, but his *United States Of America* album (Capitol) proves how fast his mind works and how deep his sword cuts. The album's still available on Capitol's budget line as is *The Best of Stan Freberg* (mostly music parodies, including "Heartbreak Hotel" and the outrageous "Yellow Rose of Texas " — and also including the greatest *Dragnet* takeoff ever took).

© Warner Bros. Records.

Button down cool: Newhart.

Radio, Radio

The second group of marv mouths is the DJ's — specifically the rock 'n' roll ones who helped birth the babe in the Fifties, swung through the Sixties and, with a few exceptions, vanished from ear range in the Seventies. The best of these deserve places in the Haywire Hall of Fame as much as the warped discs they spun. Black originators like Doctor Daddy-O, Poppa Stoppa, Jack the Cat, and Shreveport's Professor Bop spouted jive, broke crazy rhythm records, and paved the way for Alan Freed, the first white r 'n' r deejay. Despite being immortalized in the film *American Hot Wax,* Freed's radio style is hard to come by today. (Similarly missing in action: aural artifacts of such asbestos-lunged broadcasters as Wolfman Jack and the Real Don Steele.)

Thirteen of Freed's noisesome offspring are represented on the *Cruisin'* series (Increase Records): thirteen albums, each dedicated to recreating the sound of a specific year ('56 through '67), with hits of the day (and vintage commercials) presented by a hot DJ from the period. The best: *Cruisin' 1963,* hosted by then-WMCA New York Goodguy B. Mitchell Reed; *Cruisin' 1955,* with "Jumpin'" George Oxford

from San Francisco; and *Cruisin' 1957,* featuring the incomparable Joe Niagara, Philly's finest. Out of print as of this writing, the series is rumored to be returning; meanwhile, the records often turn up in cut-out bins — look for the groovy, full-color comic-type covers.

Tom Konard's Aircheck Factory offers the real thing: authentic blasts from radio's past — excerpts of actual broadcasts. His cassettes can wing you back to 1965 (or just about any other year). Pop one in your car stereo and drive around in a time warp, listening to Mad Daddy, The Real Don Steele, Jack Armstrong, or even the sounds of Britain's mid-Sixties pirate station Radio Caroline. For info: Aircheck Factory, Route 1, Aircheck Acres, Wild Rose, Wisconsin 54984.

REGULAR POTATO CHIPS

JUN26B

NET WT. 8 OZS. 227 GRAMS

Koehn

Potato Chips of the Gods

The Ultimate Junkfood Jones

by Bob Merlis

Remember the days when every hamlet had its own minor league baseball team, its own volunteer fire department, and its own brewery?

No? Me neither. Must've been a long time ago. On the other hand, if you're into potato chips, you don't have to climb into Mr. Peabody's time machine to recall the glory days of your scene. They're right now. Over two hundred "chippers" (trade talk for manufacturers) are catering to America's appetite for the most assaulted junkfood since polyunsaturated manna.

If you're chip-addicted, you don't necessarily crave potatoes. You're not strung out on salt, and you could probably care less about oil. But put them all together, fry them up, and you've got a Bronx Zoo-sized grease monkey on your back. Chips and hipsters have gone hand in mouth since Socrates ... or least since the days when Legs McNeil would celebrate the general joy of hi-cal, low-value comestibles in *Punk* magazine, right alongside cheap beer and bad records. Even now, only late blooming hippies or "health food" extremists would refuse a grab from a bag of Granny Goose.

Grease and Salt

Freshness is the key, and it's why, with the exception of Lay's national brand, chip disbursement remains a strictly local issue. The truth is, oiled spuds simply aren't that mobile. Their volume-to-weight ratio is such that they take up more room than they're worth to carry in a semi or freight car. They also don't live very long (especially in the Eighties, when preservatives have become a no-no). Fierce consumer loyalty to local brands also freezes out non-locals — real chipsters know what they want.

Around Chambersburg, Pennsylvania, they want Nibble With Gibbles potato chips. Los Angeles exports Lips Chips in cannisters festooned with Magritte-type clouds, and northern California's where you get Buffalo Chips. The toddlin' town of Chicago has more to blow its horn about than its late mayor and a Picasso at city hall. It's got Jay's, which enjoys an incredible 65 percent market share in Chi-town. Jay's are even more than their slogan "A pip of a chip" lets on. Take it from electrical engineer Dave Turner, a displaced Chicagoan who carries an empty suitcase home for the holidays in order to fill it with boxes of Jay's, which then accompany him back to Jay's-less southern California. "In a city where excellence has always been measured in direct proportion to grease and salt," says Turner, "Jay's has always been the leader."

Chicago loves Jay's. On December 8, 1941, they trashed every box of Chicago's then leading potato chip they could find. It came as no surprise that, within one month of the destruction of the Pacific fleet, Leonard Japp, founder of Mrs. Japp's Potato Chips, changed the name of his product to the more occidental sounding Jay's. Says a Jay's spokesman: "It's a no frills chip that uses one hundred per cent corn oil. Jay's was natural long before it was natural to be natural." We'll munch to that.

Hard to Get in Honolulu

The hottest chip trend these days is the Hawaiian style or Maui chip — batch fried (only about three hundred pounds at a time) with the spuds wearing their jackets. They're sliced a bit thicker than their mainland counterparts. *The* island chips, though, are the ones from Kitch'n Cook'd, made by hand in Kahului. Tycoons import 'em to the forty-eight, despite the fact that Kitch'n Cook'd are hard to find even in Honolulu. (Maybe that's why.)

If you're tired of sampling the array at your local supermarket or 7-11 and your jones has taken you beyond Lays, why not consider home delivery? Charles Chips of Mountville, Pennsylvania, maintains a nationwide network of three hundred franchised distributors who bring when you ring. Charles' key attraction: They come in a return deposit ($1.20) can which keeps the chips fresh longer. Don Gratz, vice president of sales at Charles, says "Florida's a great market for us because of the humidity. Our chips stay crisp for quite a while even under adverse atmospheric conditions."

"People become addicted to the product. Sometimes they can't help themselves when they see the truck pass," claims Charles routeman Martyn Glover, who is quite used to being flagged down by strung-out customers who hurl themselves at his van as it makes its rounds on the streets of Los Angeles.

Cottonseed vs. Peanuts

Like I said, localism reigns and loyalty rules. Chipsters will argue endlessly about the virtues of frying time or the relative merits of opposing oils. (Charles goes for cottonseed, Jay's swears by corn, and Dayton's Mike Sells brand is cooked in 100 percent peanut oil.) But two Pennsylvania chippers have argued for years over a name. Which came first: Snyder's of Hanover or Snyder's of Berlin? More than just 125 miles separate these two fierce competitors. It goes back to the early Fifties and a lawsuit and a lot of hot air, but it still goes on. In lieu of a cute slogan, each firm bags its chips with a disclaimer — S.O.H. is "not connected in any way with Snyder's Potato Chips, Inc. of Berlin," while S.O.B. steadfastly maintains, "We are not connected in any way with Snyder's of Hanover." Potato Chip Wars?

Stewart's are the only chips currently made in Saratoga Springs, New York, where America's first chips were invented ... or discovered. History books say that a cook named "Aunt" Katie Weeks accidentally dropped a piece of chipped potato in some boiling oil in which she'd intended to deep fry crullers. Saratoga chips, as they were then called, became instantly more popular than crullers. Heirs of robber baron Cornelius Vanderbilt have been claiming some involvement on the part of their forebear in the development of the Saratoga chip. Don't buy it. It was Aunt Katie who, in July of 1853, came up with the goods. Don't let anybody tell you different, even if they've got money.

Wax Bags and Wide Distribution

If you've got extra coin, you might be ready for the potato chip junkie's pilgrimage. Pittsburgh attorney Bruce Wolf advises a trip down Route Forty from Uniontown, Pennsylvania, to Hopwood, where you can't miss Ruse's Roost, a roadside stand which "COOKS POTATO CHIPS TO ORDER" while you wait. The warm chips "rival oral sex as an eating experience," says the normally staid legal eagle. Or consider the junket to Watertown, Wisconsin, where Pagel's Bakery cooks up a few chips every day and packages them in a hand-stapled wax bag. They've got a bit wider distribution than Ruse's; you can buy a bag of Pagel's not only at the bakery, but at the malt shop next door as well.

The next time you rip open a bag of Granny Goose (made in Frisco), Freshies (Seattle), Go Blue (Ann Arbor), Golden Flake (Birmingham, Alabama), Grippo's (Cincinnati), Boyd (Lynn, Massachusetts), Kuntz (Xenia, Ohio), Lance (Charlotte, North Carolina), Buckeye (Columbus, Ohio),

Chickadee (Whatley, Massachusetts), or Dentler's (San Antonio), take a moment to think about those billions of pounds of potatoes ... those millions of gallons of oil ... those oceans full of salt.

Then uncork an aluminum container of carbonated chemical beverage, find the station showing the hundred and fiftieth rerun of your favorite *Honeymooners* episode, sit back and enjoy those starch-and-sodium chips to your heart's content.

No health nut can ever know your bliss.

Swamp Dogg unwinds with a tall cool Rémy after cookin' session.

Swamp Dogg has distinguished himself in so many fields, it's hard to know from whence his latest fame derives (see *Who's Cool in Music, Who's Who in the Arts in America, Who's Afraid of Virginia Woolf?*). In the kitchen is where he really wails. The following recipes are excerpted from his forthcoming *The Cook Book That Was Heard Around the World*.

A Trio of Exalted Gastronomical Concoctions

by Swamp Dogg

CORNED BEEF CHA CHA CHA

	Corned Beef Brisket (4-5 lbs.)	6	potatoes peeled and cut in half
1	tablespoon salt	2	green peppers (quartered)
1	teaspoon pepper	12-	oz. can whole kernel corn
4	yellow onions (halved)	1	lbs. 12 oz. can tomatoes
1	lb. sweet Italian sausage	1	head cabbage (cut into 6 wedges)
6	carrots (cut in 1 inch pieces)	1	lb. can Chick peas
1	clove of garlic (chopped)	2	stalks of celery with leaves cut in 4 inch pieces

Place corned beef in a large heavy pot covered with water. Add salt, pepper, onions, and sausage. Cover and bring to a boil, then reduce heat and simmer for 2½ hours. Put in the remaining ingredients and simmer another 45 minutes. Drain off the broth into a soup bowl. Serve the broth in 8 oz. cups, then slice the beef and serve with the vegetables.

Makes 5-7 servings.

FILÉ GUMBO FATS DOMINO (3 TRACK)

TRACK I

½	cup olive oil	2	bay leaves
2	tablespoons margarine or butter	2	tablespoons tomato paste
3	onions diced	¼	teaspoon celery seed
1	teaspoon minced garlic	4	tablespoons parsley (chopped)
1	tablespoon fennel (chopped)	1	teaspoon pepper
1	teaspoon saffron	2	tablespoons salt

In a large pot heat olive oil and margarine. Add the remaining ingredients and cook until transparent.

TRACK II

3	tablespoons Wondra		Water to cover
8	chicken wings	32-	oz. can tomato puree
1	teaspoon thyme	1	tablespoon lemon juice
1	teaspoon red pepper	¼	cup dry white wine

Add Wondra to Track I and stir until you get a paste. Add all of the other ingredients in Track II with water to cover. Simmer thirty minutes.

TRACK III

	Water (cover ingredients below)	1	lb. shrimp
6	lobster tails cracked	1	lb. scallops
6	King Crab legs		Creole Gumbo Filé
2	lbs. Filet flounder		

Add lobster tails to Track II and cook ½ hour. Next add the king crab and cook 15 minutes. Next add the filet and cook 15 minutes. Stir in shrimp and scallops and cook 8 minutes more. Remove from heat.

Mix 6 tablespoons of the soup, with 4 tablespoons of gumbo filé. Put a teaspoon of filé mixture in each individual bowl. Never put it in the pot because it will become glue.

Serve with French garlic bread.

Serves 10-15.

Portsmouth, Virginia, Tomato Pudding (33-1/3 RPM)

This fantabulous dish has to be done in two steps, but the end results will make every step worth its weight in calories.

TRACK I (EIGHT CRUSTY BISQUITS)

2 cups all purpose flour	⅔ cup cold water
2 tablespoons vegetable shortening	(do not substitute milk)
¼ teaspoon salt	1 teaspoon baking powder

Preheat oven 450°

Combine flour, baking powder, salt, and shortening. Mix together thoroughly with spoon or hands. Pour in water gradually while working pastry together. When flour is soft and light, not sticky, turn out on floured board. With floured hands pat dough until smooth. Roll into an oblong and cut out 8 bisquits. Place on ungreased baking sheet, one inch apart and bake for 15 minutes.

No. Do not use canned bisquits under any circumstances.

TRACK II (PUDDING)

1 16-oz. can peeled tomatoes	1 teaspoon nutmeg
1 cup sugar	8 oz. butter or margarine (melted)

Put tomatoes in a bowl and mash with a potato masher. Add butter, sugar, and nutmeg; stir until blended. After the bisquits have baked, remove from oven and reduce heat to 400°. Wait 5 minutes and put tomato mixture in the oven for 30 minutes, in a two-quart baking dish.

Remove the tomato mixture from the oven and add bisquits crumbled up to tomato mixture. Stir and place in oven and bake until bisquits are golden brown.

This is another great dessert to serve at those times when you are bored with the norm.

Serves 6.

Mixed Drinks:

Cooler Than Celery and Cream Cheese?

by Richard Meltzer

Mixed drinks — they exist, just as do plutonium and the fifth, make that the sixth, Billy Joel LP; this much is certain and not really subject to doubt. Just as certain: their inalienable right to *do so* — to exist, persist, survive, and not be shot at by every crazy-assed loony from here to Port Bazonga. Less certain: how come some wiseguy ever introduced 'em in the first place. Are there "mixed books," for inst (cocktail onions on the page)? Are there "mixed combs" (sugar & cherries in the teeth)? Are there even, in fact, "mixed goats" (grenadine, lemon peel & Tonic water in the hairs)? No, there are not. Or if there are, they have not yet made the "rounds" of libraries, beauty salons, and barnyards, respectively. And for v. good reason: People are not (yet) that dumb.

So why izzit so many of 'em have accepted the wholesale despoilment — due to mixturization — of alcoholic bev? The answer, as anyone worth his/her gumboot will tell you, is fivefold (five reasons there are — no more, no less). (1) so "milady" (this is before the days of lib, natch) will tipple with her "gent," who, it is assumed, is already thoroughly familiar with the John Barleycorn route (but, as is far more likely in the sad, sorry "man's world" of any era, merely knows how to *fake it*); (2) so the concomitant intake of intoxicant will, perhaps, "get her hot"; (3) to aid and assist the "non-drinker" of any sex in overcoming his/her aversion to the taste of poison (a luna moth caterpillar immersed in gin will die); (4) to hip the "social drinker" to a range of options over and above the venerable shot & beer (a compass of "hard stuff" variations that is right up there with the eight-page wine list and two from column A/three from column B); (5) to give the would-be alco-gourmet adequate props for being "one up" on his/her compeers of quaff.

With 20-20 hindsight, widesight, and sidesight we can of course throw out nos. 1 and 2 for being of spurious causal ublub in the temporal confugment, as today's gals (and, say some hist'ry bks., *even yesterday's*) are fully capable of (1) drowning their livers w/ the best — and worst — of the boyboys and (2) triggering their juices *d'amour* far more functionally (w/ or w/out ethyl stimulants) than can their male colleagues in orgazgrope do w/ their own. No. 3 we still got (more on which shortly). With nos. 4 and 5 we're finally finally *finally* circling in on the proper domain of this heppest of all possible tomes: cool.

Crème de X-Y-Z

The project at hand: to explore, examine — strip-mine, as it were — the mixed-drink universe in order that we might find, discover — perchance to ingest — some such liquid comminglings that will not only not make a non-Republican cool person puke, but which are (bottom line) worth *at least their weight* in hangover. For starters, we must of necessity weed out those mixeds which pander to either (1) the thirsty or (2) lovers of the merely "delicious." (A tall stein of suds will outquench an RAF Cocktail nine times out of eight, and if you want taste-good, forget that Piña Colada and go to a juice bar — fruit & veg can be *tasty*.) Next, just to be thorough, let us reverse the coin and kiss off those that neither quench (you might as well just belt a shot) nor can be drunk w/out gagging; we thus wave a not-so-reluctant bye-bye to the Two Fifty Two (1 oz. 151 rum, 1 oz. Wild Turkey 101 — what, no gasoline?) and the Golden Sting Ray (¾ oz. Galliano, 1 oz. bourbon), which ain't nothin' but homemade Southern Comfort, that mixed-in-the-bottle vom so fond of whoring itself in the pages of *Argosy* and *TV Guide*.

While we're at it, it is only fair that we

eighty-six to the fullest extent of the law *all* premixeds, esp. those that stick to the glass on contact: Galliano, Campari, the dread S.C., crème de menthe, crème de cacao, crème de cassis, crème de x-y-zed, and the papa-oom-mow-mow of crèmes, Bailey's Irish etc. If they stick to the porcelain they will stick to you, but as with all laws, howev, there are loopholes. The rancid iodine-hood of Campari, f'r inst, can be used to "mask" the kidney punch of shitty vodka and, in so doing; give us the fabulous Zeus (1 oz. vodka, 1½ oz. Campari, fill w/ ice, lemon twist); you will surely not wanna waste your precious Stolichnaya on this godhead of "drinks," but it is not half bad for disguising the repulsiveness of rotgos like Kamchatka or Tsar Pisserooski. Likewise, the ultra-cool Golden Haze (2 oz. vodka, ½ oz. Galliano) will confuse ya enough to offer e-z access to gettin' loaded on cheapo mock Russian swill and not regret it till the morning aft. Or you can go *whole hog* and gulp down a my-t-good Three Faces (1 oz. rum, 1 oz. Galliano, ½ oz. Campari, fill w/ ice, squirt of soda, orange peel), taking full advantage of the Big G's 70 (count 'em) proof w/out having to actually taste it and upchuck your din.

Although, as shown (see above), toying w/ premixeds is not exactly the desolate, war-ravaged dead-end street many would hold it to be, such shilly-shally is beating around the bush (yanking the crank, slamming the slongo) nonetheless. Let us waste no more time at locating where the good stuff, the true stuff, the actual cool stuff is at. It is at your grocer's shelf under soda pop (club); at your fridge under ice; at your liquor cab'net under whiskey. The Highball (a.k.a. "& Soda") cannot be beat. Flavorful & deelish, plus, science tells us, bubbles speed things up in the three-sheets-to-the-wind dept., so you got the best of "both" worlds and you

got 'em good. Canadian Highball is incredible, Sour Mash Highball is incredibler still, but the most incredibly sensational of all is the Applejack Highball (1½ oz. applejack, fill w/ soda, ice, lemon twist optional). The only Highball (so named for Babe Ruth's comment, "Give me a high ball and I will slam it into the third deck of Yankee Stadium any day o' the month") that is *not* up to "snuff" is the Scotch Highball, although it is prob'ly less the fault of bubbles & ice than the heinous, horrible substance we know as Scotch (only stockbrokers would drink it).

Add the tangy flavor of caffeinated cola nuts to the carbonated *eau,* substitute rum for whiskey, and you've got yourself a nifty Cuba Libra a.k.a. Rum & Coke (1½ oz. rum, fill w/ ice & cola, squeeze of lime), which on caffeine alone will keep you awake & guzzling through your sixth tall one and on to your seventh. Fidel Castro drinks 'em, and no one is cooler than him.

While we're still on rum, there's no reason we can't talk Zombie (1 oz. lime juice, ½ oz. lemon juice, ½ oz. pineapple juice, ½ oz. orange juice, ½ oz. passion fruit, ½ oz. Falernum, 1 oz. light rum, 1 oz. dark rum, ½ oz. apricot brandy, shake, float ½ oz. 151 rum, pineapple stick, cherry, mint sprigs). Zombie is actually the finest & coolest mixed drink in the known world and is strongly advised over eggroll/bar-b-q snacks at Kelbo's or Don the Beachcomber in Cool Outpost #3 (behind New York and Buffalo), Los Angeles, California. But it wouldn't be too kind of *simple* to prepare in yer bedrm. while watching *Dallas* (disclaimer the publishers insisted we include).

Roughage & Zinc

SECOND COOLEST. Get ready 'cause it's too goddam *much:* the fantastic, fantabulous, cool-is-not-the-word

Rasputin (2 oz. vodka, ½ oz. clam juice, anchovy-stuffed black olive). Globules of olive earl on the surface make for top-notch viewing (eyeballing a mixed drink is 57 percent of the fun), and the fishy — slimy, scaly black thing on the bottom — is nothing to sneeze at (excellent incentive to "get the job done" so you can gobble the goulash and satisfy min. daily requirements for protein, calcium, roughage, and zinc). All in all, there is no finer "alternative" Vodka Martini than a properly mixed Rasputin; that is the gods' honest truth.

In closing, it is only fitting that we pay final lip service to those "purists" among us who categorically assert that *all bottled alc* is mixed — w/voluminous amts. of H_2O — or else they'd all be 200 proof! These guys're cut-ups indeed, and it is only right that we honor their name by renaming those "mixed drinks" commonly available anywhere from 80 to 100 prf. Irish whiskey: let's call it a Mick Turtle Beehive Cooler. Bourbon: a Particle Board Fizz. Rye: Dodo Marmarosa's Dream. Gin: So Tough. Vermouth: Bicentennial Dump Pump. Tequila: The Teardrop Expels. Cantalope Liqueur: Highway 101. Pernod: Jacqueline Onassis Tongue Sandwich. Underberg bitters: Castle in Croatia, Part 2. Hey, drinking is great — let's do it again t'morrow!

CIGARS
Should a Gentleman Offer a Lady...

Yes, there are dozens of ways of creatively idling away those excess hours. When you're not playing games, cooking, drinking, or walking your robot, consider one of personkind's bigger gases: vegetable matter on fire in your mouth. Or in your hand. And we don't mean cigarettes. They often smell bad and, like a bear or a runaway Killdozer, they could waste you. We also don't mean pipes. If you're swingin' the briar way, you're either a blowhard or on your way to becoming one. Six months is all we'd give you.

No, the subject is cigars. Churchill waved them; Kovacs blew their smoke in smart alecks' faces. If memory serves, Bruce Gordon chomped them in his continuing role as Capone valet Frank Nitti on *The Untouchables*. The point: They're healthy diversions (who inhales?), and they constitute one of the coolest *props* ever devised. George Sand relied on them for her strength, Lola Montez flew the White Owl, and Castro carved a profile to rival Rushmore with his stogie and fatigue cap. Style-smart folk today could do worse.

There is no such thing as an uncool cigar. A gal who puffs the cheroot — or puts up with a guy who does — that's

Four Gelasso brothers mix loud shirts and stogies in film version of *The Wanderers.*
© Warner Bros. Records

especially cool. Why not walk on the wild side of image enhancement?

Cigars take commitment. Cigarettes are a habit, and nico-addiction is a habit you'd be sharing with what? ... a select 60 million of your closest countrymen?

We suggest...

The Tiparillo. The most famous of the popular "tip" types; a good place to start for novices, esp. the femmes.

Hav-A-Tampa. Old-time tradition, genuine wood (not plastic) tips, plus that faint vanilla flavor. Watch for splinters.

Parodi. The smallest, smelliest sold. Favored by bocce ball-playing Italo-Americans for centuries. Light one in a polite room and make the antisocial move of your life.

Jamaican cigars. Forget those Rastafarian potheads, this is the island's best export — hearty "all natural" goods wrapped in real leaves. (Some domestics use dyed paper.) Look for **Royal Jamaican** and **Macanudo** above all others.

Partages. Top of the line. Next time you've got a couple of hours to kill, why

not pass them by literally lighting dollar bills and making like Churchill? These are the ones Winnie went for: 8 inches in length, 5.2 inches in circumference. The war is won.

When to smoke? "It's a boy/girl!" occasions, landing a promotion, or flunking out of bartending school. Every day's a holiday when you swing the stogie way.

Things cigars go good with: brandy, comedy (Groucho, Kovacs), driving cab, terrycloth cabana sets, Miami Beach, Western TV series (Richard Boone's Paladin, James Garner's original Maverick). Also: loud shirts worn outside the pant tops, and running a newsstand — (for instance, in Manhattan it's illegal to run one without constantly gumming a cheap cigar while making change).

Demographic upcreep suggests the most novel use yet: Younger people can smoke cigars to impersonate oldsters (soon to comprise a majority of the population). Why wait till you get there to have all the fun to which age entitles you? Do it now, before your Medicare starts. B.M., P.L.

LOUIS PRIMA

by Nick Tosches

Louis Prima, more than any other artist of his era, greaseball or no, perceived and embraced the spirit of post-heroic, post-literate, made-for-television America. His was a brave new world of chrome, not gold; of Armstrong linoleum, not Carrara marble; of heptalk, not meaningful dialogue. It was a world in which everything came down to broads, booze, and money, with plenty of linguini on the side. It was the modern world, the prefab Eden from which we, except for Bert Convy, are descended and devolved. To hear Louis Prima sing is not only to begin to understand this world, but also to begin to understand why no one in a tweed suit ever got laid within twenty miles of downtown Newark.

The great man was born on December 7, 1910, in New Orleans. He studied violin for seven years, but had turned to the trumpet by the time of his graduation from high school. In 1932 Prima and his bride, the former Miss Louise Polizzi, traveled to Cleveland, where Louis played for a while with Red Nichols. In September 1933, he went to Chicago, where he and two other men recorded two sides for the Bluebird label. These recordings, hot versions of "Chinatown" and "Dinah," were released under the fitting name of the Hotcha Trio.

In August 1934, Prima moved to New York, where he put together a seven-piece band, Louis Prima and His New Orleans Gang. They began recording for Brunswick-Vocalion in September, and by March 1935 they were playing regularly at the new Famous Door on 52nd Street.

He traveled west to Los Angeles, where he successfully exploited his musical gifts and **faccia bruta** in a series of cheap movies. The first was the RKO short **Swing It** (1936), followed by several full-length features, including one with Broderick Crawford and the Three Stooges, **Start Cheering** (1938). It was while in California, in 1936, that Prima wrote and introduced the song "Sing, Sing, Sing," which Benny Goodman cut and made famous the following year.

Returning to New York, Prima began recording for Varsity in January 1940. By now he had mastered a style the likes of which the world had not heard. It was, like his music itself, jazz-influenced, yet it struck the ears as decidedly strange. He sang in English, granted, but it was an English heavily interlarded with the Neapolitan slang of his roots. When all else failed, he simply commenced making odd sounds. Long before there was a Little Richard, there were people gathered round

> **He traveled west to Los Angeles, where he successfully exploited his musical gifts and faccia bruta in a series of cheap movies. The first was the RKO short Swing It (1936), followed by several full-length features, including one with Broderick Crawford and the Three Stooges, Start Cheering (1938).**

trying to decipher lyrics — Louis's lyrics. This was often a fruitless task, as these lyrics sometimes contained words the meanings of which were known only to the great man himself. (Take, for an example, his 1940 "Gleeby Rhythm Is Born.")

After leaving Varsity in 1941, Prima went through record companies as if they were candy: Okeh, Majestic, RCA-Victor, Robin Hood. He had one hit with each of these labels, then moved along down Gleeby Street. (He also went through wives with great alacrity. By 1948 he had been married three times.)

In 1951 Prima signed with Columbia, where he did some of his most intriguing work, such as "The Bigger the Figure" (1952), an homage to fat broads, based on the "Largo al Factotum" aria from Rossini's **Barber of Seville.** It was also in 1952 that Prima wed his fourth wife, twenty-year-old Keely Smith, a Virginia girl who had been working with Louis since 1948. By 1954 Prima and Smith were the biggest act in Las Vegas, commanding almost $10,000 a week for their shows at the Sahara.

Toward the end of 1956, Prima went to Capitol. Singing a Son-of-Sam version of "That Old Black Magic" with Keely Smith in 1958, he had his most successful record since 1950. After one more Capitol hit ("I've Got You Under My Skin"), the couple switched to Dot. By this time, Prima's career had begun to ebb, and he seemed to be losing the powers he had once had. When he cut "Wonderland by Night" in 1960, the old gleeby rhythm had all but died.

The Prima-Smith act ended in the fall of 1961, when Keely filed for divorce on grounds of "extreme mental cruelty." Slowly the great man became naught but a memory, except among the faithful who gathered before him in Vegas and Tahoe to hear him sing his words of sharkskin magic.

In 1965 he took on his last wife, Gia Maione. The next decade passed as in a dream, the great man reduced to deeds such as supplying the voice for King Louis, the cartoon orangutan in Walt Disney's **Jungle Book** (1969). In the fall of 1975, Prima fell into a coma while undergoing brain surgery. He lay in stillness in a New Orleans nursing home until, on the bright, hot day of August 24, 1978, he died — and with him not only gleeby rhythm, but much else besides.

Although Louis Prima's recordings are hard to come by these days, modern man would be wise to search them out. His Capitol album **Strictly Prima** (1959) alone can teach us more about ourselves than a thousand pork **braciole.** And that, like the existence of God and girls' underwear, is truth of the highest order.

*Saintly Relics: **Strictly Prima; Call of the Wildest; The Wildest Show at Tahoe.** Currently available budget sets: **A Tribute to Louis Prima** and **The Hits of Louis & Keely** (all Capitol).*

Michael Ochs Archives

Games are great, toys are too much. But for those moments when you are in the mood for passive electronic diversion (PED), there's just one place to go: that vast greatland and its medium cool contents. Namely the...

gone shows
TV's All-time Greatest

THE ANDY GRIFFITH SHOW (1960-68, CBS). The real stars of Andy's hick circus were, of course, Deputy Barney Fife and philosopher-king Floyd the Barber (Howard McNear) whose conundrums still baffle. What drug *was* Floyd on? (While that question goes unanswered, dozens more are dealt with in Richard Kelly's book *The Andy Griffith Show,* out now from Blaire Publishing. Plus: a fifty-page section of show summaries, including the too-hot-to-syndicate "Goober and the art of Love.")

ASTRO BOY (first syndicated in 1963). Originally created as a pro-nuke cartoon in postwar Japan, the friendly flying robot still occasionally battles Satan

and the Hog Dog Men on Saturday mornings in some cities.

BATMAN (1966-68, ABC). In its premiere it booted Ozzie and Harriet out of their prime slot. At its high camp height, it inspired dance crazes (the Batusi), hair styles (Bat Cuts) and pop-art discotheques (Wayne Manor in Sunnyvale, California). Rerun nowadays, Adam West's wooden Bruce Wayne and those sound balloons ("Argghh!!!") are twice as fun. Coolest villains: Victor Buono's King Tut, Burgess Meredith's Penguin, Julie Newmar's Catwoman. Holy shit!

BRONK (1975-76, CBS). After two decades of maiming, raping and rustling, and inciting revolution, movie baddie

Jack Palance mellowed into a pipe-smoking cop who sat on his porch wailing "Red River Valley" on harmonica as his paraplegic daughter wheeled in behind him. Kojak sucked lollipops.

THE BULLWINKLE SHOW (1961-64, NBC; syndicated).

The hippest animal riff of all: a squirrel in an aviator cap and a Steinbeckian moose. Plus: Boris and Natasha, Sherman and Mr. Peabody, Snively Whiplash, and "Fractured Fairy Tales." Gee willickers.

CLUTCH CARGO (syndicated 1959).

The animation technique was called "syncro-vox," but this cartoon oddity looked more like reverse ventriloquism. The only things that moved were Clutch

CAMPING FOR DOLLARS: Adam West's Batman fights flab over utility belt, while Burt Ward's Robin momentarily forgets how to do the Batusi. Opposite: Buono's King Tut, an ex-Yale prof who took on the identity of the late Egyptian monarch as the result of a head injury received in a student riot.

© Lorimar

Hagman's J.R.

and pals' photographically superimposed (and very human) mouths, making for a line-drawing dadafest of epic proportions.

DALLAS (1978- , CBS). Larry Hagman's J.R. weekly wrecks homes, businesses, and the ecological balance of Texas and a dozen lesser nations. The significant question was never 'Who shot J.R.?' but who'd dare try to top TV's heaviest heavy? The line is long, with Howard Duff's Titus Semple *(Flamingo Road)* up front. Coming up fast: Jane Wyman's sour wine-family matriarch, Angela Channing *(Falcon Crest)*. Hiss.

DARK SHADOWS (1966-71, ABC). "The most revolutionary soap opera" bewitched home-bound audiences with a version of ghoul cool that mated *As the World Turns* with *The Addams Family.*

DRAGNET (1952-70, NBC). TV's equivalent of cool jazz, with dialogue like a bass solo. Even later episodes

kept the groove: Jack Webb's death-ray impassivity turned crooks to stone. Best moments; Sergeant Friday lectures a Leary-type acid guru on the domino theory of hard drug addiction, straightens out a suburban mom who's out shopping for burgers when her three-year-old goes belly up in the tub, and busts pillhead Jack Sheldon for stashing benzedrine in his radio. Dum da dum dum.

Webb's Man Friday.

Photo courtesy of MARK VII LTD.

Ernie Kovacs.

ERNIE KOVACS SHOW (1952-56, NBC, CBS). More than just the "live comedy" godparent of *Saturday Night* et al., Kovacs' shows reveled in the surreal, even to the point where yuks ceased and non-phenomena took over. Kooksville cast included Percy Dovetonsils, J. Walter Puppybreath, the Nairobi Trio. Audio only: *The Ernie Kovacs Album* (Columbia Records, 1976).

FIRING LINE (1971- , PBS). William F. Buckley still the king of serpentine cool. The tongue darts. The brain engages. The eyes cast the enemy for weak spots. Zap!

FLAMINGO ROAD (1981-82, NBC). What *Batman* was to camp, Morgan Fairchild and Howard Duff's dirty little South Florida saga was to sleaze: top of the pop pile. Duff's crooked sheriff bribed, connived, wore white. Fairchild's minx vamped, overread. "Knockoff Pseud," as Tom Wolfe would say.

GEORGE BURNS & GRACIE ALLEN (1950-58, CBS; now syndicated). Burns beat McLuhan to the Global Village theory, playing God with his den TV set. He used it to spy on wife and neighbors, and asked the audience's suggestions on how to deal with Harry Von Zell.

GREEN ACRES (1965-71, CBS). To be truly cool one must genuinely understand the uselessness of logic and reason in a world gone mad. And this show understood it better than any other. Eddie Albert (ostensibly sane) spent six seasons appealing to the wacked-out citizens of Hooterville to behave in a rational and orderly manner. Naturally, he got just what he deserved — the gradual erosion of his own mental stability. Aficionados of this show like to call it surreal. I call it real life.   R.S.

HARRY-O (1974-76, ABC). Detective David Janssen took the bus everywhere and exuded a world weariness that put Rockford and Columbo to shame. The great man's theme lives, on *TV's Greatest Detective Hits* (Mercury LP).   D.S.

THE HONEYMOONERS (1955-56, CBS; now syndicated). *The* comic sitcom of all time. Lines flew almost as fast as crockery in the Kramdens' tiny apartment. "I hope you like it on the moon, Alice," yells Ralphie, "'cause that's where you're goin'!" Best episode: Ralph and Ed Norton take Mambo lessons.

JOE FRANKLIN (1951- ; syndicated). Joe will have virtually anyone on his talk show who gives him a call (he's listed, in the New York book); also has big-timers who obviously hit town too late to swing a real appearance. Has had such mixed bags as Vaughn Monroe and Buster Crabbe; deals with everyone the same (with by-the-numbers overstated, insipid tongue-tied grace that any second seems like it will collapse ... and often does). Unchallenged master of the *nolo contendere* cliche.   R.M.

THE JOE PYNE SHOW (1966, syndicated). In the Sixties, L.A.'s greatest living rightist was a razor-cut, ex-marine

ABC TV, Editors' Archives

David Janssen waits for the Number Ten crosstown in *Harry-O.*

who hosted a weekly two-hour talk show. Pyne grilled left-leaning guests and entertained "fringe" celebrities — including, once, the "king" of Aqualandia, who modestly lay claim to "all lands under all the seas of the world." Right.

LATE NIGHT (1982- , NBC). *Time* said David Letterman behaved "like a Perry Como on mescaline." They're right this time. Letterman's night-owl talk show proves that Steve Allen's

Mambo lessons precipitate family feud in all-time sitcom *The Honeymooners,* now syndicated. Editors' Archives.

Perry Como on mescaline.

soft-core surrealist mantle will once again be worn with dignity and silliness.

LEAVE IT TO BEAVER (1957-63, CBS, ABC).

Yeah, there were other idealized, sanitized, and altogether unreal depictions of Fifties family life on the tube. But this was the one that dished it out from the kids' perspective. "Theodore"? R.S.

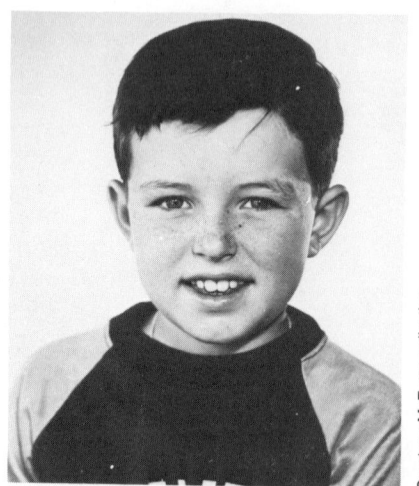

THE MAN FROM U.N.C.L.E. (1964-68, NBC).

It sold a swinging version of spy-spoof cool — plot twists and rendezvous, knee-booted "birds" from T.H.R.U.S.H., and Leo G. Carroll, fresh from *Topper*.

NAKED CITY (1958-63, ABC).

Neurotic nirvana! Each week some wacked-out "method" thespian played a gone villain to bug Lieutenant Paul Burke. Roddy McDowall was a black-turtlenecked improv actor who also killed cabbies "at the corner of Death and Transfiguration Boulevards." Cornered on a rooftop and told to surrender "because there's no audience here," Roddy places his hand over his heart, answers "Jack, I play for *myself!*" and jumps fifteen stories to his death. There were many such stories in the Naked City. R.B.

THE PHIL SILVERS SHOW (SGT. BILKO) (1955-59, CBS).

The coolest conman of the twentieth century wore sergeant's stripes and a card dealer's visor. Plus: Doberman, Colonel Hall, and Sergeant Ritzik (Joe E. Ross, later to shine as *Car 54's* Gunther Toody).

Hamerschlagg Collection

Chowder & Son Collection.

Patrick McGoohan calls TV's freakiest fan meeting to order on *The Prisoner,* ca 1968.

PLAYBOY AFTER DARK (syndicated 1960). A weekly visit with the Big Bunny in his Chi-town penthouse. Surrounded by adoring cupcakes, Hef, acting as wooden as a spanker's paddle, mingles with his "guests." Memorable meeting: 1967 episode where pipe-totin' Hugh greets a very punky, Kool Aid-refreshed Grateful Dead. Hef: "Gee, Jerry, that was a swell number. What do you call that?" Jerry Garcia: "That was 'The Golden Road to Unlimited Devotion.'" Hef: "That's great. Play us another?"

THE PRISONER (1968-69, CBS). Like members of some South Seas cargo

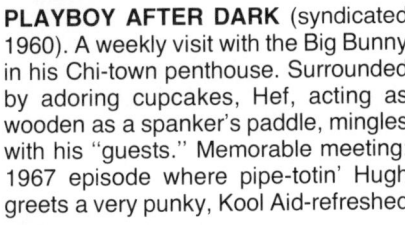

Phil Silvers' Sgt. Bilko persuades innocent miss to donate her bracelet to worthwhile charity.
Editors' Archives

TUBE

cult, fans of television's freakiest series wait faithfully for the return of Number Six. Send a self-addressed envelope (with an international reply coupon) to: Roger Goodman, Coordinated, Six Of One Club, "The Prisoner" Appreciation Society, P.O. Box 61, Cheltenham, Glos., GL 52 3JX, Britain.

ROCKFORD FILES (1974-1980, NBC). Gentleman Jim's beat message: Very few expenditures of energy are worth the effort. Like zen, man.

SECOND CITY TV (1980, syndicated; now NBC). Coolest cathode comedy yet: Prickley's cackle, Floyd & Tongue's flicks, Bittman's schtick, Willie B's butt-ins on the *Sammy Maudlin Show,* and (last time we looked) no dope jokes. "Ow-ooh!"

Decades before SCTV was a glimmer in Guy Caballero's eye, Soupy Sales elevated cheesiness to new heights. Like Velveeta.

SOUPY SALES (1955-62, ABC). Cool because it poked fun at the genre it was supposed to be part of — the kid show. Cool because it was unslick and irreverent. Cooler still for transforming its incompetence and general atmosphere of cheesiness into something really desirable. If that's not enough, how about the most god-awful puppeteering of all

Canuck cool: SCTV. William B and Bobby Bittman (left) restrain themselves as Maudlin (right) interviews rock group. Fine programming. © RCA Records. Photo: Patrick Harbron.

the *Sammy Maudlin Show*

Moe, Curly and Larry make rug-rat wit on socially redeeming episode of *The Three Stooges.*
Hamerschlagg Collection

time, delighting anyone who'd upchunked their way through countless cutesy-poo *Kukla, Fran & Ollie?*   R.S.

THE STEVE ALLEN SHOW (1956-61, NBC; 1967, CBS). The best bits were usually his own (the Question Man, Letters to the Editor, the Allen Report to the Nation), but the support crew helped: live water pistol shoot-outs at the Hollywood Ranch Market, Louie Nye's hepster Gordon Hathaway, Don Knotts, Tom Poston, Dayton Allen ("Why not?"), Bill Dana, Joey Forman. Unsung major dude, for his stand-up comic send-ups as "Lenny Jackie": John Byner. Many of Steverino's best bits are

reprinted verbatim in his book *Schmock-Schmock!* (Doubleday), now remaindered and cheap.

THEN CAME BRONSON (1969-70, NBC). Moody, mysterious, and memorable for the fact that vagabond biker Bronson usually uttered no more than three lines per bizarre episode. Michael Parks in the ultimate James Dean tribute. Mmmnnn.

THE THREE STOOGES (Independent). Noses pulled with pliers, crania clobbered by two-by-fours, sixty-year-old men behaving less sensibly than their grandchildren. The essence of

American Stupid, and, appropriately, better on TV than in a theater. Knuckleheads, dig: video cassettes, films, posters from Official 3 Stooges Fan Club, P.O. Box 266, Mt. Morris, Illinois 61054.

THE TONIGHT SHOW STARRING JOHNNY CARSON (1962- , NBC). For twenty years, America's loved what Carson cooks: cool corn from the heartland. McMahon's second banana bit is bested only by John Candy's Willie B. "You're wrong, cream-of-asparagus-breath!"

VEGAS (1978-81, ABC). Bad TV at its contemporary best. Robert Urich's performances as detective Dan Tanna could be measured in board feet, Bart Braverman's Binzer was the smarmiest sideman, and chorine Phyllis Davis' gams never quit. A laff riot: Tony Curtis as casino boss "Bernie Roth."

THE WESTERNER (1960, NBC). Sam Peckinpah's short-lived minimalist Western starring Brian Keith and his dog. On one show the two leads did nothing but sit on the roof of a house. Brian spoke. The dog was silent.   R.B.

YOUR SHOW OF SHOWS (1950-54, NBC) Never have so few given so much: ninety minutes of live lunacy every week. Once seen, never forgotten: Sid Caesar, Carl Reiner, and Howard Morris as the zoot-suited jazz combo The Three Haircuts. Caesar as Cool Cees, world's farthest-out bop musician: "Got two new members in the band, Dracula and the Wolfman," "Any problems?" "Only when I say 'Take five.' Everybody takes five minutes. Drac and Wolfman take five people."   R.B.

Sid Caesar readies the role as jazzbo Cool Cees on legendary *Your Show of Shows.* Lunar cool. © Columbia Pictures.

Cool TV is where you find it. Sometimes it finds you, as evidenced by the following report from correspondent Gregg Turner, called...

¡WRESTLING FROM PERU!

La Mumia demonstrates Lima-style choke hold on surprised opponent in recent match.
Turner Collection.

The worldwide appeal of championship wrestling has never been in question. The "sport" is a TV staple everywhere, and the thirst for its good-against-evil cartooning transcends all barriers of language and culture. To wit: in 1975, L.A.'s Channel 22 (which now serves up Korean drama and "Ask the Options Expert: Precious Metals") piped in weekly installments of *Wrestling from Peru*. Peru? Like some earlier American versions, Peruvian wrestling featured fifteen thugs with ridiculous names in comic book costumes paired off in a beat-the-champ format. But there all resemblance ceased. Where the domestic version pretends *some* semblance of legit athletics, the Peruvian import dispensed with all notions of fairness and competition.

Each wrestler approached the ring to the strains of his own theme song (a South American mail-order LP collected them all in one place and was heavily advertised) and brought with him a full complement of props and gimmicks. "El Spaceman" debarked from his space capsule behind the ring and slowly made his way to center stage zapping potential bad guys with his *raygun*. "El Weightlifter" (!) entered by hefting barbells and weights and running through calisthenics.

Another star was "The Ringmaster," with top hat, tails, and a whip, presumably to tame the wild animals he'd face in "mortal combat" (the phrase would inexplicably jump from the color commentator's all-Spanish narration). Very popular with the ladies, the Ringmaster was always greeted with flowers and kisses and good vibes from this weird clique of sleazy ringside groupies. All this, following a circus-oid calliope dance number to announce his arrival.

Conventional wrestling attire was buried under the personalized outfit each of these idiots chose for himself.

"La Mumia" (The Mummy) was the most foreboding. The image of evil incarnate, he was intended to be hideous, wrapped in tacky gauze from head to toe, arms outstretched in bandaged paralysis just like his movie namesake. He was so horrifying that the announcer could barely choke out his introduction: "Oh no! La Mumia! LA MUMIA! Aah, LA MUMIA'" And La Mumia's theme music: canned chamber-organ stuff that went on for close to ten minutes. Lots of "Oh no, La Mumia!'s" and tons of "mortal combats" from the hysterical play-by-play. As the mummy inched his way to the ring, the camera would wiggle and pitch, the picture zooming in and out like an outtake from *Dr. Tongue's 3-D House of Beef.*

In fact, La Mumia, it turns out, was so terrible, that the mere touch of his lamely wrapped paw to an opponent's forehead assured instant collapse and coma (all opponents were removed from the ring by stretcher, wet towels over their faces). La Mumia was of course always victorious. Not even El Spaceman's personality-altering raygun affected this creep's disposition!

Wrestling from Peru, on afternoons, ran approximately sixty minutes in its entirety, and the latter half of each broadcast was reserved for La Mumia (fifteen minutes to enter, fourteen to leave, about one or two to paralyze victims). His victims included two shining stars, "El Hippie Hair" — and lots of it — and Manuel Love from "Haight Ash*burg*"!

All this, and much more. And no sign of why or how or what happened when *WFP* suddenly exited a short six months after it began. Maybe it's running in your town right now. And keep an eye peeled for *Wrestling from El Salvador.* Rumor has it La Mumia's brother's holed up there, awaiting victims a with killer tourniquet.

THE FINE ART OF TV VILLAINY

Featuring J.R., JD's, Psycho-killers and Those Fun-lovin' Windbreaker Hoods

Ask anybody. The best thing about so-called "drama" on television is not deeply touching stories (there aren't any), hotshot acting (none of that either), or *auteur*-type direction (where?). The best thing is Bad Guys. And now Bad Girls. Heavies. You know, low-ball cutthroats and cheats, swindlers and crazed maniacs. They're almost always preferable to good guys in terms of pure entertainment and, at least over the last thirty years on the best cop shows — where they're over-simplified and often overacted with a finesse approaching pure art — they get the coolest lines.

Think of it. J.R. on *Dallas* throwing on that smug, happy face when he tells the cartel boys those stock certificates he's sold them aren't worth a liter of gasohol. Or those menacing pinstripe punks on *Cannon* or *Mannix* who catch their extortion victim daddy as he's leaving for work and tell him "Real nice family you got there, mister. Sure be a shame if anything were to ... *happen* to them." Heh heh heh. The sniggers echo way back to the ghoulish Cryptkeeper and all those horror comic hosts. Face it: He's not blond, but Snidely Whiplash has more fun than you'll ever have. Believe it.

Where did it all start? The Fifties, probably. Richard Boone's Paladin character on *Have Gun Will Travel* ("a knight without armor in a savage land") was a black-dressed avenging angel, a bounty hunter with a boss business card and a tendency to let his pearl-handle do his talking. This was back from '57 to '63. Even before that, TV's first cop and detective series ran with stock baddies — lots of goons with five o'clock shadow, pencil moustaches, and light ties on dark suits crimed it up on programs like *Boston Blackie*.

But it wasn't until '57 or '58 that the first significant trend in tele-villainy popped up. We're talking about the

Frank Cannon and Barnaby Jones scan the horizon for windbreaker hoods. Barnaby remembers when all the young punks wore spats. Editors' Archives.

"Hey *maan*," the Vic Morrow clone sneers as he flicks open his switchblade, "you goin' someplace?"

juvenile delinquent. He was a convention borrowed, as were most of the rest, from the movies *(Blackboard Jungle, The Cool and the Crazy, High School Confidential)*, and from '57 through about '60, he was hurriedly written into every cop show script that required thoroughly repugnant antisocial behavior and a touch of relevance. "Hey *maan*," the Vic Morrow clone sneers as he flicks open his switchblade, "you goin' someplace?"

With its usual style, television softened even these hard guys in the name of family interest. If the widescreen version was puff-faced John Chandler Davis and pals swaggering down the sidewalk casually kicking over a baby carriage in *The Young Savages* (people scream and flee; the buggy cradled only a doll), TV was Edd "Kookie" Byrnes hot-wiring a T-bird and skating for the malt shop. It's not widely known, but Byrnes, Mr. Cool to millions in '59 and '60, began his *77 Sunset Strip* career as a JD. In the pilot episode, he played a psychopathic teen killer who watched color cartoons in between mayhem sprees. Even as a heavy, Kookie was such a hit that the show's producers were forced to bring him back as a regular — a reformed hood who parked cars rather than stole them.

From there, it was only a matter of ten years before the Fonz blew into town, proving that, just because a guy wore a ducktail, engineer boots, and ratty black leather, there was no reason he couldn't counsel teens and patch up domestic discord like some free-lance Danny Thomas. Heeyyyy...

Real JD villains vanished from the air as the Sixties dawned. A final few were located idling outside rural greasepits along *Route 66* or harassing surfers in *The Aquanauts* and *Malibu Run*. They were politely ushered out with a wave of the hand when the fall '59-spring '60 season arrived, bringing with it a little Desilu number, a period piece on organized crime fronting the greatest wooden actor of all space and time, Robert Stack. Stack was Eliot Ness, Ness was the tough talking Federal Prohibition agent, and *The Untouchables* became the first Sixties cop show smash. In its

He might be a psycho Viet vet trafficking joy pills, a small-time con running a harmless fatcat fleece, or some pimp engineering May-December marriages and accidental deaths for quick policy payoffs.

favor, the program made more creative use of petrol-powered vehicles crashing through doors, walls, and abandoned warehouses in a single episode than *Dukes of Hazzard* has in umpteen seasons. And its heavies — great thundering bad-asses such as Bruce Gordon (as Frank Nitti), Neville Brand (as "Scarface" Capone), and Nehemiah Persoff (as the slimy Jake "Greasy Thumb" Guzik) — were tops, real mad dogs among mad dogs.

But wait! They all wore suits! Suits?! Right. Double-breasted, vested, tailored two-hundred-buck jobs. Regular guys they were, oiled crumbs just up

180   Rehabilitated JD Kookie (center) confronts crime wave with Efrem Zimbalist, Jr. and Roger Smith on *77 Sunset Strip.* © Warner Bros. TV

from the rackets, and — granted, Greasy Thumb and Bugs and Big Al were now well off, but suits? — they looked downright respectable.

And, unlike the sadismo hoods of '57-60, these guys weren't kids. Pretty soon, every cop series was full of natty mobsters, manicured, pedigreed punks, dapper middle-aged cats who looked as if they'd just as soon buy a new Eldorado and move wife and kids into that big split-level down the block as slit your throat. Call Welcome Wagon; here they come — right next door to you. Like, what's happening?

What happened was inevitable. In no time, the cop shows themselves mutated into lawyer shows, and the criminal element moved further uptown, into courtrooms on *The Defenders* and its imitators. Upscale thugs ruled. Increasingly, their wrong-doing became more genteel, less violent. It wouldn't be long before *Bracken's World* (1969) and subsequently *Executive Suite* (1976) replaced knife-wielding scumbags with white-collar crooks, setting up audiences for J.R. Ewing's dastardly but graciously performed deeds.

The late Sixties did make one invaluable contribution to tube villainy, when they momentarily reversed the gentleman gangster trend in a single stroke and created a monstrous generic meanie, a character type I call the California Windbreaker Hood. He was surely a cousin to the juvie, and his emergence was certainly a nod to the westward tilt of the world. He might be a psycho Viet vet trafficking joy pills, a small-time con running a harmless fatcat fleece, or some pimp engineering May-December marriages and accidental deaths for quick policy payoffs. But one thing's sure: He trashed the three-piece heavies with what has got to be the coolest, most casual style to ever stalk the scanlines.

The California Windbreaker Hood!

No ones knows the exact point where he first appeared, mind you, but there are clues. Like that '67 or '68 *Mannix* episode "A Step in Time." A young woman is abducted by two thugs on the Malibu sand. Mannix and Peggy drive out to a seedy coffee pad (the Freak Out) to check leads. Peg: "Joe, this is where all the weirdos up and down the beach come to groove." Then it happens. Joe and Peg locate a witness who cops: "I saw them. One of them had on a longish black leather jacket. And the other had on a ... a ... a windbreaker!"

You bet he did. The navy MacGregor model, 100 percent cotton, with the midnight-blue knit collar and the two-button neck strap, the narrowed knit cuffs and alloy Talon Claw zipper. Like Ike wore battling the Nazis, but civvie, lightweight, and cool blue. And the creep would invariably have on the rest of the ensemble — white chinos, immaculate crew neck t-shirt (white), five-eyelet Ked deck shoes in blue, and impenetrable Balorama shades. And he'd have short hair. Neat. Cut clean. Like a block of ice. Suburban.

Looked like the kind of guy you'd meet Saturday morning buying lawn seed or polishing the Evinrude on his power boat. But no. The ranchwagon exterior concealed an evil so insidious, so unpredictably malevolent, he was the closest image match TV has yet devised to Tony Perkins' tidy little Norman Bates in *Psycho*. Eventually, these sunburnt California bully boys took over televillainy, cropping up on *Cannon, Barnaby Jones,* every other *Mannix,* and most Quinn Martin shows.

In fact, the all-time Windbreaker Hood performance was given by the late Steve Inhat on Q-M's *The F.B.I.* Inhat, a pioneering character heavy who played a chilling game of wits with detective Richard Widmark in the movie *Madigan,* buttoned up his Mac for dozens of CWH parts in the late Sixties. But here he leads a pack of leering jacket-boys into the Mojave Desert to hold all twelve inhabitants of a touristy ghost town hostage in a decrepit old house. Efrem Zimbalist, Jr., and company get the scent, so Inhat's gang plays a waiting game. They unzip their windbreakers to half mast, keep their pistols trained on their sweating hostages. When a distraught young woman begs Inhat to let her take one hostage, an infirm old geezer, to the nearest hospital, Inhat growls "Nobody leaves!"

The woman decides to go for it and breaks for the door with the dying geezer. Inhat catches them, the old man stumbles then falls to the floor, conked out. "You killed him!" screams the woman. "It's your fault! He's dead!" Tight shot on Inhat's face. He breaks into a grin, looks at the hysterical gal. "People die," he says.

Looked like the kind of guy you'd meet Saturday morning buying lawn seed or polishing the Evinrude on his power boat. But no. The ranchwagon exterior concealed an evil so insidious, so unpredictably malevolent, he was the closest image match TV has yet devised to Tony Perkins' tidy little Norman Bates in *Psycho*.

From there, it's all downhill. The last Windbreakers broke out on *Starsky & Hutch* and occasionally on *Vegas*. Nowadays the action has moved else-

where — to Sunbelt power corridors where J.R. Ewing wheels and deals, to Denver where Blake Carrington's books, not his hands, run red with heinous deeds. Over on Flamingo Road, the maniacal Michael Tyron dabbled in voodoo, home-wrecking, and senator-buying, while Howard Duff's Sheriff Titus Semple bugged whorehouse bedrooms, framed innocent victims, and waved his cigar in the air while referring to all males as "Bub." Mild stuff.

If the Eighties have vanquished the great goons, they've at least provided equal opportunities for women.

The past two or three seasons have witnessed the overdue arrival of a strong breed of female cutthroats — scheming sex kittens like *Dynasty's* Fallon Carrington and *Knots Landing's* Abby Cunningham, and the doddering gothic matriarch Angela Channing of *Falcon Crest*. But, above all the rest: Morgan Fairchild as Constance Carlyle on *Flamingo Road,* whose moist lips speak lust *and* larceny, and Joan Collins' satanic Alexis Carrington *(Dynasty).*

Collins' treachery knows no bounds; she's carefully plotted the ruin of ex-husband Blake's marriage and his business career, successfully caused Blake's new wife to abort, and, in the spring '82 season closer, literally loved Blake's archrival to death. In a steamy bedroom scene just this side of hard X, Collins bedded the obsequious Cecil Colby inside Blake's on-premises guest house. The lovemaking grew too intense for middle-aged Cecil, who expired in the sack after a heart seizure. "You can't die on me now!" shouted Collins. "You've got to help me get back at Blake!"

Good stuff. And, hopefully, there'll be more to come, if low Nielsens and Moral Majoritarians don't intervene. Like some infernal bad seed, evil grows on in television land. Viva villainy.

Now It Can Be Read!

"THE LOST NECK-TIE"

The Suppressed Teleplay of Oozy Nullson!

Nowadays there's lots of talk about television's "Golden Age," which supposedly took place in the early and mid-Fifties when the medium was young and restless. While many of the shows then aired had real merit, the truth is that most merely look brilliant when compared to the current cretinous fare. Then, as now, any program with an original concept found it hard going. (Ernie Kovacs' tribulations are well known; in the Sixties, Stirling Silliphant and Howard Rodman drew flak for their adventurous work.) The avant garde has always taken its lumps.

Such was the case with the writer of the well-remembered family sitcom The Nullsons. Although his first efforts were conventional enough, the always present Absurd elements soon began popping up unexpectedly until gradually a kind of comic nihilism came to dominate most later scripts. Naturally, such a thing could not be allowed into the nation's living room. Not only was Oozy Nullson's work misunderstood (his well-meaning agent once told him to "Stop all this loony crap"), but it created outright hostility.

Predictably, after all efforts to get Nullson "back on the track" failed, hacks were brought in and told to bury the author's unique vision with criminal deletions and alterations, all in the name of making his script more "acceptable." Week after week this butchery continued until The Nullson's death (1966). Sadly, most of the original teleplays were destroyed several years ago by the writer's own hand.

Yet recognition is on its way. And what better place to bestow that recognition, than in this Catalog? Already an underground cult hero, with this publication of one of his best unexpurgated works, the real Oozy Nullson is for the first time available to the public in all his cosmos-probing glory...

THE LOST NECKTIE
Original screenplay by Oozy Nullson
© 1958

(The skeletal frame of a two-story house. In back, stairs lead upstairs. The kitchen is to the left and contains some chairs and a kitchen table. The living room is to the right and contains some stuffed chairs, a couch, a coffee table, and a TV. Oozy, dressed in cardigan sweater and slacks, sits in a stuffed chair looking at the dead TV and absent-mindedly playing with himself. Henrietta, his wife, is in the kitchen stirring something. All actors wear a black-and-white photograph of the character's face they are playing. The photographs are mounted on cardboard with holes for eyes, nose, and mouth. The masks are attached to one's head by two elastic loops over the ears. All masks have noncommital, pleasant expressions, except for neighbor Horney whose false face expresses lunatic joviality. After about five minutes of silence Riggy, Oozy's youngest son, walks into the house area through the front door, wearing a 13-year-old's mask. He walks between the kitchen and the living room in the hallway. Oozy jumps out of his chair and greets him nervously. Pacing stays leisurely throughout the page. There is usually a pause between thoughts. The atmosphere is warm and folksy – very relaxed.)

Oozy:	Oh . . . uh . . . uh hi, Rig.
Rig:	Oh hi, pop. (Oozy *sits down and* Rig *walks around the hall area looking for something. He finally goes into the living room and comes up to* Oozy.) Uh, gee, pop, could I ask you a question?
Oozy:	*(Jumping up.)* Well, I don't see why not. After all, I am your father. Heh heh heh. Fire away. (Oozy *doesn't stutter exactly, but he lingers haltingly over consonants as if perpetually "collecting his thoughts." His manner is always apologetic.)*
Rig:	Have you seen my striped tie? (Rig *mumbles, so* Oozy *must listen carefully.)*
Oozy:	Striped tie? Gee — uh, no, Rig. I don't think so. Not recently anyhow.
Rig:	Well, when was the last time you saw it?
Oozy:	Oh, uh, let's see now. Hmmm. Oh sure, now I remember. Davy had it on.
Rig:	That sure is funny. I didn't know Davy liked that tie.
Oozy:	Oh sure. He's worn it lots of times. As a matter of fact, now that I think of it, so have I. In fact I think it's my tie. Heh heh heh.
Rig:	I don't think so, pop. My tie has wide gray stripes and thin brown ones. Besides, you spilled ice cream on yours.
Oozy:	Gee — that's right. Darn it. Now I can't remember which one I saw on Davy.
Rig:	Well then, all I have to do is ask Davy. *(He turns to go.)*
Oozy:	Wait a minute, Rig. Aren't you forgetting something?
Rig:	No sir. I don't think so. What is it, pop?
Oozy:	You're going to have to find him first.
Rig:	Yeah, but I thought he was upstairs.
Oozy:	I don't think so, Rig. I was up there some time ago, and I didn't see him.
Rig:	Gee — I don't want to go up there if he's not there.
Oozy:	I know what you mean. Well, I don't think it's anything to worry about. Here's your mother. Maybe she can give us a hand.
Henrietta:	*(Entering, stirring something.)* Hi, fellas. What's all the commotion? *(Her speech is dry and nasal, yet pleasant.)*
Rig:	Hi, mom.
Oozy:	Hi, Henrietta. It's really nothing, but Riggy seems to have a kind of a problem.
Henrietta:	Well, I'll help if I can, but I'll have to know the problem first. *(To Rig)* What is it, dear?
Rig:	Well gee, Mom. I can't find my striped tie. And Davy might know where it is, but we don't know where to find him.
Henrietta:	Well, if that's all the problem is, you should have come to me long ago.
Oozy:	Well, what do you mean?
Henrietta:	The mystery is solved.
Oozy:	Well, how can that be?
Henrietta:	Because I know where that tie is. In the basement. I just finished washing it today.
Rig:	You did?
Henrietta:	Yes, I did. It took quite a while, though. There was this big ice cream

	stain on it. I'll go get it now. *(She turns to go.)*
Oozy:	Uh, wait a minute, Henrietta.
Henrietta:	Something wrong?
Oozy:	Well, uh — No, nothing's actually *wrong* except for the fact that that's not Riggy's tie. It's my tie. Heh heh.
Henrietta:	Your tie?
Oozy:	Well, yes — y'see it was my stain — not Riggy's.
Henrietta:	I'm afraid I'm lost.
Rig:	Gee Mom, let me explain. Pop's tie is the one with wide brown stripes and thin gray ones. Mine has thin brown stripes and wide gray ones. Pop spilled ice cream on his.
Henrietta:	Well, that's all very clear, but I'm afraid it doesn't help matters. There weren't any stripes on this tie. It was sort of streaked. Very attractive and modern.
Oozy:	What colors were the streaks?
Henrietta:	Hmm. Let me think. Oh! I'm sorry, dear, but I'm afraid they were gray and brown.
Oozy:	*Darn!* The man who sold it to me said it wouldn't run. It was hand-made in Italy.
Henrietta:	Well, it certainly is distinctive now. I sort of like it.
Rig:	Excuse me for interrupting, Mom, but I still have to find my tie. Do you know where Davy is?
Henrietta:	Well, now that I think about it, I haven't seen your brother in a long time. He must be upstairs. You know how quiet he is.
Rig:	Pop was just up there, and he didn't see him.
Henrietta:	Well, then I'll bet he's at the malt shop.
Oozy:	Say, that's a great idea. I'll go right down there and find out.
Henrietta:	Now, Oozy!
Oozy:	Aw gee, Henrietta. If I don't find him, I'll come right back.
Henrietta:	That's nice, dear. You really should be doing other things instead of hanging out at that malt shop.
Oozy:	OK, Henrietta. Heh heh. You win. Coming, Riggy?
Rig:	Gee, I'd sure like to, Pop, but I promised some girls I'd sing for them today, and they're due any minute. I better go tune my guitar. Excuse me Mom, Pop. *(He goes off.)*
Henrietta:	And I'm going down to get that tie. I'll show it to you when you get back, and you see if you don't think it looks much better. *(Goes off. Oozy leaves house.)*
Oozy:	*(Sotto voice.)* Hey, Horney!
Horney:	*(In shorts and a beany, enters.)* Hiya, Ooze! What's up?
Ooze:	Hi, Horney. I'm just going down to the malt shop. I thought you might want to come along.
Horney:	Sorry, Ooze. The answer is no. I've been banned from that place *(nudges him)*. I got into a little trouble down there.
Oozy:	Trouble? I don't get it.
Horney:	Well gosh, Ooze, it's kinda embarrassing but . . . well, don't talk about it to anyone, but one of the girls down there claims I got fresh with her, and they made a big thing out of it. So it's off limits for me for at least a week.

Ooze:	Gee, Horney, that's too bad. I'll bring you back a macaroon to cheer you up.
Horney:	Gosh, *thanks,* Ooze! That's swell! Hurry back!
Oozy:	Okay, Horney. Take it easy. *(Turns to leave.)*
Horney:	Hey, Ooze!
Oozy:	What is it, Horney?
Horney:	Behave yourself!
Ooze:	Heh heh heh. Oh...OK, Horney, I'll do the best I can. Heh heh. What a guy. *(He leaves). Several girls come to the door and ring the buzzer. Henrietta, carrying the tie over one arm as she stirs something, answers the door.*
Henrietta:	Oh, hi, girls.
Sue:	Hi, Mrs. Nullson! We came to hear Riggy sing. Is he in?
Henrietta:	Yes, girls, he's expecting you. If you'll wait in the living room, I'll go call him. *(Squeals of "Sure!" "Swell!" and "That'll be fine.")*
Sue:	Gosh, what a dreamy tie, Mrs. Nullson. Is it Riggy's?
Henrietta:	Oh, I'm glad you like it, but I'm afraid it belongs to Mr. Nullson. Riggy can't seem to find his.
Sue:	Oh that's a shame. Maybe I can help. I'll get the other girls to look. *(The others have now joined her in the living room.)*
Henrietta:	Well, that certainly is very nice of you. I'm sure Riggy will appreciate it.
Rig:	*(Enters wearing a 17-year-old's mask and carrying his guitar).* Sorry I'm late. I was tuning my guitar. *(Henrietta smiles at them both and goes.)*
Sue:	*(Walking into the living room with* Rig.) Hi, Riggy! I just love your mother.
Rig:	Thank you.
Sue:	Hey, everyone! Here's Riggy! And he's ready to play! *(Shouts and cheers fade to excited whispers as the girls arrange themselves in a seated semi-circle and Riggy makes some last minute adjustment to his guitar. He is wearing now, as in the beginning of the play, a windbreaker. Before he starts his song he turns the collar up. As the song progresses — it is pantomimed to a record — the girls sway from side to side, eyes sparkling.)*

It just Ain't Right!

(Spoken at first, then building in intensity and rhythm)

Pin-up pictures over my bed,
Filthy thoughts goin' round my head,
Don't know what I'm gonna do
Losin' my mind over you, you, you!

(The following stanzas are sung to the tune of "Too Much" by Elvis Presley.)

I want to touch-a-bye your lovelies with my lips,
Squeeze 'em and tease 'em — give 'em flips,
Put my love to you with all my might,
But unh unh baby — It just ain't right!

(Last line repeated for echo effect.)	Every time I see you it's to my regret.
	My crotch gets itchy and I start in to sweat.
	I'm lovin' up my pillow most every night,
	But unh unh baby — It just ain't right!

Sue: *(After tumultuous cheers and applause.)* OK, girls, we've enjoyed Riggy's singing. He's done something for *us!* Now let's *us* do something for *him!* He lost his tie, and maybe we can help him find it! What does it look like, Rig?

Rig: *(After putting down his jacket collar.)* Gee, girls, thanks a lot. It has wide gray stripes and thin brown ones, and the last one to have it on was my brother, Davy.

Sue: OK, girls, you heard him. Now let's go into action! *(The girls search the living room making remarks about how beautiful all the furnishings are.* Henrietta *enters carrying a tray with bowls and bottles on it.)*

Henrietta: I thought you might like some refreshment after all that exercise, so I made some Coca-Cola and potato chips. *(She puts the tray on the coffee table.)*

Girls: Wow, what a spread! Gee, this is *swell*, Mrs. Nullson. Dig in. This is delicious. You shouldn't have.

Oozy: *(Returning through the front door and bumping into* Henrietta *as she is leaving the living room.)* Uh, hi, Henrietta. What's all the commotion?

Henrietta: Just some friends of Riggy's. Was Davy there?

Oozy: No, he wasn't — and nobody's seen him either. Gee, I'm tired. I guess I'll go up and lie down till dinner.

Henrietta: Oozy Nullson! How many sundaes did you have?

Oozy: Aw gee, Henrietta. Just a little scoop of vanilla ice cream and a spoonful of chocolate syrup. Don't worry about me. Heh heh. I'll eat my dinner.

Henrietta: Well, I certainly hope so. We're having butter pecan parfaits. The ones you married me for, dear.

Oozy: Heh heh.

Girls: *(Walking past* Oozy *and* Henrietta *as they are ushered out the door by* Rig.*)* We had a great time. Sorry we couldn't find your tie. Let us know if it turns up. Bye! Bye!

Sue: *(To* Rig *before she goes.)* Bye, Riggy. I just love your father.

Rig: I'm glad you could come. Bye. *(Turns to his father.)* No luck, pop?

Oozy: Gee — I'm awful sorry about this, Rig, but Davy wasn't there.

Henrietta: *(Showing the tie on her arm.)* Could I interest you gentlemen in this tie? It's yours, Oozy.

Oozy: Say that does look kinda nice at that. Hey, I've got a great idea.

Henrietta: Well, tell us, dear.

Oozy: Well, it's actually very simple. Riggy can wear my tie. Is that OK with you, Rig?

Rig: Well gee, pop, I'd sure like to, but I was sort of counting on wearing my own. No offense.

Oozy: I know how you feel, son. I always feel better wearing my own tie, too. Must be a real heavy date.

Rig:	I guess so, pop. But to tell you the truth, I was just sort of looking forward to putting on some new clothes.
Oozy:	Gosh, that reminds me — I better change my cardigan for dinner. Don't give up, Rig. After I change I'll come down, and we'll give one more search.
Rig:	OK, thanks, pop. I better put this away. (Rig *leaves with his guitar and* Oozy *exits upstairs.* Henrietta *goes into the kitchen. After a pause neighbor* Horney *comes up to the front of the house and rings the buzzer.)*
Rig:	*(Entering with a twenty-two-year-old mask and opening the door.)* Oh, come on in, Mr. Horney.
Horney:	Hiya, Rig! Is your pop back yet? He promised to bring me a macaroon. (Henrietta *enters from kitchen, stirring something.)* Hi, Henrietta!
Henrietta:	Oh, hi, Horney. What's this I hear about a girl getting fresh with you at the malt shop yesterday?
Horney:	Oh now just a minute, Henrietta. I don't —
Oozy:	*(Rushing down stairs.)* Henrietta! Riggy! I found Davy *and* Riggy's tie!
Henrietta:	Goodness, dear, you sound a little excited.
Horney:	Hiya, Ooze.
Oozy:	Hi, Horney. Now look, Henrietta, don't get upset, but Davy's dead.
Rig:	No kidding?
Oozy:	Well I'm afraid so, Rig. Y'see, I went into the spare closet just now to get another cardigan, and in the back, where all those heavy coats are, I saw Davy hanging by your tie.
Horney:	Ooze! That's terrible!
Henrietta:	Well, all I can say is if he had told us, we could have done something about it, and all this wouldn't have happened.
Oozy:	It sure is an awful thing, alright. I guess we'll just have to do the best we can. Riggy, would you get my camera for me? It's in the basement.
Rig:	Sure, pop. *(He goes.)*
Henrietta:	Oozy! Don't you do anything foolish.
Oozy:	For gosh sakes, Henrietta, there's absolutely nothing to worry about. I just want to get a picture so Riggy can have his tie back in time for his date. Then we can see what has to be done.
Horney:	Gee, Ooze, this is an awful thing — for you and Davy. I want to be the first to offer my heartfelt sympathies.
Oozy:	Thanks, Horney, I appreciate it. *(Shouting.)* Hey, Rig! Can you find it?
Rig:	*(With effort.)* I've got it, pop. I'm coming back up. *(He enters with a thirty-five-year-old's mask.)*
Henrietta:	Riggy, you look so much *older.* I must say it makes me feel sort of ancient.
Rig:	Gosh, Mom, it must be the dampness down there. I better not leave here anymore. *(Fade to black.)*

THE END

R.B.

When it comes to TV, the going gets rough. It's not as easy to get your hands on vintage video as it is to score back-issue mags or even out-of-print books. Syndication is just about the only salvation. As we went to press, for instance, *Dark Shadows* was creeping back into selected markets, and if you got up early enough Saturday mornings in Los Angeles, you could watch *Leave It to Beaver.*

The problem is, reruns syndication is locally administered and you'll never know what secret sitcoms are running in Muncie or Sarasota. (Enterprising TV collectors have been known to find sources in other locales — often through publications like *Videophile* and *Video Swapper* — and exchange tapes of old shows across the country.) If you do get the bug and find yourself lusting for *any* info on *Naked City* or *Green Acres,* try *TV Guide Specialists* (Box 90-T, Rockville, Maryland 20850). They carry *Guides* all the way back to '48. For $3, they'll send you their latest catalog of available issues; for a stamped, self-addressed envelope,

they'll answer inquiries about specific articles in *TV Guides.*

Once you've looked up your fave lost show in Brooks and Marsh's *Complete Directory to Prime Time Network TV Shows* or Vincent Terrace's *Complete Encyclopedia of Television Programs,* you can find exact dates the programs aired. Ordering *TV Guides* from the period, you'll get program descriptions and will at least know the names and content of the episodes you're after.

Comprehensive episode break-downs, as well as informative features on such topics as the *Beverly Hillbillies'* Jane Hathaway, *Our Miss Brooks,* and Clint E's *Rawhide* are found in *Reruns* ("the magazine of television history"). Published bi-monthly, at P.O. Box 832, Santa Monica, California 90406-0832; $12 for a year's worth.

We'd be remiss if we didn't mention the most penetrating, entertaining, vital, exciting, iconoclastic, level-headed, straight-talking television column going — James Wolcott's, weekly in the *Village Voice.* It's called "Medium Cool."

It's endured years of losing teams and bad jokes
("second prize, two weeks in Philadelphia"). It
discovered Fabian and Ben Franklin. To hear Mr. "C"
tell it, you ain't been nowhere till you've been there
and fully dug.

HIP CITY, U.S.A.
The Real Philly Story

by Joe McEwen

The Geator is barely in control. Johnny and the Hurricanes' "Sheeba" crescendoes in the background, and Jerry Blavat cannot contain himself. His feet twitch convulsively, spasms rock his wiry body, and his high-collar white cotton shirt is already drenched with sweat. But it's his mouth that commands attention, a gaping abyss that emits a nonstop stream of yowls, groans, gurgles, and barely decipherable syllables. "Come on, South Philly," he hisses, swallowing air in gobs like a man who has just done fifty push-ups. "Come on, come on, West Philly, come on, South Jersey, come on, yon teenagers everywhere. Hit that thing now. Hey, hey, ho, ho. Let me say greetings and salutations. Welcome to the biggest of all big-time ones. Once again, yours truly, the Geator with the Heator and, of course, everybody here, swingin', tick-tock-rockin' with the big time Chez-Vous tower of power. The toughest dances in the entire world! Let's kick it off the big time, Du-Ettes — 'Please Forgive Me' — oooohh!" For Jerry Blavat, in 1966, a night at Upper Darby's Chez-Vous has just begun.

In the *Rolling Stone Illustrated History of Rock*, Phil Spector rattled off a marvelous, manic description of Philadelphia in the Sixties ... "Philadelphia was just the most insane, most dynamite, the most beautiful city in the history of rock and roll and the world. Its energies were just phenomenal. Everyone you met was raging and racing, 24 hours a day, seven days a week, and existed for nothing but hype. They existed to pull strokes, conjure deals out of nowhere, juggle hits off nothing. Money was a lot of it, of course, but there was something else as well, a real glee involved; a purist's love of hustle for its own sake."

Fore those who grew up there, Jerry Blavat's arcane, machine gun prattle only seemed normal, a natural back-

Jerry Blavat

© Lost Nite Records

ground for the raucous dances and frenetic Motown grooves that served as background music to everyday teenage life.

Offbeat, askew in time, the junk food capital of the world, a paradise for sports fans whose teams fold in the clutch, Philadelphia rarely seems to escape its past and always seems doomed to repeat it. Philadelphia has never been like anyplace else.

These, the biggest of all big-time ones, are the reasons why:

Cheese steaks. The roll is the key — hard-crusted on the outside, soft on the inside. Essential ingredients: chopped minute steak, onion, cheese. Grease.

Douse liberally with ketchup. But don't try to make it yourself — head for Pat's Steaks, South Philly.

Hoagies. Again, the roll makes it, with thick tomato slices, Italian cold cuts, provolone, thick onion slices, lettuce, olive oil, and hot peppers.

WDAS. "Soul music fills the air, I smell soul food everywhere!" Its motto is "the station that raised you," and for black and white Philadelphians, this is indisputably true. Home to Butterball, Jocko, Georgie "the Guy with the Goods" Woods, Jimmy Bishop, and a host of other radio legends.

Kensington and Allegheny ("K & A"). The city's white ghetto. The place where Jerry Blavat could standup and scream "the toughest dances in the world!" and mean every word.

K & A Breakfast. Tastykake chocolate cupcake and Frank's orange soda. White soul food and a balanced meal that's served Philly school kids well for twenty-five years.

Connie Mack Stadium. One-time home of the Phillies, which meant the home of last place. Destroyed by urban renewal, not, strangely enough, by hard-bitten fans.

Georgie Woods

Bunny Sigler. Once a wacky, offbeat soul man ("Theme For 'The Five Fingers Of Death'"). His version of "Tossin' and Turnin'" remains one of pop music's undiscovered masterpieces.

Dave Zinkoff. Public address announcer for Philly's pro basketball teams dating back to Joe Fulks' era, with a style alternating between elongated bursts and cavernous rumbles. When Julius Erving scores, Zink reacts with an emotional roller coaster of barely connected syllables. Rarely has the public good been better served.

Joe Niagara. WIBG's "Rockin' Bird." His warm jive and heartfelt sales pitches made even Muntz TV commercials seem like displays of civic pride. ("What're you watchin' right now? Ten-inch? Twelve-inch? How'd you like to step up to bigger than life, sixteen-inch television? Tonight, fight night, when the man says 'What'll you have?', tell him a *Muntz TV!* Call now...")

And more. Ortlieb's Beer ... Wilt Chamberlain ... Overbrook High ... the Uptown ... 69th Street ... the Temptones, Daryl Hall's white soul band from '67 ... the Intruders ... Chuck Bednarick—the Eagles' "Concrete Charlie," still dancing over Frank Gifford ... Krass Brothers clothiers ... Richie Allen ("Crash") ... Harvey Holiday, Hy Lit, Ed Hurst, Frank X Feller, and South Street ("where all the hippies meet") ... John Facenda ... Roy Rubin: nine and seventy-three, with help from Kevin Loughery ... Sally Starr, the low-budget Captain Kangaroo hosting a kids' show with "Chief Halftown" ... Thom Bell ... By Saam ... McCoy Tyner ... the Big Five ... Sonny Hopson ("The Mighty Burner"), scrapple, Cuban heels and Wildwood ... Brenda & the Tabulations ... soft pretzels ("with mustard") ... Louise Williams ... Wagner's, home of the Wagner Walk, which the Geator probably in-

vented ... Yo-Yo, Phillies perennial superfan (after thirty years of loyalty, he didn't live to see them finally win big in '80) ... Cool Earl & Cornbreak, the graffiti kings ... Willow Grove Park, Eddie Gottlieb, Sandy Grady, Sid Mark and his "Fridays with Frank" and Sundays with Sinatra" ... the Troc: Arch Streets hot nightspot, providing entertainment for the whole family. Take it all off ... major Coxson ... WIBG ("Wibbage, Radio 99!), Pancho Herrera, the Delfonics, John Bandy, WHAT, George Michael ...

Of course, these proper and not so proper nouns reflect only a small part of Philly's hall of fame. For now, they, and it, remain solid: the last bastion of doo-wop culture in a McDonald's world.

The SOUL SURFERS
radio 148

CARL · BUTTERBALL · JOCKO · LARRY · JIMMY · KAE

SOUL SOUND SURVEY

WHEELS

Cool people and cool cars have always had eyes for each other. Kookie Byrnes parked them, "Big Daddy" Roth customized them, James Dean and Jayne Mansfield drove them to their deaths. Whether you're bound for Hip City or beyond, the secrets of automotive cool run deep. Bob Merlis reveals a few of the best...

DAGMARS, FANTA-FINS & HIGHWAY HI-FI

Fall 1956. Ike and Dick are about to sock it to Adlai and Estes. You open your morning paper, and there it is! — a ten-point headline screaming: "SUDDENLY IT'S 1960!"

No, you haven't tripped into lysergic awareness or the Twilight Zone (neither will be invented for three more years). It's '56 all right. "Love Me Tender" is in the Top Ten, Jack Kennedy's been standing in line to see **Bus Stop,** and the guys at Chrysler Corp have unilaterally decided we'll all be better off if they flush what's left of the Fifties down the toilet. The future's been expected in autodom since VJ Day, and now it's here, courtesy of the flipped stylist cats and ad copywriters now gigging with Chrysler. Tomorrow's cars today, starting with the righteous 1960, er 1957, Imperial.

The '57 Crown Imp convertible: 4820 pounds of joy. Elvis and Lizabeth Scott cruised in one in Loving You. Let's have a party!

Ever seen one in full wallow? Check out the wildest towering fins this side of a B-47. Dig those crazy acres of panoramic windshield — like widescreen. And the quad headlamps and "gunsight" taillights, Torqueflite push-button-activated three-speed automatic transmission (standard, Jack). Hey, isn't this the first production car with compound curve side glass? You can bet the Teamsters' pension fund it is. The '57 Crown Imp convertible: 4820 pounds of joy. Elvis and Lizabeth Scott cruised in one in **Loving You.** Let's have a party!

The new wave hit in '56, but it had been heading Detroit's way since war's end. Back then, Henry J. Kaiser, fat from his Liberty Ship business, took on Motor City's Big Three with the help of designer "Dutch" Darrin. Darrin, famed for his swoopy Depression-era movie star/gangster Packards, was told to come up with something avant for Henry J. He did; his flattened out '47 Kaisers and Fraisers looked like no prewar buggy anyone'd ever seen.

At Studebaker, they tossed history to the wind and turned loose Ray Loewy. Raymond Loewy, the most cosmic industrial designer since the Bronze Age, who'd already blown minds with his boss blue Ritz cracker box, with Lucky Strike's red-and-white bull's-eye packs and Coke's streamlined fountain syrup dispensers. Loewy's late Forties Studeys don't even resemble cars. They look like trains. To be exact, they look like the Pennsylvania Railroad's GG-1 locomotive, which Ray just happened to have dreamed up a couple of years earlier. You've seen it: a bullet-shaped engine intended to haul in either direction to avoid switching.

Applied to autos, the "is-it-going-or-is-it-coming" design made Studebaker

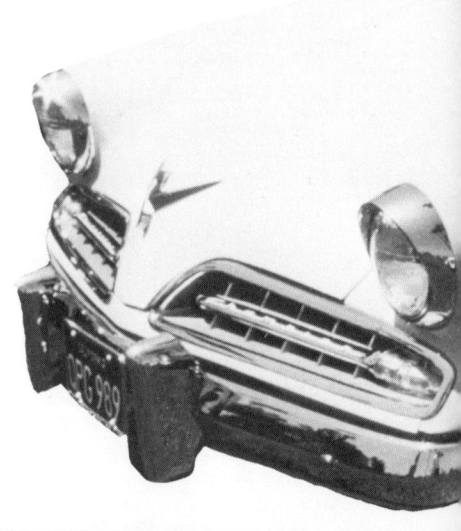

Commanders and Champions bad joke fodder for years. But no one could deny the cars' look was futuristic. How better to suggest the far-flung shape of shorts to come than with 180-degree wrap-around rear windows and, on those '50-51 Commander Starlite coupes, what for all the world resembled a propeller nacelle from a P-38? Loewy had only succeeded in transforming a car inspired by a locomotive into a fighter plane with a few bands of metal and chrome appliques. Voila! And just in time for Korea.

Other independent car makers experimented, too — Nash's revolutionary "bathtub" models and those bulbous Packards that came on like bumper cars with the mumps. In the end, the "safe" styles of Chrysler, Ford, and GM carried the day, and the indies were squashed. But those wild train-, boat- and plane-derived models made their mark, and the majors got the message: You **could** put a rocket ship on the road, even if you had no intention of going to Mars. Move it, Ming, the light just changed!

Simply, the coolest land cruisers ever to sit on four Firestones rolled off American assembly lines from '56 to '67. What follows is a guide to the swingin'-est wheels, the ones whose presence once insured their country's unquestioned superiority in things cultural. Think about it, citizens.

The most beautiful car ever made: Loewy's low-boy, circa '53.

Chowder & Son

General Motors

CADILLAC. First with the fin, and their finest may rest on the '49 Coupe De Ville, Caddy's original "hardtop convertible." "Dagmars," dual chrome-plated grill protuberances with a marked resemblance to a statuesque Scandinavian starlet of the day, began to sprout in the early Fifties, and grew into actual rubber-tipped mammaries by '58.

The absolute apex of chrome-choked jukebox style was reached the following year with garish mutant models that looked like they'd been zapped in the womb by the same lethal radiation that got Godzilla. And who could forget Paul Newman, bottoming out the mushy suspension of his '58 Cad in **Hud?** No wonder Patricia Neal went ga-ga for that ratfink.

The next (and last) Caddy worth breathing heavy over is the '67 Eldorado. This massive machine was lean and razor-cut. Not surprisingly, it became the proto-pimpmobile for the Superfly generation.

BUICK. The future started in '59 for Buick, when they chucked years of fat-cat wagons with names like Special, Century, and Roadmaster. Here came the LeSabre, the Invicta, and Electra, with Eurasian headlights and wide-angled fins aiming up and out. For the Sixties, the medium cooled — chrome

"Dagmars," dual chrome-plated grill protuberances with a marked resemblance to a statuesque Scandinavian starlet of the day, began to sprout in the early Fifties, and grew into actual rubber-tipped mammaries by '58.

grew scarce, shapes got slippery. Buick's hippest move was the Riviera (especially '63-'65): two-door hardtops with bucket seats, sharp looking from every angle. Inspiration apparently struck style chief Bill Mitchell one foggy night in London town — a coach-built Rolls sliced through the mist, Bill flashed, and the Riv was born.

Like too many good things, it was downhill from there on out. The only cool late Riv is the boat-tailed '71 "Batmobile" model, which has its points. (Mainly a very large one — at the base of the trunk, a fan-shaped growth appears to swallow a good three-quarters of the chassis.) These fastback beasts still look menacing. Gary Busey hauls Jodie Foster's teenage ass around in one in **Carney.**

Paul Newman is out of sight. So is his rubber-tipped **Hud**-mobile, the incomparable '58 Caddy convert.

1958

Undercover Catperson purrs on passenger side of the '71 "Batmobile" Riviera.

Buick Division, GM

Sharper than a Paul Sargent continental suit: the razor-cut Riviera, Buick's hippest move.

Buick Division, GM

Cadillac Motor Car Division, GM

OLDSMOBILE GM's "image car," Olds was the first to feature hydramatic, front-wheel drive, turbochargers. Fifty-six was a great year, thanks to the yawning shark's mouth grill treatment. The car looks like it's slobbering, but the overall effect is very strong. In '66, the original Toronado (the first American front-drive car since the Thirties' Cord) looked more like a fastbacked tank than an Oldsmobile. It moved: 135+ mph was not out of the question.

PONTIAC. Until '59, the year they invented "wide track," Pontons were strictly Little Old Ladiesville. Just what was "wide track"? A surrogate for testicular fortitude: the wheels were spaced a bit farther apart for a more macho stance. Sixty-three's Grand Prix, with chrome-free slab sides, concave rear window, and buckets is the slickest Big Indian that ever was.

CHEVROLET. So many have frothed freely over the '55-57's that there's no point in doing it again. Nomads were a weird hybrid (station wagon crossed with sports car), Corvairs have a nice nerd appeal, but if you're talking strictly cool, you're talking about one Chevy and one Chevy only: the '63 Corvette Sting Ray "split window" coupe. Never has a car emulated marine life so closely. The split rear window, a throwback to the early Forties, was dropped within a year, but that peculiar design quirk, coupled with the fastback neo-powerboat tail roof line make this 'vette the very hippest.

The Cousteau vibe even extends to foldaway headlights hiding out in fenders punctured by gill slits. This plastic-bodied grouper was the fastest in its school, thanks to fuel injection. A dream car you could buy. The Beach Boys pose with one on the cover of **Shut Down Volume 2;** Jan & Dean try the same on the flip of their **Dead Man's Curve/New Girl in School** album.

Ford Motor Company

LINCOLN. The neoclassic heritage spawned by the original tire-in-the-back Continentals of the Forties haunts the marque to this day. The dinner jacket look of the first Connies was revived in '56 and '57 with the Continental Mark II, the first car from a modern major to break the $10,000 tag! Even at that

Continental Mark II: Bring your tux, and ten thousand clams. Ford Motor Co.

steep tariff, these were built solely for prestige: A thousand clams were lost on each one sold. By '61 the Marks were over and the New Frontier and Great Society ('61-67) swung with the understated four-door sedans and converts

Jaws-ville: Fifty-six Olds Super "88". Oldsmobile, GM

Out of water, '63 Corvette Sting Ray awaits Brian Wilson's arrival. Chevrolet, GM

simply called Lincoln Continentals. The early four-doors with the rear door hinged at the back (they open "out," like the classics) are the ones to have. Just the car to drive when making a withdrawal from your neighborhood school book depository.

Ford must've had some remorse

about scrapping the old Mark II's, so they reincarnated it in '69 as the Continental Mark III. Popeye Doyle and his cronies dismantled one one winter's eve in **The French Connection.** (Didn't anybody think it a little odd that a frog had his American car shipped to the U.S.? How many of us give our LeCars round-trip tickets when we vacation in Nice?)

MERCURY. Lincoln's little brother has always demonstrated a flair for the far-out. In '57 Mercury used its real-life dream car, the Turnpike Cruiser, as a kind of stalking horse for the forthcoming Edsel, offering hardtops and convertibles with a boatload of wild extras — a gold anodized inlay along the indents on the rear fenders, reverse slant

power windows, quad headlamps in hooded over-hanging nodules, and "Seat-O-Matic" control, which offered the driver a choice of forty-nine "power" seat positions! And don't forget those dual dummy antennae jutting out from pods atop each side of the windshield. These pods were completely practical, of course — they were extremely helpful in permitting large amounts of water to enter the passenger compartment during the rainy season. The Turnpike Cruiser, like the Edsel, was a bomb, but a beaut.

Semi-cool: The original Cougar, Merc's "pony car," started as a Mustang sidekick in '67. Taillights automatically signalled the direction of your intended turn by flashing sequentially. Wow.

FORD. Fifty-seven Skyliner retractible hardtops. Are they converts or hardtops? Only their five motors, ten solenoids, thirteen switches, nine circuit breakers, and 610 feet of wire know for sure. Fifty-eight and '59 T-birds: big, square-mouthed, appealing in a violent sort of way. Mustang: like Dobie Gray says, the original is still the greatest — '64's and '65's only. Join the In Crowd.

Corvairs have a nice nerd appeal, but if you're talking strictly cool, you're talking about one Chevy and one Chevy only: the '63 Corvette Sting Ray "split window" coupe.

One of the greatest looking pieces of machinery ever designed, 1962 Jaguar XKE coupe.

Jaguar Rover Triumph

Chrysler Corp.

IMPERIAL. Once shorn of their (late Fifties) fanta-fins, Imps were never again cool, but consider Elwood Engle's redo on the '64's. The former Ford man gave them a Lincoln influence by impressing a tire shape onto the trunk lip and lower bumper. The shape was on the square (as in non-round) side. Really, Elwood.

CHRYSLER. Innovation struck in '56 with the introduction of "Highway Hi-Fi": your favorite tunes played at 16 2/3 rpm right under the dash. Mambo to go. Fifty-seven's 300-C is one of the greats. Its "Suddenly it's 1960!" fins and yawning egg crate grill make it say "Get the hell out of my way" even when it's parked at the market. Three hundred ninety horses. ¡Maron! the '60 300-F's were pretty scary, too, boys and girls (400 horses @ 5200 rpm).

DODGE. Like the Pontiac, an old lady's car that was put on a hormone program in the late Fifties. Just uttering the name of 1957's top of the line can take your breath away — "Dodge Custom Royal Lancer D-500." Cops loved 'em, at least on TV. Broderick Crawford fishtailed all over hell in one every week on **Highway Patrol.** In '66 Dodge kicked off the "brute car" brawl with the Charger (check McQueen's classic Frisco car chase in **Bullitt**). In the Seventies there was a Dart hardtop called the Swinger. It wasn't.

PLYMOUTH. Hard to imagine that a car whose emblem is the *Mayflower* introduced a model named for a cartoon

Innovation struck in '56 with the introduction of "Highway Hi-Fi": your favorite tunes played at 16 2/3 rpm right under the dash. Mambo to go.

character in '69. Beep beep. Sixty-four's Barracuda was a crazy fastback that filled in a missing roofline slope with a giant piece of contoured glass. Fishbowl fun! Rear-seat passengers broiled, courtesy of the solar "greenhouse effect."

Studebaker-Packard

Perennial also-ran Studebaker (merged with Packard in '56) consistently came up with the most gone attempts at covering those market slots the Big Three ignored. Dig: '53 Loewy Starliner coupe, without question the most beautiful car ever made in the U.S.A. True. Not until the Seventies did any major domestic maker attempt anything as rakish. Loewy's lowboy was

facelifted into the hawk line by '56 and flew until '64.

Studebaker picked 1963 as the time to give America the family sports car — the Avanti, an eccentric Loewy creation cooked up at the master's Palm Springs retreat. The fastest production car ever built stateside, a kind of four-passenger Corvette with a sharp collection of circles and reverse curves and planes for a body. Shortly after the Avanti's arrival, Studebaker was forced into Canadian exile. You can buy a new Avanti II today (no longer made by Studebaker — they use a GM drive train).

Also gone, but never to be forgotten: the Packard Hawk, freakish stepchild of the S-P union — fish-faced chromeless cavity for a grill, with dual Dagmar tusks, towering fiberglass fins, and upholstery on the **outside** of the door. Too hip, baby.

Foreign Bodies

Sure, U.S. iron is best, but fairness forces us to admit that some boss sets of wheels traveled by sea before hitting land. Various un-American examples of auto-cool have come and gone, but one sterling example remains, one of the greatest looking pieces of machinery ever designed, regardless of intended purpose.

Forget about that classic wind-in-the-face sports car stuff that makes old square-radiator MG's and Jag XK-120's so cher-chez'd. The Jaguar E-types ('61-74) are the only foreign made movers ever to run with the 'vettes and to be storied in song ("Deadman's Curve"). Despite the overt phallic symbolism of its hood, the E would turn on someone who'd been neutered. The Dave Clark Five stood inside an E on the cover of their **Try Too Hard** album. This is the car to drive down Carnaby Street. England swings...maybe for the last time.

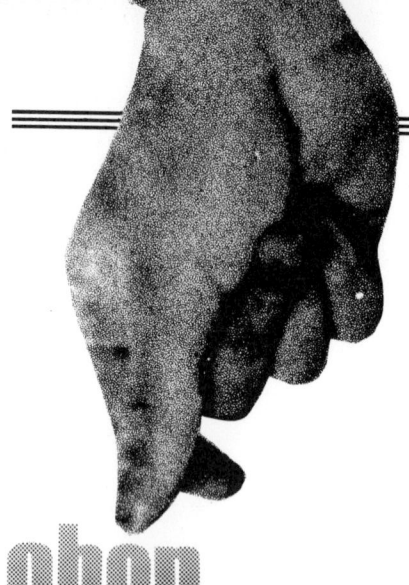

shop around...

Getting your hands on cool wheels today isn't as rough as it looks. It'll only cost you time and money, and what better way to use both than to cop a '62 Studebaker Gran Turisimo Hawk? What are you waiting for? Start searching, pilgrim.

Now that you've decided to put a car of the past in your future, just how do you latch onto one of those junkyard angels? If you live in the Sunbelt, consult your local classified. The scourge of older iron, namely rust, isn't much of a problem in the Southwest, but it's the very thing that can turn your dreammobile into a holy nightmare if you live where the snow falls and the salt spreads. If you're a Snowbelt resident, consider a vacation to Arizona, California, New Mexico, or Nevada. You'll only need a one-way ticket and you can line up a buy before you fly by combing through one of the many national periodicals that cater to hardcore car nuts.

The best is a fat monthly called **Hemmings Motor News.** It lists everything from Amphicars to Wartburgs, plus it features tons of great parts and service ads, all alphabetically by make. Twelve issues for $13.75 to: HMN, Box 100, Bennington, Vermont 05201.

Old Cars is a weekly newspaper covering the scene with classifieds and a helpful listing of prices recently paid for old cars at auctions. It's a good guide to how much you should be willing to pay for what you want wheelwise. Fifty-two issues for $15 to: **Old Cars Weekly,** 700 East State Street, Iola, Wisconsin 54990.

If you're stuck making payments on an '81 Celica (chump!) or just aren't in a position to take responsibility for the care and feeding of a real car, you might take the Lowell Thomas way out and armchair it with **Special Interest Autos,** a well written glossy bi-monthly that covers the cars that made a cultural impact regardless of sales volume. Six issues for $7 to: *Special Interest Autos,* Box 196, Bennington, Vermont 05201.

There's also **Car Exchange,** another monthly specializing in American autos of the Fifties and Sixties. Twelve issues for $9. Write *Car Exchange,* 700 E. State St., Iola, Wisconsin 54990.

One last note of caution: be careful of the current "replicar" phenomenon. Replicars are (generally) newly manufactured caricatures of real cars, many built on Volkswagen floor plans. They're primarily for rich drips who don't know the difference. You do, so don't bother. You might keep in mind that it could conceivably cost you less to score the real thing than one of these new forgeries. The '57 Thunderbird replicar looks like a '57 Thunderbird, but it isn't a *'57 Thunderbird.* If you dream about wheeling around town, top down, in a T-bird, try to find a way to get one. Does anyone dream about replicas of T-birds? Hey...

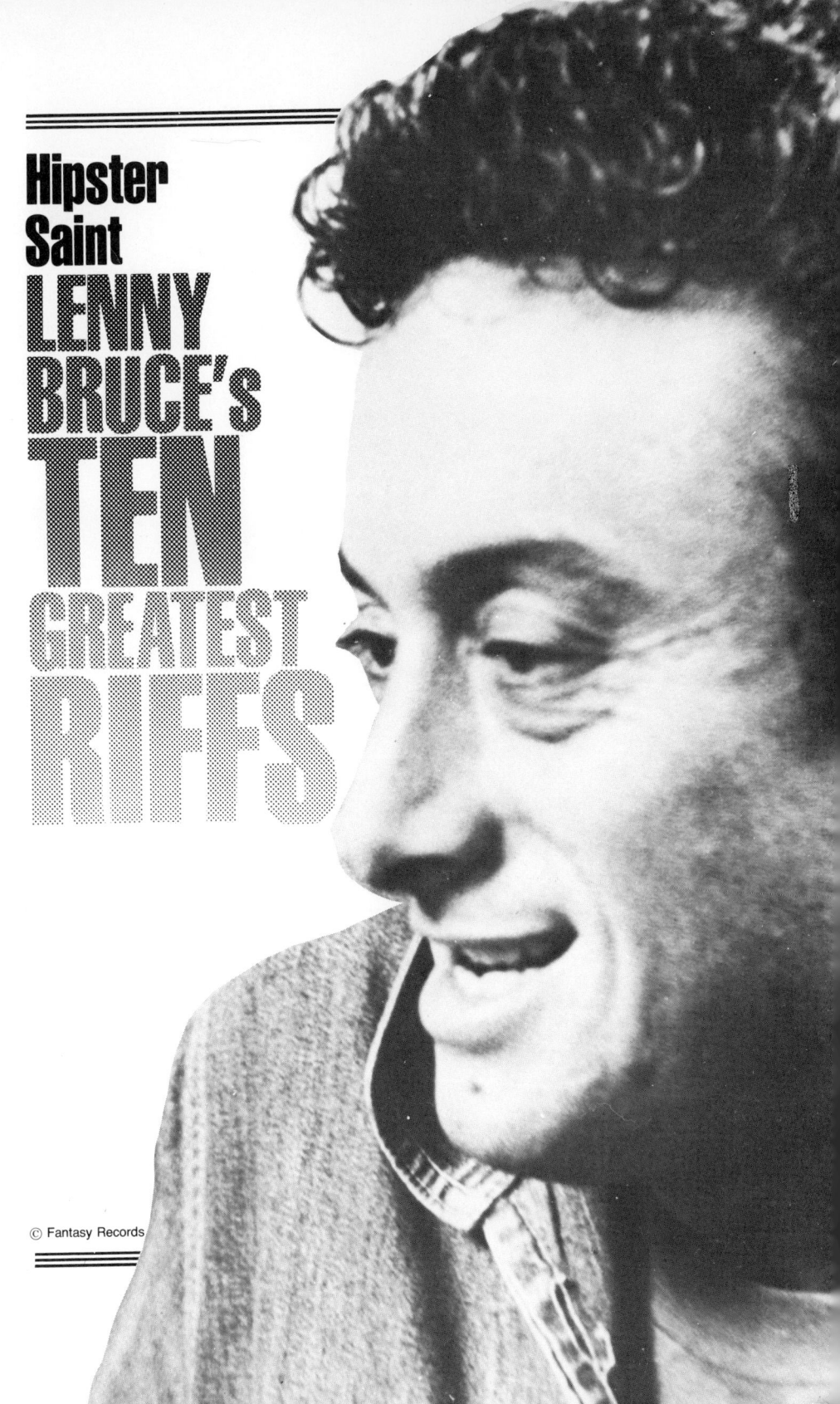

**Hipster
Saint**

LENNY
BRUCE's
TEN
GREATEST
RIFFS

Lenny Bruce. The wisest Jew since Solomon. Wait a minute. What kind of wisdom does it take to skin-pop controlled substances? Not that kind of wise, schmuck. Dig: "wise" as in wiseguy.

Who needs all that hippie twaddle about Father Bruce being the conscience of America? Later for the Cliff Gorman-Dusty Hoffman tortured martyr portrayals. And let's not even bother, shall we, with Albert "Little Elvis" Goldman's sinsational bio-fantasy. Leonard Schneider is part of this *Catalog* not because his scalpel-sharp tongue lanced the boil of hypocrisy (a cool move, no one's arguing), but because he was a dyed-in-the-sharkskin Hipster, a narrow-lapeled pointy toad, spittle-on-the-lips sharpster who somehow made Borscht Belt *schpritzing* into a conceptual art form the likes of which no one since has come within an ID bracelet's dangle of.

The fact that he occasionally used common A-Saxon (as well as Middle European) expletives is of no real concern. There've been scores of "blue" comics before and since St. Len's coming. As he explained it, "I don't do motel jokes." What he did do was topical, was cinematic, was Cool Entertainment. He was an actor who wrote himself the farthest-out parts. Show biz meets underground. Groove.

Sure, he thought segregation was a drag; only a *putz* or a Georgia cracker would have taken issue with that stand. Nuclear war? Definitely out, but we're talking about Lenny Bruce not Bertrand Russell. Here's a Brooklyn smart aleck who could somehow get a laugh with one quick turn of phrase — a snappy "Shut up, you nut!", a belligerent "Don't bug me, man." Stuff that, out of the mouth of a pre-fab beatnik like Maynard G. Krebs, wouldn't get a laugh from

anyone who actually believed Bird died for our sins. When Bruce's mile-high jazz musician says it was "like a really swingin' scene, can you dig?", you (a) laugh and (b) better believe it was a really swingin' scene. Dig?

The Bruce reliquary is stockpiled with enough holy *schtick* to keep a comedy store in business through the next mil-lenium and a half. Hey, I'm sorry as the next guy he was hounded by the heat, had a costly hot bottlecap hang-up and all that depressing news. The riff remains the same: Bruce can swing for you, and he'll swing better if you don't get hung behind the b.s. maudlin reverence scene. Herewith the rundown on Lenny's licks...

1. On the culpability of the Jewish race for the death of Christ: "OK, we did it. We found a note in the basement: 'We did him in. Signed, Morty.'"

2. Uttered by the kid who discovers airplane glue fifteen years before the Ramones: "I'm the Louie Pasteur of junkiedom!"

3. Ice-breaking suggestion from the bit "How to Relax Your Colored Friends at Parties": "That Bojangles. Christ, could he tap dance!"

4. Legend on novelty cocktail napkin hawked at conventions at "Religions, Inc.": "Another martini for Mother Cabrini."

5. Chairman of the Board of Religions, Inc., on the phone to the Pope: "Johnny baby, what's shakin', sweetie? Billy wants to know if you can get him a deal on one of them dago sports cars."

6. "YADADEYADA, Warden!" (response of Dutch, the desperate con, to the suggestion he give himself up, in "Father Flotski's Triumph").

7. "Did you hear that, you bitches in Cellblock Eleven? He's giving it all up for me. I feel just like Wally Simpson" (Kiki, the festive prison hospital attendant in the "Flotski" saga).

8. Warden to prison guard who is about to start taking lead: "You knew what this gig was about — only hope your old lady swung with Mutual of Omaha!"

9. Theatrical agent contemplating Hitler's mug after discovering him painting a wall at MCA (Mein Campf Arises) agency: "Look at zat face! Is zis an album cover? Vat a veirdo!"

10. "Adolf, baby, you'll make more money in a minute in the dictator business than you can make with that Chem-tone jazz in a year" (same agent).

11. TV used-car huckster in "Fat Boy": "Folks, this car was just used once in a suicide pact; there's just a little lipstick around the exhaust pipe."

The bits live on, here. Most of his albums are still in print. And each one comes with two flip sides...

THE REAL LENNY BRUCE (Fantasy). A double album with most of the great riffs plus six pages of Ralph Gleason notes and a number of manic-looking photos of the man himself. A real OD.

BEST OF LENNY BRUCE (Fantasy). Some of the same material as *Real* on a single LP. Gleason's de rigueur liner,

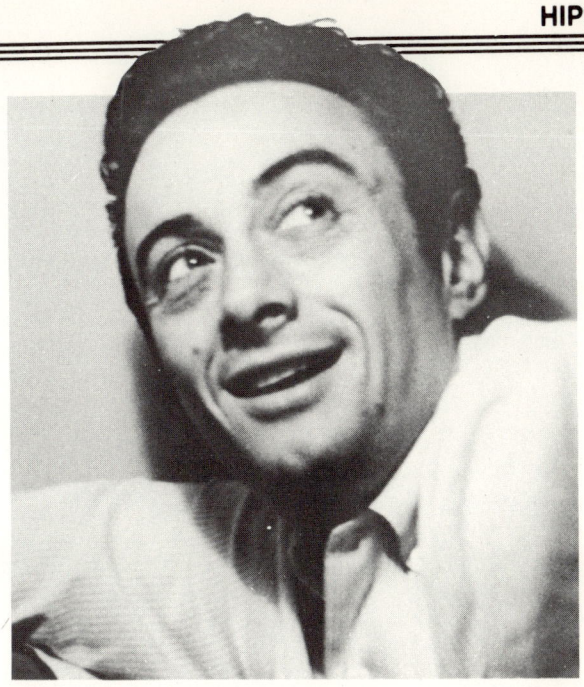

but the package was put together pre-mortem, so you can fool your friends into thinking you've had it in your collection for twenty years or so.

Fantasy is also the home of **THANK YOU MASKED MAN,** a compilation of early bits; the three-record **LIVE AT THE CURRAN THEATER;** as well as **LENNY BRUCE — AMERICAN; TO-GETHERNESS; INTERVIEWS OF OUR TIME;** and **THE SICK HUMOR OF LENNY BRUCE** — worth getting for the cover of our hero having an ethnic picnic on a cemetery grave. Like irreverent!

Further study might take you to Bruce's autobiography *How to Talk Dirty and Influence People* (Playboy Press) or *The Essential Lenny Bruce* (Bantam), a series of transcriptions of his routines. The latter book's index reads better than most chapters in straight literature: I. Blacks; II. Jews; III. Religions, Inc.; Catholicism, Christ &

Moses, and the Lone Ranger; IV. Politics; VII. Pills and Shit; VII. Fantasies, Flicks & Sketches; IX. Balling, Chicks, Fags, Dykes & Divorce; and XIII. Spotting Heat and Understanding Judges and Lawyers...

Modern technology puts Lenny on your home screen (a medium he wasn't allowed to massage too often during his lifetime). Vestron Video has recently released *The Lenny Bruce Performance Film,* and they're at P.O. Box 4384, Stamford, Connecticut 06907. And Fred Baker Films offers vid versions of the documentary *Lenny Bruce Without Tears* and *Lenny on TV.* The latter compiles his various television appearances, including his Steve Allen shots and the rare pilot for his never-was CBS series. Various distributors have handled these two. For up-to-date info on who's got them in your area, write Fred Baker Films, 347 West 39th Street, Suite 404, New York, New York 10018.

Since the Stone Age, people have gone to some very creative lengths to distinguish themselves from other people. Upscale or low, lingo's the thing that usually does the trick best; custom jargon keeps the stevedores from the stewardesses. It can seal outsiders out or let insiders into the party in progress. The "Haywire Hall of Fame" in our Sounds section mentioned a few of the more notable recorded efforts at defining "hip talk."

There have also been several dictionaries of hip or "bop" phraseology. Cab Calloway wrote one as early as 1938. Texas disc jockey Lavada Durst still hawks his *Jives of Dr. Hepcat* ($6.50 to 1408 Ulit Avenue., Austin, Texas 78702). One of the best, *Dan Burley's Original Handbook of Harlem Jive* laid it out straight on the page in 1944, parsing such magnificent mumbo-jumbo as "Uncle is hipping a whole lot of cats as to what to do when the action gets off the track."

For those who've yet to connect with Dr. Hepcat or Burley's handbook — or Slim Gaillard's or Babs Gonzales' or Del Close's records — we've corraled the following nouns, verbs, and all-purpose Voutyisms, all currently in usage somewhere in the U.S.A., to come up with our own version of the glossary called...

(With special thanks to Tom Vickers, Ned Klaflan, George Clinton, Lord Buckley, Kookie, Tim White, Jeep Rice, and the Nagle-Mathews Institute for Advanced Studies.)

(to) arc out (verb): To overcome a bothersome obstacle, to clear a barrier with ease. "The math exam was a bear, but I arc'ed out."

beard (noun): Cover or disguise, in the form of an object or person. Dean and Ehrlichman were Tricky Dick's beards at Watergate.

Betty's world (noun): Referring to any geopolitical event occurring during the reign of Elizabeth I (1558-1603). "That Shakespeare was the swingin' prose king in Betty's world."

HOW TO SPEAK HIP

(the) Big Deuce (proper noun): World War II.

bogue (adj.): Bogus, uncool. Strictly fakes-ville.

bourbon (adj.): Lost in space, a general state of fuzzy-mindedness. "I just can't think straight. It's straight bourbon."

cheese (adj.): Top of the line in its class. The 1958 Eldorado is unquestionably "the cheese Caddy." (From Nagle-Mathews)

(to) cop and blow (verb): To make a purchase and split the scene. "Let's make it to McDonalds, cop and blow."

(to) dig (verb): to understand implicitly. Also: to appreciate or like.

(to) do it like Mommy (verb): To come on domestic in a big way. "This morning I cleaned house, vacuumed, ironed. I did it like Mommy." (From the record of the same name by Simtec & Wylie.)

Doll City (adj): Physically attractive in a standard-issue way. "Those Hemingway chicks with the Brezhnev brows are Doll City. I'll freeze."

(to) douse the Edisons (verb): To turn out the lights.

drug (adj.): *(From the past tense of* drag). Worn out, tired. "I'm too drug to climb those twenty flights just now," said Eddie.

in Fat City (descriptive phrase): Rich, well-off financially, satisfied. "Since the inheritance came in, she's in Fat City."

full tour (noun): Same as three-hour tour.

geepie (noun): (Pronounced with hard "g"). An underage hipster, a funk-bopper of either sex. (From Bootsy Collins)

gettin' the mohawk (verb form): Building up irritation to a major level, causing one's hackles to rise. "There was nothing on at seven except for *Family Feud*. I was gettin' the mohawk." (Nagle-Mathews)

gig (noun): Job, vocation, temporary assignment.

grove (verb): Past tense of *groove* (itself a corruption of *grok* — to orb enthusiastically). "The rebirth sequence in *2001* was too much. I grove the colors."

(to) have eyes for (verb): To want badly. "Eddie Cochran had eyes for that '49 Ford in 'Somethin' Else.'"

hip (adj): Aware, having acute perception.

hit me and cut the rap (directive): Hand over whatever you came here to give me, with no backtalk. (From the P-funk)

hung (adj.): Needy. "He's really hung for bread."

I'll freeze, Bill (phrase): A polite turndown. "Thanks for inviting me to that Pia Zadora flick, but I'll freeze, Bill." (From *The Price Is Right* TV game show, per Tom Vickers)

jacked up (adj.): Upset, anxious, held in suspension while the sundial ticks. "I got jacked up over my rent. I'm hung for the dough and can't make it."

(to) kiss (verb): To skip, pass, shine on. "She told me she'd rather just go to the mountains and kiss the city altogether this weekend."

(to) Kojak (verb): To find a usually unavailable parking space. "I can't believe it: a spot right in front of the hotel. I Kojaked!"

(to) Kreskin (verb): To intuit or foresee. "I Kreskined that you'd call before noon."

lamb-time (noun): Spring.

lean green (noun): Loot, dough, scratch. Money.

Leo-time (noun): August.

luggage (noun): Bags under the eyes.

(to) make the legal move (verb): Get married. Einstein, says Lord Buckley, found his woman, "made the legal move, rang the bells and out of this union were born two swingin' Marsheads."

Mister Ed (noun): 1. An unimpeachable inside source. "Woodward and Bernstein had a Mister Ed."
2. A reliable sidekick or confidant, as in McMahon.

Motel Hell (adj.): Characteristic of a bad place to stay, as in a souring love affair or dead-end job. "Man, I'm quitting; the gig is Motel Hell."

(to) Orb (verb): to eyeball or look at. "They orbed the window, then walked into the store and copped."

to pile up the z's (verb): To sleep.

puppethead (noun): Square person, esp. one who lets others pull his or her taste strings. (A typical puppethead remark: "Wow, I just paid forty bucks for tickets to see Devo. I've never heard them, but they're supposed to be rilly neat.") Synonyms (Tim White, 1978): **cement-head, chowder-head.**

queeb (noun): A small hassle or unavoidable screw-up, often mechanical. "Sorry I'm late. I had a minor queeb with the starter on my car."

rooster time (noun): Early morning.

rumor (noun): Something kaput, over with, ancient history. "Man, after Waterloo, Napoleon was a rumor. Finished."

scramble (noun): According to Nagle-Mathews, the peculiar effect achieved when a balding male combs what hair he's got left on the sides up onto his top. Hence, any attempt to stretch a thinning resource. Full scrambles: deficit budgets, the careers of Muhammed Ali and the Rolling Stones.

(to) senior out (verb): To tire, become too weak to function. To do it like an oldster. "I couldn't make the late movie. I seniored out, went to bed at ten."

Shovel City (adj.): Deeply dug, much appreciated. "You enjoying the music?" "It's too much: Shovel City."

(to) sit down (verb): To make an impression, to suggest lasting impact. According to Klaflan (1982), a good idea or great music "will definitely sit down, kids."

Sue City (descriptive phrase): Involved in a court action or otherwise engage in legal matters.

(to) swing (verb): To achieve the highest state of well-being. To soar free and clear. Bobby Rydell attended a "Swingin' School." Bruce and Sinatra graduated.

(to) swing like sixty (verb): To perform at peak, to freak freely or wail radically. "That girl's the cleanest when it comes to threads. The dress she wore last night swung like sixty."

Swiss (adj.): Neutral. Having no opinion or preference. From Vickers (1980-82): "I don't care where we go tonight. Dinner? Flicks? I'm totally Swiss."

(to) take the bus (verb): To do something in a low-cost, no-frills fashion. "When it comes to shoes, I take the bus — I shop at K-Mart."

(to) take the scenic route (verb): To perform a task with an eye toward enjoyment rather than efficiency. "Fun will take the longer way around," sayeth P-Funk. "Clinton takes the scenic route often."

three-hour tour (noun): A drag, especially any experience that takes longer than expected. From the Gilligan. "Waiting in line at the bank was a three-hour tour."

T-zone (adj.): Blissed out, unaware, spaced. "I'll never go out with him again. He's strictly T-zone."

under house (adj.): (From *under house arrest*) State of being uncontrollable, out of hand. Wildy frustrated. "Once Batman got hip to his scene, Penguin flipped. He was under house."

vines (noun): Clothes, threads.

Wall Street didn't jump (descriptive phrase): Indicating an action which fails to draw the anticipated reaction; creating no ripples on the pond. "He told the finance company he'd be inheriting a million bucks in six months. Wall Street didn't jump."

in Wig City (descriptive phrase): Caught in the township of the flipped, just outside sanity and peopled by mad daddies and moms.

wrapping (noun): Threads, vines, esp. women's.

Z-bird (noun): A loser. Last in line, hence the squarest. Prominent Z-birds: the Schmenge Brothers.

WRITE IF YOU GET HIP

We're beat
and ready to
split for Wig City.
But we can't do
that without
asking you to
write us with
your suggest-
ions for what
should go
into the
next
*Catalog
Of Cool.*
If you've
got some,
straighten us
'cause we're
ready.

Write:
"Cool"
Warner Books
75 Rockefeller Plaza
New York, New York 10019

216

RD 9M